Crisis in the Sahel

Other Titles in This Series

Food, Politics, and Agricultural Development: Case Studies in the Public Policy of Rural Modernization, edited by Raymond F. Hopkins, Donald J. Puchala, and Ross B. Talbot

Appropriate Technology for Development: A Discussion and Case Histories, edited by Donald D. Evans and Laurie Nogg Adler

Governments and Mining Companies in Developing Countries, James H. Cobbe

Technology and Economic Development: A Realistic Perspective, edited by Samuel M. Rosenblatt

The New Economics of the Less Developed Countries: Changing Perceptions in the North-South Dialogue, edited by Nake Kamrany

Protein, Calories, and Development: Nutritional Variables in the Economics of Developing Countries, Bernard A. Schmitt

Economic Development, Poverty, and Income Distribution, edited by William Loehr and John P. Powelson

The Military and Security in the Third World: Domestic and International Impacts, edited by Sheldon W. Simon

A Select Bibliography on Economic Development: With Annotations, John P. Powelson

Credit for Small Farmers in Developing Countries, Gordon Donald

The Emergence of Classes in Algeria: Colonialism and Socio-Political Change, Marnia Lazreg

Boom Town Growth Management: A Case Study of Rock Springs--Green River, Wyoming, John S. Gilmore and Mary K. Duff

From Dependency to Development, edited by Heraldo Muñoz

Migration and the Labor Market in Developing Countries, edited by R. H. Sabot

Agricultural Credit for Small Farm Development: Policies and Practices, David D. Bathrick

Westview Special Studies in Social, Political, and Economic Development

Crisis in the Sahel:
A Case Study in Development Cooperation
Noel V. Lateef

An examination of a unique international program of rehabilitation in the Sahel following the tragic drought of 1968-1974, this study is especially important for its predictive value about the kinds of synergistic measures that can be orchestrated to ward off future threats of famine throughout the world. Dr. Lateef pays particular attention to the role of the United States in the Sahel Development Program; his accent is on the changing nature and determinants of official U.S. response, and his conclusions are directly relevant to the present congressional debate concerning the role the United States should play in implementing the objectives of the Sahel Development Program and other programs of its kind.

Noel V. Lateef is director of the Law and Development Program at Yale Law School and has been program officer for AID in Dakar, Senegal, as well as special assistant to Ambassador Jean Wilkowski. He was also a National Science Foundation fellow at John F. Kennedy School of Government, Harvard University, during 1978-79.

Crisis in the Sahel: A Case Study in Development Cooperation

Noel V. Lateef

Foreword by Michael Reisman

Westview Press / Boulder, Colorado

Westview Special Studies in Social, Political, and Economic Development

Published in 1980 in the United States of America by
Westview Press, Inc.
5500 Central Avenue
Boulder, Colorado 80301
Frederick A. Praeger, Publisher

Library of Congress Cataloging in Publication Data
Lateef, Noel V.
Crisis in the Sahel.
(Westview special studies in social, political, and economic development)
Includes bibliographical references and index.
1. Sahel--Economic conditions. 2. Sahel--Economic policy. 3. Economic assistance, American--Sahel. 4. Technical assistance, American--Sahel.
I. Title.
HC1000.L37 338.91'73'066 80-36798
ISBN 0-89158-991-0

Composition for this book was provided by the author
Printed and bound in the United States of America

TO A REVERED TEACHER AND FRIEND,

JOHN P. LEWIS

Contents

Tables and Maps

Tables

Maps

Foreword: National Development as International Development

Every territorial community is challenged to develop: environmental transformations and changes in substantive demand constantly require authoritative community institutions to reclarify and perhaps revise goals, identify new conditions, and invent new strategies. In comparative scale, the observer may distinguish different stages of development competence and different development pathologies. The most minimal form of development will result when the territorial community lacks institutional or functional means for locating itself, with some degree of realism, in a global time and space perspective and of clarifying and projecting the goals which it must or should pursue as a common endeavor. Such nondevelopment does not derive exclusively from lack of institutional articulation; in the deepest sense, it reflects perspectives--in particular, demands and expectations about the impossibility of human-initiated change--shared by key segments of the population. When some feature of a theretofore routinized environment--in which the trusted old ways "worked"--is threatened by an unexpected natural or human factor, catastrophe looms, for the nondeveloped community cannot plan and adapt.

In the case of more advanced development competences, the more frequent pathology is that of the territorial community whose institutions are capable of clarifying relevant goals but unable to implement them because of the lack of resources and skills. "Cargo cults" are not limited to Pacific islands; expressions of them may be found in the platforms of more than one political party in industrial democracies.

At the far end of the spectrum, one encounters the social pathological condition of "hyper-development": communities replete with articulated development bureaucracies, whose inventiveness for dealing with new circumstances is strangled by crystallized institutions wedded to past goals and practices or commenities paralyzed by a crossfire from conflicting pressure and interest groups. Historical examples are the overbureaucratized systems found in certain periods in the Roman and Chinese Empires. Whether the industrial and science-based civilization we have reared falls into this category remains to be seen.

Properly understood, the optimum goal of a community is not development, in the sense of achieving a static capitalization and allocation of values conforming to transient demands, but rather, as Noel Lateef points out, the establishment of a viable, ongoing, development process, responsive to environmental changes and challenges, capable of reformulating goals and inventing new institutions and strategies to achieve them, and performing all the other decision functions for the maintenance of satisfactory community order.

Indispensable to understanding, let alone implementing this task, is a broad contextual approach, and this is one of the strengths of Lateef's book. Because social process is a manifold of interacting events, development, even in the smallest communities, must be assessed with comprehensive contextuality. Ecological, international, regional, national, and local levels must all be used as provisional foci for development, for what can be achieved in any one community is, in measure, a function of all the greater or lesser communities of which it is a part or which compose it. Development strategy invention, as Lateef shows, may often involve programs integrating the skills and resources of many different communities--at many different public and private levels--in existing or innovative institutional arrangements.

Similarly, as Lateef points out in a number of examples, development must be conceived in terms of all values, and never in terms of a single allegedly "key" variable, often adopted because of its presumed mensurative advantages. Certainly, characterizations of development exclusively in terms of a single value, for example, wealth--an increase in GNP, a favorable trade balance, a change in median income, economic infrastructural growth and so on--is completely inadequate. The development significance of such changes depends upon the aggregate of goals projected and the coordinate or independent changes in other value accumulations. The implementation of the principle of contextuality requires heuristic conceptions for different aspects of social and community processes and for the different values of public order, so that manifest change in a single category can be tested for the often latent contextual effects in many others.

Lateef's review of the Sahel and its human-induced and other changes underlies the point. Rivers may be deepened or redirected, swamps drained or filled, mosquitoes eliminated, irrigation and transportation canals dug and so on. None of these changes is discrete; each, as Lateef points out in a number of cases, may precipitate myriad social and ecological changes which may cumulatively, intentions notwithstanding, deviate even further from goals. Hence the necessity for regularly considering the ecological dimension--either as a direct target of change or as an inevitable receiver of the impacts of other changes--in all development programs.

By the same token, prospective and actual changes must be located in the community and, in particular, in the power context. The realistic developer is perforce concerned with identifying changes in groups with effective power in the target community: the formation of new or the dissolution of old coalitions and the coalescing of entirely new power groups. Because the cutting edge of development is political, those with effective power must be persuaded and recruited or neutralized. Assume one's target is the neighborhood of an American city: the formation of a new gang and its coalition with a political group or with a sector of the police force may constitute a critical change in the power process which can be used for or against preferred development. In a landlocked Latin American country, a bandit chief may, under the stress of events, become the head of a peasant army, with major changes within that country and perhaps in the continent and the world. Note, again, that a change in one phase of the power process can induce many changes in other features of the context. Adhesion to a peasant army, for example, may involve enormous personality changes in members of formerly prepolitical population strata, with coordinate changes in the constitutive process of the community and in aspects of its public order. Comparable interrelated changes must be charted in the constitutive process and in all the value processes of the community's public order: wealth, enlightenment, skill, well-being, affection, respect, and rectitude.

Most of all one cannot lose sight of the integrality of a "local" problem with a global system. Development is conventionally framed in terms of value capitalization and allocation _within a particular territorial community_. But, political boundaries may often be a comparatively minor factor in the delimitation of development processes. It is the interchange of values relevant to the process and the institutional decision patterns necessary to deal with them that demark the boundaries of a development process. In a world of intensely interdependent component communities, which interlock at many points and levels, the only useful perspective is the most comprehensive and global one. Lateef's felicitous emphasis on integrated development and the design of his study could not be more apt. The intellectual and practical implications are substantial.

One can conceive of micro-social development in which the establishment and operation of indispensable decision-making institutions appear to be extremely limited in geographical scope. The division of functions within a nascent family group, for example, seems to involve only allocations of extremely mundane and spatially close-range activities in order to establish a micro-development process: fulfillment of the value needs of the family members, capital accumulation to buy a house and so on. But the efficacy of this micro-development process may depend in great measure on the effectiveness of a larger development process, which has produced human beings with sufficient well-being to work; which has acculturated them to capacity for giving and receiving affection without which the nuclear family could not have been formed; which provides gainful employment sufficient to support the family members; which gives them sufficient self-respect so that they can relate positively to other family members. If the nascent family depends upon these supporting struts of a national social and economic system, the national system itself will depend upon a regional and global system with which its macro-economic activities are interdependent. Participants involved in these processes may perceive boundaries that seem to insulate them from other processes, but observers and development planners will be struck by the illusory or porous character of such boundaries.

Many of the major and most basic development challenges of the immediate and distant future will defy conceptual boundaries, although they may indeed benefit from administrative delimitations in the concrete realization of the solutions proposed. Consider the pressing problem of environmental maintenance and improvement. A single municipality or nation-state may legislate for the minimization of air pollution in its immediate area, but much environmental deterioration is aggregative. Hence more ambitious prophylaxis and amelioration will require many, and for certain problems, all governments as well as other effective actors, to participate in planning and execution. Other problems may require transnational collaboration on a regional basis, with participation dictated by such factors as the ecological unity of a river valley. In many cases, the apparent geographical boundaries of a problem will be exposed as no more than "mind-forged manacles" and will be pierced by the necessity for the incorporation of external values: foreign capital, foreign know-how, and so on.

Happily, Noel Lateef's very admirable and eloquent case study and appraisal of the joint and separate international and national responses to the Sahel disaster does indeed trace many of these interrelationships. The value of the work is increased by the insights he draws and the recommendations he offers for new foci, strategies, and fundamental structural changes to increase the future effectiveness of international crisis abatement and development response. It is a pleasure to introduce the book and to congratulate its author on a major and important accomplishment.

Michael Reisman
Yale Law School

Acknowledgments

The personal investment in the embryology of an international effort to bring the Sahel "up to speed" can be traced to a close association with sub-Saharan Africa. For three impressionable years, punctuated by such epiphenomena of the great drought as famine, massive human migration, and political upheaval, I lived in Niamey, a piquant base for frequent travels in the region (Timbuktu, situated in neighboring Mali, is a day's journey by Landrover). In the ensuing years, periodic visits of several months' duration were made to Lagos, Nigeria, and Dakar, Senegal. In 1976, I worked for the U.S. Agency for International Development (AID) mission to Senegal, and the following year, I was awarded a McConnel Foundation Scholarship by Princeton's Woodrow Wilson School of Public and International Affairs, permitting an extensive tour of Senegal and Mali. I am grateful to AID/Dakar, particularly the mission director, Normal Schoonover, and his deputy, Arthur Fell, for a valuable "apercu" into the donor perspective on foreign assistance. It is likewise incumbent upon me to record my gratitude to the Wilson Woodrow School for yet another opportunity to acquire and apply interdisciplinary tools. Let me further particularize my debts.

While the desire to do the present study has been percolating for many years, when the opportunity presented itself, the sheer psychological weight of intimacy with the region, as well as the substantial accumulation of materials caused me to teeter apprehensively. The encouragement of the Wilson School's John P. Lewis, presently with the Development Assistance Committee (DAC) of the Organisation for Economic Co-operation and Development (OECD), helped to put an end to my vacillation. His counsel and criticism subsequently bolstered the enterprise immeasureably. Another individual to whom I am grateful for having found the time to read the entire manuscript is Robert Gilpin.

For their guidance at various stages of this project, I am also indebted to Fouad Ajami, Richard Falk, Alvin Felzenberg,

Gerald and Lou Ann Garvey, Philip Hamburger, Albert O. Hirschman, Arthur Lewis, Paul Sigmund, Donald Stokes, and Julian Wolpert, all at Princeton. To a tolerant group of freshman advisees I am very grateful. Several sections of the study were enhanced by stimulating seminars at Harvard with Graham Allison, Harvey Brooks, Samuel Huntington, Mark Moore, John Montgomery, and Joseph Nye. Their general helpfulness, given the many demands placed on them, will always be remembered. I especially appreciate the incisive comments made by Professor Huntington on key chapters.

A good portion of the study was written on the metroliner while shuttling between Princeton and Washington where, at the State Department, I served on the staff of Ambassador Wilkowski. The flexibility and interest shown by Ambassador Wilkowski and her deputies, Donald Toussaint and Jim Stromeyer, are much appreciated. I should also mention that a meeting I was asked to organize at the United Nations Secretariat, bringing together Hans Einhaus, Guy Gresford, John Lewis, Gustave Ranis, and Jean Wilkowski, had a felicitous effect on the research in progress.

The AID/Washington "old hands" contributed greatly to my research. I am grateful to Donald Brown, Lois Hobson, Princeton Lyman, and David Shear. The staff of the Sahel Office and the AID Reference Center, particularly Helen Davidson, provided efficient and friendly services of which I am most appreciative. They made available to me a Niagara of hallmark documents and ephemeral papers. Surprisingly, however, the present effort represents the only shot at a comprehensive compedium despite the interest generated by the Sahel. As a compedium, I have drawn heavily on past research, including several studies that I prepared previously for AID and the State Department.

Acknowledgements to individuals in the "field" go far back in time. In Niger, my involvement in Peace Corps activities led to friendships with hard-working villagers from many ethnic groups for whose fortitude I have the utmost deference. It bothers me that these people--the Sahelian silent majority--are normally treated sparingly, and "textually" at that, in works such as this one. Unfortunately, I am no less culpable of this kind of oversight, however deliberate. In narrowing the scope of inquiry, I fall back on the lame excuse of having recorded oral traditions of two Sahelian ethnic groups. I have also published several ethnographies and analyses of Islamic and animist influences on Sahelian conceptual systems. I hope to address in greater detail some of the social processes that have salient interfaces with political and economic development in a forthcoming book on law and development.

To my West African hosts I extend heartfelt appreciation for their hospitality during a lengthy sojourn that would have strained the welcome in most other parts of the world. Moreover, few doors were closed. I benefitted from meetings with Presidents Hamani Diori and Leopold S. Senghor, with whom I shared a useful exchange of correspondence. Several individuals of vast experience were particularly helpful. They include: Samir Amin, Haroana Bembello, Manga Boulama, Sory Coulibaly, and the sagacious Boubou Hama. Among the Sahelian institutions whose facilities were graciously made available to me were Niger's Centre National de Recherche Scientific et Humaine (CNRSH) and the University of Dakar's Institut Fondimentale d'Afrique Noire (IFAN). The resources of several international organizations represented in the Sahel were tapped, including those of the United Nations Development Program (UNDP) and the Food and Agriculture Organization (FAO). A key contribution to this project was made in the course of informal sessions with several U.S. Ambassadors to West African countries, including Rudolph Aggrey, Donald Easum, Roswell McClellend, John Reinhardt, Robert Smith, and Terrence Todman. I owe them and their aides my profound gratitude.

Before closing this haphazard and futile effort to thank all who lent a hand, a shoulder, or both in this enterprise, I would like to cite the enthusiasm of my editor, Miriam Gilbert, whose communications, oral and written, buoyed my spirits. For a ruthlessly efficient typescript, I am grateful to Jody Kennard. Finally, I would like to acknowledge my foremost source of inspiration and renewal--my family. Although I frequently taxed their patience, they showed tolerance and understanding. They provided a decompression chamber when I sought one, and more often, they made possible a cross-fertilization of ideas that is at the heart of any kind of development. One cannot quite express one's gratitude for this kind of reinforcement. I am particularly grateful to Nora Lateef, whose participation in this enterprise as a "de facto" research assistant was indispensable. In trying to acknowledge this contribution, I am reminded of the Latin dictum: "Tacita quaedam habentur pro expressis." (Things unexpressed are sometimes considered as expressed.) This dictum does not pertain when it comes to responsibility for the final product. "Ergo," the failings of this enterprise, and--were it otherwise--there are many, rest entirely at my doorstep.

Noel V. Lateef

Introduction

The Sahel is unlikely to recede far into the recesses of global consciousness soon. At an international symposium in Bonn, West Germany, climatologists unanimously agreed that a new climatic pattern characterized by extreme variability in weather conditions will persist for several decades, posing a severe threat to world agriculture. Nowhere has this erratic fluctuation been more evident than in the Sahel. For the past ten years the rains have come to the Sahel too early, too late, or not at all -- creating a wholesale embranglement in Sahelian food production. In almost every Sahelian country, the normal spring-summer monsoon rains for 1977-1978 did not arrive on time or were insufficient to permit normal maturation of crops. A fact-finding team for the U.S. Agency for International Development (AID) reported:

> Based on information available to us at the end of September, it appears that neither Niger nor Mali will require emergency food aid in the year ahead, and that Chad and Upper Volta may benefit enough from the late rains to avoid any large-scale emergency food aid requirement in 1977-78. The same claims cannot be made for the western Sahel countries of Cape Verde, Mauritania, Senegal and The Gambia, however, for in each of these countries the rainfall has been totally inadequate in 1977. To date, Cape Verde, Senegal and The Gambia have made official requests to the United States for emergency food aid to help tide them over until the harvest of 1978. In addition, Mauritania and Togo will require some emergency food assistance in 1977-78.

Again, wetter rainy seasons since the disastrous 1968-1974 drought have proved to be only mild reprieves.

As Malthusian scenarios gain credence in a world experiencing population pressure and shrinking resources, a record of the international response to the Sahel's difficulties is important for its predictive value about the kinds of synergistic measures that can be orchestrated to ward off future threats of famine abroad. Because of its leadership role, the United States figures prominently in this account and the accent is on the changing nature and determinants of the U.S. Government's response to the Sahel's plight.

As in other impoverished developing areas, the time-frame for Sahelian development is so open-ended as to be a major political hindrance. The mobilization of financial, technical, and human resources needed to effect a transformation of the social and economic life of the Sahel will require considerable staying power -- at least a generation of concerted donor-recipient effort. What must not be glossed over in the course of setbacks and attendent frustrations is the brute empirical fact that regional food security and self-sustained economic growth in the Sahel is not "gleam in the eye." However, the reluctance of donors to transcend the one-dimensional world of crisis politics is not limited to the Sahel.

The absence of staying power is perhaps one of the greatest pitfalls in the deployment of foreign assistance. It can be argued that the piecemeal approach to development assistance is one of the reasons that the business of development assistance seems to be characterized by a mindless thrumming devoid of worthwhile results. More often than not the job is not bungled but half-finished. The ensuing dissatisfaction produces the drag effect of political unpopularity that plagues foreign assistance at home and abroad. Rarely, is the root cause of this malaise with foreign aid seen as a problem of commitment.

Reluctance on the part of the U.S. Government and, in particular, the Congress to make commitments to development projects abroad and to give these initiatives continuity is reflected in the policy shift on contributions to the international financial institutions, a policy which was changed two years ago from multi-year commitments based on executive branch negotiations and authorization legislation to one year commitments based on appropriations legislation. This holding back can be problematic in cases like the Sahel, where "esprit de corps" and psychological momentum is necessary despite congressional perceptions of the desirability for leeway in adjusting foreign aid programs to political vagaries. There is almost universal agreement that insulation of the Sahel from the effects of future drought is, "ex vi termini," a long-term proposition. Yet, no attempt is made to factor into fiscal calculations the interaction of variables in long-range programs affected directly or indirectly by present appropriations systems.

Can it be otherwise? The arguments favoring reconsideration of present procedures in the case of the Sahel are preponderant. Constance J. Freeman in testimony before the Senate

Subcommittee on Foreign Assistance has said:

> It is complicated, if not inconsistent, for a country to agree to participate in a long-range program but still insist on limiting its actual commitments to a year at a time. This procedure is likely to encourage other donors to do likewise for fear the United States will decide to pull out and leave them with an untenable burden. Similar reasoning prompted the institution of the "spring" mechanism for the International Development Association (IDA), which prevents IDA from using contributions from all donors until the U.S. contribution has been made. Insecurity about the availability of funding for long-range efforts also makes recipient countries reluctant to invest in the planning necessary for regional cooperation and real development. They are likely instead to continue undertaking any project which a donor agrees to fund, regardless of its rationality or the wider ramifications of its implementation. The world is full of examples of the negative ecological, health and economic results of this kind of procedure.

Freeman proposes multi-year appropriations that would cover the costs for the life of all projects starting in that particular year. Inflation and cost overruns might necessitate supplemental appropriations, but the U.S. commitment to foreign aid ventures would be less suspect. Especially important would be the positive signals emitted by this strategy to other donors. Indeed, in 1976, the U.S. authorization for the Sahel was a multi-year authorization. This kind of reassurance in no way implies that donor input will be taken for granted. On the contrary, it facilitates policy conditioning by the donor in sensitive areas like agriculture pricing policy and population growth since recipient governments are confident that they are not dealing with fly-by-night con-artists in the game for no more than an inning.

From the donor perspective there is no dearth of suspicions as well. Development becomes a negative-sum game and a developing area is inherently chaotic until proven stable. Donor policies rest on underpinnings of short-term political risk which may be amended if the prospects are good for programs with more extended time horizons. Length of commitment becomes a key indicator of the firmness of that commitment. However, only after both recipient and donor demonstrate that they are like-minded can the kind of chemistry requisite for a successful development outcome evolve. With enhanced coordination, the probability is good that duplication will be minimized -- a sore spot in the history of development assistance.

By the same token, lively, albeit corrosively cynical, arguments are put forward decrying a bureaucratic vested interest in securing the longevity of foreign aid programs by exaggerating crisis dimensions so as to effectuate a good-doer full-employment plan. According to James Q. Wilson, crises, no matter how small, are very exploitable vehicles for bureaucrats who would build empires: "...any crisis must be solved; if it must be solved, then it can be solved -- and creating a new organization is the way to do it." However, the focusing function of crisis should not be deprecated. Despite a penumbra of uncertainty, for that is the character of the decision problems being confronted, governments are expected to bear up to more proximate time horizons for action. Most important, the government's record-keeping process encodes new entries which, as the Sahel illustrates, set a long-term chain of responses in motion. A new set of behavior rules, i.e., standard operating procedures, are learned enhancing government capacity to act in the future. The arousal of bureaucracy is of course symptomatic of a wider shift in common perception. In essence, a new mood is generated, and mood politics begins to hold paradigmatic sway. The interlocking of the many factors that contribute to a new mood defies crisp analysis. However, particularly in the penetration of administrative structures, the mobilization of political resources not controlled by regular participants in the political process appears to be critical.

Nongovernmental organizations (NGOs) have played a key role in sustaining the prominence of Sahelian development as an issue. By seeing the pattern of recurring droughts as an international problem requiring remedial measures, NGOs spearheaded the crucial business of constituency creation. A recruitment process was initiated to sensitize people on the periphery. With a critical mass of organizational support, a growing network of organizations marshalled resources, issued timely status reports, and generally countered apathy in the developed world. As this network contributed to a new mood that inexorably seeped into the worldviews of individual governments, the establishment of new action channels historically deemed expensive in terms of political capital no longer seemed too costly. The inception of a new mood, intangible in substantive terms as it may be, must be seen and evaluated at this time for what it is.

The Sahel Development Program embodies this new mood. Formulated with the recognition that the enormity of the challenge calls for long-term programming, the strategy is bifurcate:

Priority I: Activities directed at improving the capacity and productivity of existing resources such as manpower and agricultural lands, planning for the development of the river basins, and improving the health, education, and nutritional status of the population in the near term.

Priority II: Activities aimed at achieving self-sustaining growth by the year 2000 which in addition to expanding Priority I objectives will focus on phased river basin development, completion of major transport links, expanded capacity for the export of livestock and agricultural products, and growth of light industry.

This division is sound and what bones critics have to chew with the overall strategy pertain to the need for a relevant radicalism within the framework of the present conception. However, comparative assessments of development assistance strategies are valuable, and the Sahel must be carefully considered. From the recipient perspective, evaluation may not seem necessary since the donors are friends and what they give seems free. Robert Klitgaard asks: "Why look a gift horse in the mouth?" From the donor perspective, evaluation can often degenerate into an exercise in futility. Albert O. Hirschman observes:

> . . . [T]he project analyst ... cannot even pretend to classify uniformly, for purposes of decision making, the various properties and probable lines of behavior of projects, as either advantages or drawbacks, benefits or costs, assets or liabilities ... Upon inspection, each project turns out to represent a unique constellation of experiences and consequences, of direct and indirect effects.

A 1979 report to the Congress issued by the General Accounting Office quaintly depicts the Sahelian context for these "unique constellations":

> The magnitude of AID project managers' tasks is enormous. They are to manage the transfer of technical assistance -- new knowledge and technology -- to the Sahel people. Yet many Sahel people are poorly educated and are oriented to tribal customs not all AID development programers fully understand. They live in harsh environments endemic to crippling and even killing diseases, having little or no means of outside communication. Achieving significant program objectives quickly is extremely difficult when these environmental problems are coupled with such other project implementation difficulties as the (1) Sahel Governments' inability to

> adequately support project goals, (2) slow arrival of equipment, supplies, and technical expertise, and (3) ineffective use of the AID project evaluation system.

A $70 profit, a new plow, a few more hectares added to a farmer's field -- these are some early signs that the Sahel Development Program is already touching, and improving, the lives of poor Sahelian villagers. But they are just signs -- superficial, short-term phenomena -- that cannot be used to measure the overall success of projects and the large, long-term development effort being carried out by AID and other donors. The simple fact that a farmer grows a new variety of millet is not a definitive benchmark of success, particularly if it does not improve his diet and his income or, is not cost-effective, and fails to encourage him to adopt the new farming techniques required to grow the millet.

Hirschman has posited that the art of promoting development may consist primarily in multiplying the opportunities to engage in "dissonance-arousing actions and in inducing an initial commitment to them." Indeed, there is need to go one step further and involve the target group in the actual process of development planning. This can come about once development agencies cease to be preoccupied with building economic models that are impervious to social and political dimensions of development. The bulk of historical evidence suggests that there is little possibility of escaping actions taken in these realms. Often, donors seem to be inadequately concerned with introducing fundamental processes of decision that characterize a democratic society, namely decision by impartial policymakers and by the vote of representative bodies. Plainly, the conception of economic development as a unidirectional assertion of control over human behavior is not a view congenial to political construction in the parliamentary mode. By the same token, it is difficult enough to make development more democratic and to bring about desired attitudinal shifts much less to evaluate them.

Why evaluate in the first place? To get a better handle on the ratio between outputs and inputs, i.e., productivity and efficiency, is the standard response. The commonly overlooked danger is that too much scrutiny can have the opposite effect of what is intended. As I have written elsewhere, on a more general level: "By effectively demystifying nature, the science-centered conceptual system enables the individual to see, with what amounts to a sort of x-ray vision, the full dimensions of the problems confronting his society. This gloomy scenario hardly suggests the emergence of an activist epistemology ..." A diagnosis that magnifies the warts to the exclusion of everything else can extinguish precious reserves of enthusiasm. Georges Sorel simply vetoed what is today called project evaluation: "We should be especially careful," he said, "not to make any comparison between accomplished fact and the picture people had formed for themselves before the action." Moreover, in many developing countries technical evaluations are eclipsed by questions of political expediency and feasibility. Therefore, the premium must be on the prevalent mood and its political vitality. The wisdom of leaving some things unexposed hinges on a cost-benefit analysis that weighs positive mood erosion against efficient implementation. Frequently, some miscarriage in the development process will create a situation in which it is impossible to escape some compromise of positive mood, so that the essential task is to reduce the dimensions of that compromise. The need to minimize this trade-off is at the heart of my recommendations for closer collaboration among all parties to development programs. One Sahelian official emphasized: "It is evident that solutions arrived at jointly have much more chance of being accepted and applied by the parties concerned than solutions presented as prescriptions." This cooperation is currently taking place in the Sahel between administrators and experts with Sahelian, European, and North American backgrounds. It has come to characterize the approach to long-range planning and programming for and commitments to a unique development program.

Analysis of the many complex factors in this unfolding venture provide not only a stimulating challenge to the social sciences, but also a compelling invitation to greater interdisciplinary cooperation. In pursuing an interactional theory of development, one of the critical challenges is to seek the appropriate frameworks within which to view "material phenomenally disparate in such a way that its very disparateness leads us into a deeper understanding of it." Thus, there is an internal logic to examining the Sahel for its own sake. As Hirschman has reminded us on many occasions, the social sciences are sufficiently capacious for a type of endeavor unrelated to the search for regularities, i.e., model building. Gunnar Myrdal sets the example for disciplinary eclecticism which guides the present effort when he states: "It will mean that the problem itself will be allowed to determine the discussion, without regard to the limitations of specific methods of a particular discipline." I quote gratuitously his qualifying comment: "It is more difficult to do this competently than to keep within one of our established social science disciplines; the difficulty may warrant a greater degree of indulgence to shortcomings."

Perhaps the greatest frustrations attendant to an endeavor of the sort undertaken here stem from the drive to maximize depth of treatment in addition to breadth. My concern has been to achieve coherence without sacrificing nuance. The words of a Peace Corps administrator working in the Sahel come to mind:

> Most of the stories I read about the drought were sensationalism. It was dis-

> couraging because the development problems are so complex and subtle, and all of a sudden you couldn't turn around without bumping into somebody who wanted pictures of people eating sand or of dead cattle. Time published a photo of a woman in a tree picking leaves and captioned it as if this was what she was reduced to eating because of the drought. In fact, people eat the leaves anyway and cook special sauces to go with them.

A story on the Sahel in the Chicago Tribune opens with a catchy if stretched image of Tuareg pastoralists spending their days searching the semiarid countryside north of Niamey, Niger, for anthills that might contain grain stocks. "The anthills were virtually the only food supply left for the Tuaregs, and they were running out of anthills to raid." Perhaps this is the only way to draw attention to the Sahelians' plight. However, sometimes even the most vivid portrayal of tragedy is unconvincing. When an AID official unveiled a major development proposal for a "Sahel Development Investment Fund" before the African Studies Association in San Francisco a few years ago, one sceptic scoffed that the proposal was the brainstorm of desperate AID employees afraid of losing their jobs. In his words: "A lot of Viet Nam AID people are showing up here now with big plans of expanding programs in the Sahel. AID has had to cut back a lot since the end of the war, and now the Sahel is giving them a chance to come back." Of course, much more is involved in the Sahel than a full-employment plan for AID workers.

At a time when the world around us is increasingly specialized and, hence, fragmented, there is an overwhelming need to see things whole. The fragmentation that often seems to characterize matters developmental has impeded concerned parties from addressing comprehensively the diverse but intertwined dimensions of integrated development. The crisis in the Sahel illustrates powerfully the dangers that inhere in economic development efforts that fail to acknowledge the interconnectedness of the many variables that form the whole. The introduction of vastly improved veterinary practices must be accompanied by an overhauling of livestock production systems if the increase in animal population is to be compatible with ecological equilibrium.

Sahelian governments have elected to play it safe this time around by viewing their development efforts in "horizontal" as well as "vertical" terms. For example, increased food production is a vertical function of the irrigated and dryland agriculture sector. Its horizontal functions -- outcomes manifested in other sectors -- might include better nutrition, increased resistance to disease, increased cash flow, improved marketing, and better water retention of the soil. A reservoir built for irrigation may also serve as a watering-hole for cattle, or, if appropriate, a source of drinking water for human beings; these are among its horizontal functions. The complementary aspects of these horizontal functions as they overlap among sectors can be identified and incorporated into project designs. While not a cure-all, this is a crucial strategy to combat fragmentation. To marshal the latent energies of those who would improve their lot, development architects must front numerous and intimate details of social ambience, and they must empathize with the aspirations of communities rarely monolithic. In a somewhat different, but apposite, context, Napoleon would boast with little exaggeration: "I make my plans with the dreams of my sleeping soldiers."

The attempt to find new ways to resolve the competing claims of modernity and tradition, of strong government and individual liberty, of national unity and group autonomy, and of social justice and economic growth, is an overarching challenge of our times. Societies the world over face a new synthesis of an uncertain kind. In this task of transformation, there is no room for self-imposed parochialism. Isolationism -- the desire to leave alone and to be left alone -- imperils Western as well as Third World capacity to cope with those problems that only the human species as a whole can hope to solve. The concatenated variables that compose the spectrum of integrated development will preoccupy not only Sahelians, and new political systems and ideologies will emerge. But these systems will continue to have in common, sometimes for appearance's sake -- so strong is the pressure to conform -- the conceptually ambiguous goal of modernization. In developing therapies of modernization, all peoples can truly collaborate as equals, in combining research, resources, and action. It is becoming increasingly difficult for mankind to shirk the central feature of the normative challenge proposed by Richard Falk: "an acceptance of human solidarity and all of its implications."

Malleable, syncretistic, and above all, tentative, the Sahel's socioeconomic development has left the author little choice but to attempt to detect reason in all claims in the conflict of social change and to recognize the particular legitimacy of each. The author would be less than candid, however, if he did not acknowledge his bias for economic growth, which is also a bias for hope in the struggle to enhance human welfare in developing areas of the world. To present yet again the case for economic growth would be tautologous and sadly ineloquent in the distinguished company of scholars and practitioners who have delineated this strategic assumption on many occasions. Suffice it to say that economic growth is especially germane to the Sahel, for it can give the inhabitants of this perenially drought-stricken region greater control over their environment and thereby increase their range of choice.

We cannot know why the world suffers. But we can know how the world decides that suffering shall come to some persons and not to others. While the world permits sufferers to be chosen, something beyond their agony is earned, something even beyond the satisfaction of the world's needs and desires. For it is in the choosing that enduring societies preserve or destroy those values that suffering and necessity expose. In this way societies are defined, for it is by the values that are foregone no less than by those that are preserved at tremendous cost that we know a society's character.

--Guido Calabresi and Philip Bobbit,
Tragic Choices

Human-reality everywhere encounters resistance and obstacles which it has not created, but these resistances and obstacles have meaning only in and through the free choice which human-reality is.

--Jean-Paul Sartre,
The Transcendence of Ego

Crisis in the Sahel

1
The Sahel: Breadbasket or Basket Case?

The growing literature on the Sahel abounds with extensive discussions centering on the fragility of the Sahelian eco-system, the region's abject poverty, and the plethora of "constraints" to economic development. Presentations of this kind of material are well-grounded in fact, but there is more to the economies of the Sahel than rehearsals of disheartening statistics would suggest. Even now the Sahelian economies show evidence of progress in amending structural impediments within their economies and in mobilizing more domestic resources for development purposes. While the problems associated with food production are genuinely formidable, other sectors of the Sahelian economies have expanded and diversified even during the traumatic period of the early 1970s.

John W. Sewell writes in The New York Times:

> An American visiting the Sahel -- the sub-Saharan region of West Africa -- for the first time carries the mental images of the great drought: barren land and emaciated children. It comes as a shock when reality does not match the image. The Sahel has survived its worst drought in fifty years, and the region's prospects are promising if the countries of the area and the industrial world make the necessary commitments. Only a few short years ago, many people maintained that the area was beyong hope and should be abandoned. Why the difference now? The answer is that under the impact of catastrophic drought most of us forgot that the Sahel countries are not entirely without resources of their own.[1]

A frequent misconception underpinning the gloomier scenarios of economic stagnation and ecological collapse derives from the characterization of the Sahel as "underdeveloped" when it is, in fact, largely "undeveloped." In the present state of knowledge, such features of global morphology as the polar caps and the great deserts are not properly to be regarded as underdeveloped areas unless that term is to be used synonymously with undeveloped. The very meaning of the nomenclature "Sahel" denotes "coast" in Arabic and, in effect, the arid band between 11 degrees and 24 degrees North latitude across the African continent from the Atlantic Ocean eastward some 2,600 miles constitutes the southern shore of the Sahara Desert. This is not to say that the Sahel should be relegated to the category of "empty spaces," which it is not in anyone's interest to have filled. On the contrary, the Sahel's 28 million inhabitants prove the region to be habitable. What the human condition indicates, however, is that without special measures economic productivity will continue to falter, and the prospect that it will ever attain Western levels will grow increasingly remote.

The majority of Sahelian peoples are compressed into three ecological zones which "in toto" are approximately 200 miles wide. The Sahara presses from the North and in the South such diseases as onchocerciasis (river blindness) and trypanosomiasis (sleeping sickness) deny use of the richest arable land in the Guinean zone. The disease barriers limit the population to areas of thin soils of mediocre fertility, which are cultivated with implements and techniques that have not changed significantly since pastoralism was abandoned at some unknown epoch in prehistory. In a labor-intensive agricultural system, each adult typically suffers two major debilitating diseases per lifetime. The agricultural food output of the Sahel is 8.5 tons per year, yielding considerably less than 2,000 calories of food per day to people who earn their livelihood from physical labor.

Gauged by Western standards, the absolute level of economic welfare seems so abysmally low that it is hard to imagine that anything really encouraging can be taking place. Nonetheless, the standard of living in the Sahel is much understated by ordinary statistics. National income statistics cannot easily register the value of unbought services since these do not leave tangible traces in accounting records. The textbook instance is that national income falls when a man marries his housekeeper, and rises when instead of shaving himself he goes to a barber. But in Sahelian villages, householders build their own adobe huts and entertain one another with song and dance without buying the services of theatrical performers with the exception of a wandering "griot" every now and then. They live in a tropical climate that -- albeit stifling to the sensibilities of the uninitiated -- does not require prodigious energy consumption to simply sustain life. Large blocks of leisure time make life more eupeptic, less harried, and ephemeral.

When one views the Sahel as an area whose inhabitants have an age-old habit of helping themselves, who have been making considerable progress in the face of great adversity, and who (just as they are, even without further education and better health) have much greater productive capacities than are presently being tapped, there is room for optimism about the prospects for economic development. Given this perspective, however, it is plain that development's top priorities must be reserved for programs that promise directly and fairly quickly to expand physical production -- agricultural and otherwise. From the beginning, some improvements in education, health, and general wellbeing must go hand in hand with the expansion of commodity output. But in the longer run the adequacy of these public service programs (and their effectiveness in stimulating new gains in productivity in the still longer run) will depend upon the size and strength of the local economic base that has been built under them.

It has been observed that the fundamental problem of development is "not to create wealth itself but to create the capacity to create wealth."[2] Given that capacity, major disasters and long depressions will interrupt, but not essentially interfere with, cumulative growth. Infrastructure, the framework for systematic and concentrated activities creating investment opportunities, is strategic in the development process. Once a developing country has acquired this capacity to produce wealth, it can cope with economic and socio-political challenges, i.e., it can react with an adequate response. Hence, there will be a tendency for a middle-income country to begin closing the gap with more advanced countries. But where this underlying capacity to create wealth is missing, neither economic challenges nor economic windfalls create the kind of response which will lead to a closing of the gap.

Many low-end developing countries have characteristics similar to those in the Sahel -- they are landlocked, are not rich in natural resources, and are exposed to harsh environmental conditions. Above all, they are linked in development experience by a common denominator of woefully inadequate infrastructure. While the Sahel presents a demographic patchwork which often defies generalization, more than anywhere else, the map of economic development is still "tabula rasa." Herein lies a singular challenge to design and implement a development program which provides for short-term emergencies and long-term contingencies, that addresses a wide range of urgent, cross-cutting issues, and whose development implications may be transferable to the Afghanistans and the Bolivias.

At a time when the concept of limits to growth has become an increasingly central feature of Western ethos, a reassessment of so-called "marginal areas" is long overdue. Sub-Saharan Africa, with only 50 percent of its suitable farm land currently being used, could play an important role in meeting future worldwide food requirements. The Sahel, with only one-fourth of its arable land cultivated (partly because of the threat of disease in the more fertile areas), could be transformed into a greenhouse since it stradles ecological zones that permit two, three, and even four crops a year. There are tremendous potentialities in the region's major water-drainage systems (Niger, Senegal and Lake Chad) but there is presently little water management. Less than one percent of the Sahel's arable land is irrigated.[3] Methods to predict patterns of staple crop yield and to adapt crop strains to Sahelian conditions have not been attempted. In an average year, the odds are 40 percent that a Sahelian farmer will have a poor crop and 20 percent that his crop will fail. Transportation and marketing systems, which could permit mutual support within the region, are among the most rudimentary in the world.

While most visitors to the Sahel are immediately struck by the infectious optimism that pervades the ranks of both recipient and donor institutions involved in the business of realizing the Sahel's potential, there are a goodly number of pessimistic observers and defeatist participants. A drought follow-up article that appeared in The Economist observes despairingly: "Experience since 1975 has shown that no grand design is going to transform the marginal savannah lands of the sub-Sahara. Modifying the climate, growing a "green wall" of trees across the desert or piping desalinated water from the sea all belong to the realms of science fiction. The land is going to remain inhospitable and the only people capable of exploiting its natural resources are pastoral nomads."[4] Undeveloped, the Sahel might qualify as a basket case; developed, it could become a breadbasket. This is the unambiguous conclusion arrived at by a series of studies commissioned by development assistance organizations.[5] These studies posit that the means are available to overcome the primary problems and that the Sahel could achieve food self-sufficiency and sustained economic growth within the next 15-25 years. The studies also agree that the piece-meal, short-term, and uncoordinated development efforts of the past cannot achieve Sahelian development objectives. Rather, it is necessary to undertake coordinated, comprehensive, long-term, regionally integrated planning if development action is to have an impact sufficient to overcome the multiplicity of constraints.

DROUGHT AS A DEUS EX MACHINA

American awareness of the Sahel greatly expanded as a result of the drought and subsequent famine that threatened the region with permanent economic retardation in the years 1968-1974. By 1972, the decline in rainfall had blighted all but a fraction of the region's two million square miles (approximately two-thirds of the area of the continental United States); 25 million people faced starvation and malnutrition, disease, and social disruption. The suffering of these hardy people gained the world's compassion. A massive relief effort was mounted and carried through the end of the drought in 1974. Donor participation at the crescendo of this humanitarian symphony included innumerable private, government, and international assistance organizations; many donor countries who had no African aid field presence, such as the Netherlands, Germany, Belgium, Japan, and the OPEC states were induced to participate as well. Although the cost of the drought relief was staggering, a monumental human disaster was averted. Even so, drought-sustained damage was catastrophic. The Center for Disease Control in Atlanta, Georgia, undertook a nutritional survey in 1973 which estimated that as many as 100,000 may have perished.[6] The cattle and farms on which much of the economy and social structure rest were devastated and whole populations were displaced.

The Sahel has experienced multi-year droughts before. A severe one occurred 50 years ago, and there have been periodic droughts since. However, the great drought of 1968-1974 may well have been the worst in recorded history due to a confluence of events. During the last 20 years, human and livestock populations had grown greatly, straining the region's limited resources. Levels of agricultural productivity had fallen, prompting farmers to extend cultivation into more and more marginal lands to meet the demand of an increasing population. The encroaching Sahara had overrun an estimated quarter of a million square miles of arable land in the past 50 years[7] Thus, the drought only accelerated the deterioration of the eco-system and the physical resources upon which the people depended. As reserves of grain, including seed stocks, were exhausted, thousands of refugees congregated in urban centers, overtaxing facilities, and adding the region's cities to the list of drought victims.

Procedures for rendering emergency assistance to the Sahel during the drought forcefully illustrated the region's weaknesses. With staple foods chockablock on the wharves of West African coastal ports, the problem was inland transportation. The limited railroads could not move the food on a timely basis. River transport had not yet evolved a capacity adequate for the food shopments involved. With few paved roads and barely perceptible tracks leading to the outlying distribution points where pastoralists congregate, timely transport was further impeded by few trucks, and problems of their maintenance. Even in the principal cities of the interior, lack of storage facilities precluded the accumulation of depots for long-term distribution. Airlifts were needed and provided by several donors -- with the U.S. Air Force carrying out sorties in Mali, Chad, and Mauritania.

The drought highlighted the ineffectiveness of the present agricultural production framework. Despite infusions of foreign aid in the past, the ability of the Sahel to produce food has been declining and its vulnerability to the vagaries of nature is growing. The scope of traditional foreign aid efforts did not adequately address this vulnerability. Although many laudable development projects were inaugurated after the majority of Sahelian countries received their independence from France in 1960, the benefits accruing from these projects have proved incapable of reversing the process of deterioration which precipitated the most recent crisis. With the cost of aid growing, should there be another crippling drought, it has been estimated that a relief effort comparable to the one carried out in 1968-1974 would cost the international community $3 billion by 1985.[8]

Aside from the direct loss of production and capital by farmers and herdsmen, the drought also resulted in decreased foreign exchange earnings from exports, increased demand for food imports, decreased tax revenues due to the decline in production, increased demand for government expenditures for famine relief, and decreased savings as people try to maintain their consumption standards at the same time that their incomes are reduced. Some indication of the magnitude of these effects can be seen from the percentage changes from 1972 to 1973 shown in Table 1. The loss of production of about 15 to 20 percent in the agricultural sector was very severe for people who are already very poor and who had already suffered a previous drop in production from 1971 to 1973. This average hides, moreover, important disparities between regions which resulted in some people losing virtually everything. In sum, there was extensive human suffering and loss of life.[9] Indeed, it would be impossible to assess the full extent of damage inflicted by the drought. There may also have been significant psychological damage to some children because of malnutrition during this period, which could have an effect on their future well-being and productivity.[10] Finally, declines in the size of livestock herds and changes in their age/sex composition resulting from the drought will affect production of meat and milk for many years.

There were important indirect economic effects as well. Although government revenue actually decreased only in Chad, as seen in Table 1, the rate of increase for the other countries was generally less than it had been in previous years. In addition inflation accelerated to about 10-15 percent per year and, thus, the real value of this revenue tended to decline. At the same time, current government expenditures, except for Senegal, grew more rapidly from 1972 to 1973 than did receipts, exacerbating the problem of budget deficits, especially in Chad and Mali. Furthermore, the rise in government salaries was greater than that of materials and supplies, indicating some decline in government effectiveness. With respect to exports, the drought had a decidedly depressing effect, considering that quantity declines, due to yield losses in some areas of 30 to 40 percent, were offset by commodity

TABLE 1

EFFECTS OF DROUGHT

	Chad	Mali	Mauri-tania	Niger	Sene-gal	Upper Volta
Change in real output 1972-73 (%)						
GDP	n.a.	-6	+1	n.a.	-19	-9
Agriculture	n.a	-21	-13	n.a	-20	-16
Change in government revenue 1972-1973 (%)	-13	+9	+10	-	+9	+11
Change in current government expenditures 1972-73 (%)	+2	+10	+33	+9	+8	+16
Change in value of exports in 1972-73 (%)	-6	_11	n.a.	+1	-19	n.a.
Change in current account surplus as a percentage of imports						
1972-73	+22	-5	+7	n.a.	-11	+3
1973-74	-22	-35	-5	n.a.	+14	-45

SOURCE: Elliot Berg, The Recent Economic Evolution of the Sahel, Center for Research on Economic Development, University of Michigan, June 1975.

price increases on the world market and that the expansion of non-agricultural exports, such as phosphate in Senegal and iron ore in Mauritania, helped offset the decrease in agricultural exports. With expanded demand for food imports, there was a sharp deterioration in most countries' balance of trade. Although the change in current account balance was positive for some countries and negative for others from 1972 to 1973, it was negative for all but Senegal from 1973 to 1974. The deterioration in this balance was especially severe for Mali and Upper Volta. The effects on current account were offset somewhat, however, by debt cancellation and relief and by external emergency assistance of various sorts.

One source of instability in foreign exchange earnings became especially apparent during the drought: concentration of exports on a few primary commodities. Senegal and Mauritania had the advantage of having minerals in addition to agricultural products or livestock as major exports. Though this did not directly benefit people outside the mining sector, it gave the governments additional access to public revenue and foreign exchange to help cope with the emergency. Upper Volta was also aided by substantial remittances from its workers in the coastal countries. All the Sahelian countries, however, have at least 50 percent of their exports concentrated in no more than two commodities. As a result they are vulnerable to fluctuations in world market prices as well as weather conditions at home.

In comparison with past droughts of similar magnitude, especially that of 1913-1914, the region seemed better able to protect itself in 1968-1974. Whereas loss of livestock and shortfalls of crop production were very severe in some areas, this was partially due to the period of abundant rainfall during the 1950s and early 1960s which encouraged people to settle in normally drier areas and which allowed the livestock population to expand to the limits of the carrying capacity of the rangeland, a phenomenon which was also aided by improvements in animal health care and by water development. Human mortality was reduced during the drought, however, because "better roads, greater commercialization of the whole region, more awareness of what was happening assisted by modern communication and administration, national governments, and massive international relief efforts all helped the people's own efforts and reduced a potentially murderous period into a very painful one."[11]

A fairly persuasive argument can be made for the catalytic role of drought on the development plane. Calamity is an important concomitant of reform if for no other reason than the need for immediate action in the face of more proximate time horizons. It has been remarked that "crisis concentrates attention," and it is not infrequent that some problems fail in ordinary times to be addressed effectively, not for lack of knowledge, but simply for lack of attention. Albert O. Hirschman posits: "Crisis may stimulate action and hence learning on a problem on which insight has been low and which for that very reason has not been tackled as long as it was in a quiescent state."[12] The basic proposition of The Strategy of Economic Development is that "development depends not so much on finding optimal combinations for given resources and factors of production as on calling forth and enlisting for development purposes resources and abilities that are hidden, scattered or badly utilized."[13]

Perhaps the most productive aspect of crisis is explicitly destructive. Partial crises can be accommodated with little or no innovation by man's capacity to adapt -- even at a cost to the human condition. Wholesale damage and persistant environmental pressure on the scale of the Sahelian drought, on the other hand, entail a radical undermining of living standards which could lead to counterpressures, i.e., fundamentally new activities designed to restore the traditional living standards of the community. These activities undertaken by the community to resist extensive erosion of its living standards can result in a greater ability to organize for development and, ultimately, to exploit opportunities for economic growth that existed previously but were left unutilized.

Of the many psychological hurdles that punctuate the development process, inhibition to change is one of the most obstructive. Crisis, in the Darwinian sense, is a ruthless challenge to the "status quo." People either drown or learn to swim. Such trials can result in the awareness that encounters with the unexpected lead not solely to frustration but to new understanding and to a perception that the environment can be managed. When a community acquires this conceptual handle on the world at large, the prospect of resolving a dilemma is attractive; problems are grappled headlong rather than evaded; and a growing array of "modi operandi" for addressing problems may evolve.

DETERMINANTS OF THE U.S. RESPONSE TO THE SAHELIAN CRISIS

By October 1972 the governments of the Sahelian countries realized that their people were facing a widespread crop failure. A clear message had been relayed to the authorities when in January of that year grain storehouses in Bamako, Mali, came under attack by hungry urban mobs. Most of the Sahelian countries made requests for external assistance bilaterally. Mauritania, however asked the World Food Program (WFP) to coordinate whatever assistance might be available. In neighboring Chad some technocrats were aware that a crop failure occurred, but the leadership initially refused to admit the problem existed.

Appeals for assistance, when the proportions of the situation became indisputably evident, were backed by weak supporting data. Some countries, moreover, were careless in pleading their cases. A credibility crisis ensued when Chad finally made its request for aid, which amounted to 100 kilos of grain per person for the entire population. This failure by the Sahelians to come to grips with specificity was compounded by donor misreadings of the situation. For instance, the French, who maintain a strong presence in the Sahel, failed for some time to appreciate the extent of the problem, which they assessed as another of the recurrent misfortunes Sahelians have had to endure with some belt tightening. U.S. ability to undertake independent verification of the magnitude of the threat was hampered by implementation of the Korry Report recommendations in the late 1960s providing "inter alia" for the withdrawal of regular AID staffs from all Sahelian capitals except Dakar and Niamey.[14] Reports by some State Department officials were discounted in Washington where, since the Korry Report, skepticism had developed "vis-a-vis" special pleas from U.S. Ambassadors trying to end run restrictions on U.S. bilateral assistance. Hesitation in Washington to indulge U.S. embassies with politically potent but expensive forms of aid, e.g., airlifts in U.S. military transports, derived too from awareness that two-thirds of the disaster relief funds available for fiscal year 1973 already had been taken for use in Vietnam.

Although individual Sahelian Ambassadors accredited to Washington, in particular the Nigerienne envoy, made repeated requests for more aid to their countries, they were generally even more poorly informed than their home offices about the dimensions of the impending crisis. With the exception of a few joint public appearances, the Sahelian envoys who attempted to enlist support for greater U.S. assistance preferred to act individually. By November 1972 their efforts contributed in part to the formation of a Drought Emergency Task Force composed of representatives of AID, the State Department, and the Department of Agriculture. That same month a memorandum calling attention to the need for a major international effort to resolve the Sahel's chronic dependence on foreign succor was transmitted to then Secretary of State William Rogers. In addition to recommending shipment of additional grain to the Sahel, the Task Force sought to stimulate the interest of the United Nations Food and Agriculture Organization (FAO) in playing a key role in coordinating assistance to the Sahel.

Initial FAO involvment has been described as follows:

> Although it also took time for the FAO to realize the seriousness of the drought, an FAO working group was created in February 1973, and within the FAO the WFP both forecast a deficit greater than commonly expected and identified the Sahel's rudimentary transport infrastructure as the principal bottleneck to the distribution of relief supplied in time to avoid starvation. The relationship between the U.S. and the FAO was highly interactive during the Spring, with AID officials

> suggesting FAO should be focusing more attention on the problems and subsequent FAO statements calling attention to the situation. These statements then were used by AID to stimulate greater interest within the Administration and Congress.[15]

By the end of 1973, State and AID officials could cite the pleas of the Sahelian countries and the FAO, as well as the emergency relief operations initiated by several other donor countries, in requesting approval to ship an additional 100,000 tons of grain. The October visit of Upper Volta's President Lamizana to the White House helped dramatize the crisis, and confirmed for the Sahelians their suspicion that with foreign aid, when it finally rains, it pours.

For most Americans, the discovery of the Sahelian crisis began as a media event with press and television coverage driving home the magnitude of Sahelian needs. With its sympathetic coverage of the drought, the media became the core of a pro-assistance constituency. This did not come about overnight. After an initial article of December 3, 1972, The New York Times neglected the Sahel until May 13. For The Washington Post, the hiatus was between January 20 and May 16. During these peak months of the drought, AID, the only other practical source of information on the Sahel in Washington,made no press releases on the conditions prevailing in the drought-ravaged countries. It was not until the following year that details of the crisis began to make their way into print. By June-July 1973, media coverage of the Sahel neared the saturation point. The New York Times carried five stories on the Sahel in May, eight in June, and nine in July. In The Washington Post, there was a single article in May, but seven in June and ten in July. Most of these stories (34 out of the total of 40) reported on actual or threatened human suffering as a result of the drought; 13 contained reports that up to six million people might die from starvation; and 12 advocated or reported advocacy by other sources of greater economic aid to the region. These stories were picked up by newspapers throughout the country. Soon a high volume of mail to government officials evinced public support for expanded assistance to the region. AID reported receiving 300 letters per day at one point, and much of the correspondence was believed to come from Black Americans. Some of the Sahel mail was addressed to the Secretary of State and the volume was sufficient to be reported to him in the "Weekly Report of Correspondence" prepared by his office. The first of these reports which listed mail on the Sahel famine was the report for July 2-6, 1973.

The influence of a network of concerned non-governmental organizations cannot be minimized. By July 1973, American Friends Service, Care, Catholic Relief Services, Church World Service, the Red Cross, Africare, and other agencies were active in soliciting funds from private and/or government sources, including efforts to pry more resources from AID to be funneled through their own relief programs in the Sahel. Black American groups comprised another major element in the Sahel constituency. In addition to Africare, which concentrates on relief and development projects in West Africa,and among the most significant Black groups working for more aid to the Sahel, is R.A.I.N.S. (Relief for Africans in Need in the Sahel), a coalition group which formed in mid-1973 out of 18 existing Black organizations. In his "Report to the President" of both August 10, 1973 and September 27th, Maurice Williams (the "President's Special Coordinator for Emergency Relief to Sub-Saharan Africa") cited the activities of these organizations, particularly those of Black groups as evidence of "increasing public concern in the United States" for aiding the victims of the Sahel disaster.[16]

Soon AID adopted an advocacy role. It became AID policy to stimulate concern about the Sahel and also to cultivate support in Congress. For example, in June 1973, AID's Assistant Administrator for Africa, Samuel Adams, worked with staff assistants to Hubert H. Humphrey, Charles C. Diggs, Jr., and other interested Congressmen to help develop a $30 million aid authorization for the Sahel, which Humphrey and Diggs introduced in their respective chambers of Congress in July. AID formally endorsed this authorization request in a memorandum of July 17. The same memo supported the principle of long-term assistance to the Sahel, and by early August the Agency was lobbying the White House and the public for substantial assistance in the immediate post-crisis or "Rehabilitation and Recovery" period.

FITTING THE SAHEL INTO THE U.S. FOREIGN POLICY FRAMEWORK AND AN AFRICAN POLICY

Foreign economic assistance is rendered for a variety of reasons, including East-West rivalry, international leadership, political impact, special relationships with former colonies or deputized allies, domestic and international economic interest -- the relative weight of these considerations changing measurably over time with each country and region. John P. Lewis has observed:

> American anxieties since World War II have skipped fleetingly from country to country and continent to continent -- from Greece and Turkey to Western Europe to Iran to Korea to Vietnam to Formosa, Quemoy, and Matsu to the Near East to Hungry and Poland to India and Pakistan to Cuba to the Congo and Subsaharan Africa to Algiers and Northern Africa to Berlin to Laos and Vietnam to Latin America to Western Europe and back again -- usually at the beck of some new (or renewed), immediate, and demanding crisis. [17]

This skimble-scamble approach to external assistance ignores quiet crises until they erupt and take their toll in violence, deprivation and human misery. Innoculations of aid at the height of crises are costly and since men cannot be immunized from economic want, this nonpolicy is increasingly on a trajectory out of the orbit of plausibility.

For several decades ecologists and range specialists issued warnings to little avail about the growing pressures being placed on delicate arid environments like the Sahel, but their perception did not penetrate very deeply into the priorities and working programs of governments and development agencies. According to some specialists, the number of grazing animals maintained in the Sahel by 1972, as the drought reached its culmination, approached double what the area's ranges could sustain without damage. At the intellectual level, at least, the tragedy of the Sahel has had a catalytic impact comparable to that of the American dust bowl of the 1930s. At the more pragmatic policymaking level of the development administrator, understanding of the extent and causes of desertification, however incomplete, is by now far too documented to be ignored. The 1977 United Nations Conference on Desertification deepened both the technical knowledge and the political awareness of this global challenge.

Aid to the Sahel must fulfill many functions. For the U.N. Secretary-General, Kurt Waldheim, who uttered the celebrated if slightly exaggerated words: "The encroachment of the desert threatens to wipe four or five African countries from the map," foreign aid must stave off the Sahara.[18] This popular, somewhat sensationalized perception of a tangibly receding front line must not translate into a geodic concern that focuses on the periphery at the expense of the vacuous center. In the first place, official aid to the Sahel is needed to fill gaps in economic and social infrastructure until it works with enough impetus to attract sufficient private investment. The expansion of public services such as power, transportation, communications, banking, credit and marketing facilities, technical and professional education, agricultural and administrative services exerts a powerful, if incalculable, multiplier effect on economic development. They expand a country's capacity to absorb capital profitably but until they are advanced to a certain point their profits are too slow to mature and too diffuse to attract much private investment. In addition to heavy local costs, large expenditure of foreign exchange on imported capital equipment and technical know-how is necessary to strengthen infrastructures, and, of their very nature, these are tasks mainly for the public sector.

This brings us to a second overriding reason for aid to the Sahel. Aid is needed to bridge the gap between the region's foreign exchange gain from foreign trade and private investment and the amount it needs to pay its foreign debts and achieve a reasonable rate of growth. This need is increasing; and if the flow is not maintained consistently, development grinds to a halt, the countries' own efforts are frustrated, and their political stability imperilled.

Important development and humanitarian objectives notwithstanding, the case for aid to the Sahel is neither essentially philanthropic nor is it as recipient opinion at times suspects--neo-colonialist; the argument revolves around enlightened self-interest arising from a multiplicity of mutual benefits to donor and recipient countries. U.S. participation in the development of the Sahel is an expression of increasing U.S. interest in Africa, an interest which can be expressed in very positive ways to the direct benefit of the continent's low-end poor.

The U.S. posture toward Africa, long disembodied and drifting with events, has in recent years become more focused. U.S. interest in Africa picked up shortly after the arrival of Soviet arms and Cuban forces in Angola in the fall of 1975. At the time, President Gerald Ford issued threats to Moscow to stop backing the Cubans or risk the collapse of detente. The threats failed but U.S. determination to eliminate superpower conflict from Africa hardened. In pursuit of this goal, the Ford Administration adopted a twin approach: brandishing a verbal stick at the Soviet Union and Cuba to deter future Angolas while giving new emphasis to calls for majority rule in southern Africa and economic development across the continent. The Carter Administration insisted early on that it recognized the great variety of political situations in Africa and that it would press for "a progressive transformation of South African society." After the second invasion of Zaire's Shaba province by Katangan exiles from Angola, the Carter Administration articulated U.S. objections in the strongest terms, treating the American people to a fiery display of verbal pyrotechnics even as it sought to seal Africa off from overall East-West competition. This verbal offensive was bolstered by attempts to explain what is at stake for the United States in Africa. Such an explanation is central to the question: "What are the requirements of American policy in Africa?" Moreover, we need to go one step further and ask how such a policy can be made more purposive. The failure to identify in specific terms U.S. interests in Africa has in part contributed to the lack of policy focus and a situation in which past administrations have shown concern not so much for Africa itself as for the outsiders and the outside consequences of events in Africa.

Overlooking economic, diplomatic, and cultural links and sticking with geopolitical concerns for holding the Soviets at bay, an historical review of U.S. policy shows a naive underestimation of African astuteness in choosing foreign bedfellows. In 1957, Vice President Richard Nixon visited Africa and came home sounding the warning that imminent independence for many African states might prove a breeding ground for Communism. This paternalistic attitude was overtaken by a policy of nonattention momentarily reversed when a crisis cropped up. Now the most natural way to get attention in this relationship is to cry wolf. Senegal's President Léopold Sédar Senghor detects not only a concerted attempt by the Soviets for hegemony over Africa, but in reverse progression of the Allied liberation of Nazi-dominated Europe, Senghor believes the Soviets are spearheading their advance from Europe and that their ultimate destination is North America. The invasion forces will be launched from West Africa this time, and the soft underbelly of the Western hemisphere is Latin America.[19] All the same, Senegal's neighbor, Guinea, once considered a Soviet outpost, has recently cut back drastically on the amount of Soviet naval and air activity it will permit to originate from its territory. The Soviets have also lost their base at Berbera on the Somali coast and are playing a tightrope act in Ethiopia since they have been reluctant to help do in the Eritrean separatists, who previously enjoyed their support. These Soviet setbacks are indicative of the fact that African countries have grown-up governments that can manage for themselves. Their ability to see through geopolitical designs, however, cuts both ways. This is why past U.S. policy was dysfunctional, indiscrete, and inopportune. It failed to establish and maintain American credibility. Needless to say, it did not escape the notice of African leaders that U.S. concern with their affairs coincided with Soviet adventurism. In short, the traditional U.S. attitude toward Africa has been myopic in its limited purpose. For instance, when former Secretary of State Henry A. Kissinger was abruptly asked hours outside of Accra not to visit Ghana, the cancellation was attributed to mythic "Soviet agitation" rather than Ghanian displeasure with American policy toward Africa.

To be more coherent, an Africa policy requires a strategy, at least in the loose sense of the term, a sense of priorities, and an appreciation of the interaction among the different dimensions of the relationship. Plainly, whatever Moscow's aims, the United States will be a major factor in Africa's future. African economies are inextricably bound to the United States and Western Europe as fluctuations in raw-material prices and oil have amply demonstrated in the past, Indeed, the 1973 quadrupling of oil prices dramatized the dire poverty of most African countries and portended their sinking into even deeper economic difficulties. On the diplomatic front, these two economic issues were beginning to forge desperate countries into diplomatic unity against the United States. This is certainly a relevant context in which to frame a more purposive policy toward Africa. It is in this climate of growing despair that foreign aid to Africa must be viewed.

The fallacy of dealing with aspects of the U.S.-African relationshop in isolation suggests that concern for integrated development should supersede attention to Soviet penetration. Such a strategy would have enormous preemptive value. Stressing development could have precisely the opposite impact on Africa described by Secretary of State Cyrus Vance in his July

1, 1977 St. Louis speech when he said: "If we try to impose American solutions for African problems, we may sow divisions among the Africans and undermine their ability to oppose efforts at domination by others."[20] The Sahel, therefore, should be perceived as a cornerstone of any Africa policy worthy of the designation. American participation in the Sahel's recovery is a direct response to the number one priority of Sahelian countries: their own economic development. This healthy preoccupation with national deficiencies has engendered much cooperation while obviating conflict in the region. In point of fact, fences have been mended where predrought relations were chilly, e.g., between Senegal and Mali and between Mali and Upper Volta.

At a time when great tensions are plaguing the African continent, foreign aid can contribute to political stability by encouraging regional integration, preempting cleavages such as those that have invited foreign involvement in southern Africa and in the Horn. This is not to say that the West does not have strategic interests in the Sahel. It should be noted that Niger's uranium deposits have had an alluring effect on the Peoples Republic of China. There are sizeable Chinese and Soviet presences in Mauritania, the Sahelian state most well-endowed with natural resources. Moreover, the Sahel's austral neighbor, Nigeria, has become the second-largest supplier of crude oil to the United States. In flexing its economic muscle, Nigeria has shown dogged persistence in advancing two foreign policy objectives "inter alia:" (1) majority rule in southern Africa, and (2) a sustained infusion of external assistance to Africa's poorest nations. The Soviets do not figure prominently in the Nigerian system of priorities. Niger's deposed President Hamani Diori observed: "For starving people, capitalist and marxist ideologies are like footprints of a flying bird."[21] Indeed, there is a danger that the United States may overestimate Soviet interest in the Sahel. In describing an international aid program for the Sahel "to roll back the desert," while on a six-nation tour of Africa in May 1976, Kissenger noted that the Soviet Union would not be excluded.[22] So far there have been no takers from the Communist bloc. To return to our earlier perspective,

> Even if all Communist organizations were wiped from the face of the earth, the very poverty of the underdeveloped countries would present a fundamental long-run threat to the security of rich countries, including especially the richest, now that the poor nations have become self-determinating and have acquired massive appetites for material improvement.[23]

This major dimension of international life has snowballed in prominence in recent years -- so much so that Rajni Kothari among other Third Worlders sees the fulcrum of world power shifting noticably from the East-West to the North-South axes.[24] These individuals point out that it is in the interest of the North to address inequities in the international system while it is still possible to make a peaceful transition to a more stable world order.

The U.S. economy has become intertwined with that of the developing countries, and we can expect this trend to continue. The United States presently exports more to the developing countries than to either the European Economic Community or Japan. Almost half of direct foreign investment by the United States in 1978 went to the developing countries. The United States is also dependent on some of these countries for the supply of certain crucial raw materials. However, interdependence with developing countries extends beyond such economic connections. Widespread poverty abroad can increasingly affect the quality of life in the United States. Looking to the end of this century, the National Academy of Sciences concludes that "unless the productivity of agriculture is increased in developing countries the United States may face higher costs of food production and higher food prices for consumers."[25] Some diseases which thrive where there is malnutrition and unsafe drinking water know no borders. A Brookings Institution study concludes: "As this planet shrinks, the U.S. interest in the use of the global commons must grow. The manner in which the ocean's resources and atmosphere are managed will have a profound effect on the quality of Americans' lives. The ability of many developing nations to collaborate in addressing these problems will be affected by the responsiveness of the wealthier nations to their critical internal problems."[26]

U.S. commitment in international fora to a new international economic system for the low-end poor has particular relevance to the Sahel. Here we have eight of the poorest and most rural countries in the world. Due to its vast resources, the United States plays an important leadership role in the international donor community. The Sahel provides a rare opportunity for drawing together a diverse array of donors including the Organization of Petroleum Exporting Countries (OPEC) with their considerable financial resources, the OECD countries, and Third World states in a common development objective. OPEC assistance to the Sahel increased nearly 45 percent between 1974 and 1979 (from $84 million to $120 million), an increase of considerable importance in view of the relatively limited interests of the major oil producing countries in the Sahel. The United States has actively sought ways to encourage the oil producing nations to share their wealth with the poorest countries. For the Sahel, a well-drawn development program provides the opportunity.

The political significance of the Sahel countries is not circumscribed by the economic, security, or international weight of the eight countries or the size of their population. Rather it is a question of whether United States interest is served in refusing to join in an international effort with major recipient country commitment in tackling one of the most critical development problems in the developing world today; in being identified in assisting only those countries which are well endowed; in being identified as under-cutting an important international development effort after providing one-quarter billion dollars in emergency assistance. It is not a question of alternative investment choices with possible better pay off.

CONCLUSION

In the past, the ethos underpinning foreign aid has vacillated with a singular constancy. "Should foreign aid represent simply a generous attempt to alleviate human poverty or should it be a calculated instrument reserved strictly for furthering the national interest?" and "How altruistic can a rich country afford to be?" entail hard-boiled economic and foreign policy analyses. But, "Where is the line drawn between efforts to extend succor and 'triage'?" is a tensile moral question. Increasingly, the philosophy of foreign aid is being framed in terms of a balance of benefits doctrine informed and weighted in the direction of a moral commitment to some form of distributive justice -- if not in circumstance, then at least in the opportunity for the neediest people to better their circumstances.[27] The evidence is in that an absent-minded international economic system that creates a "tunnel effect" whereby only the privileged can progress inevitably seals the fate of travelers on all lanes. One of the hallmarks of the so-called New International Economic Order (NIEO) is the growing consensus that equity and not just efficiency must figure into development strategies. Demonstrative of this new outlook is the shaping of an international development policy that is more clearly directed at the achievement of certain minimum standards of living prior to the end of this century. A number of donor countries, including the United States, have opted to orient their own policies and programs in support of a basic needs strategy of development that could eventuate in the eradication of the most blatant forms of poverty.

Prescriptive actions are not infrequently quite disparate from their normative counterparts. Gunnar Myrdal has commented that Americans are sometimes reluctant to own up to their generous impulses. He remarks: "Reality is studied from the viewpoint of the ideal. The practical problem is how or by what policy means reality can be made to approach the ideal."[28] Theoretically, many of the teasing problems in aid strategy would solve themselves if only the volume of assistance could by sufficiently increased. Unfortunately, this easiest solution is the hardest from the standpoint of the donors' politics. However, the question of absorbtive capacity aside, the view that capital is not everything is more than just a handy rationalization. There are matters of unilateral causation which can keep a country poor, e.g., insufficient water or barren soil, which can be overcome only with enormous capital accumulation a la Saudi Arabia. Unless the face of fortune smiles upon the region, it is unlikely that the Sahel will be the recipient of great wealth. In any case, the caveat should be entered that to accumulate capital, no matter how a country comes by it or the size of the mattress it fills, means necessarily to defer current consumption. William Letwin admonishes: "As men can be short-sighted, so too can they be excessively long-sighted; they can cheat the present as easily as they can cheat the future, and in that sense more capital is no better than less."[29]

The task cut out for development professionals is to concentrate on finding ways of getting the maximum impact from a limited aid flow. In other words, the question of improving the aid allocation aside, we need to improve the forms in which it is given; to upgrade coordination between the activities of donors and recipients; and to persuade recipients to use it more effectively. Efforts to assist in the recovery and rehabilitation of the Sahel have generated an unprecedented degree of consensus among the developed countries about the goals and methods of their policies "vis-a-vis" a developing community of nations. Several organizations described in the ensuing chapters have emerged in the Sahel as a result of the need to fix priorities between bilateral and multilateral channels.

It is more apparent today than at any time in the past that the Sahel is not a wasteland. The U.N. Food and Agriculture Organization believes that dryland agriculture in the Sahel might be made efficient enough to produce the equivalent of 24 million cereal tons a year compared to the present annual production of about 5.5 million tons. With irrigation from the Niger and Senegal Rivers and Lake Chad, plus some smaller streams, another 20 million tons of cereals might be added -- as well as a major cattle-feeding industry. The U.S. Bureau of Reclamation and various French and African organizations are considering the potential for a two-dam hydroelectric and irrigation project in the Senegal River Basin in Mali and Senegal. Should these and other long-awaited projects meterialize beyond the planning stage, and this is beginning to happen with outside financial help, the Sahel can produce enough food to meet its own needs and those of neighboring countries.

American commercial interests in the Sahel can be expected to grow as a result of the U.S. bilateral program being carried out within a multi-donor framework. American input in the region's development, however, transcends dollar-and-cents calculations of particular interest groups and is consonanant with domestic concern for assisting the world's poorest inhabitants. No single international issue has united the American Black community as did the 1968-1974 drought. Aid to the Sahel is a direct response to the Congressional mandate that U.S. development assistance be directed to the poorer regions of the world. As the poorest, the Sahel also benefits from the Carter Administration's priorities on meeting basic human needs.

2 Profile of the Political Economy

The still hours before dawn were shattered by gunfire. Word spread through the capital city of Niamey that several truck loads of troops from nearby garrisons had surrounded the President's palace and demanded that the Niger head of state surrender to them peaceably. Instead, under the direction of the President's wife, a proud Fulani, the executive bodyguard resisted the assailants until the woman who prodded them on fell mortally wounded. While the bloody "coup d'état" which took place in the Niger Republic on April 14, 1974, had an unreal quality, it brutally marked the toppling of Niger President Hamani Diori's 14-year-old regime. By nightfall, all the cabinet officers and high ranking members of the sole political party, "Parti Progressiste Nigérien," had been rounded up and sent to desolate military camps in the country's vacuous interior; the constitution had been dissolved; and the national assembly abolished.

The fall of Diori's government by a "coup d'état," the twenty-fifth in Africa in eleven years, conferred on Niger the additional distinction of being the eighth republic of former French Africa to come under military control. A major causal element in the demise of what was considered to be one of Africa's more stable governments has been traced to Niger's relations with France. Richard Higgot and Finn Fuglestad state:

> Throughout the life of the regime, the continued French involvement in all aspects of Niger's economic and political life was a constant focal point for resentment. The Government's unwillingness (and in many cases inability) to modify this influence, especially with regard to the French military presence, was to be a major factor in its downfall.[1]

Diori had long been regarded as solidly pro-French. He had steered Niger into the French African Community after De Gaulle's referendum, outmanoeuvring his opponents who wanted immediate independence from France. He had maintained his authority with French financial, technical, and military aid. However, shortly before the coup, disagreement broke out over the terms of French exploitation of Niger's principal natural resource, uranium. In a coalition initiated by Diori with uranium-producing Gabon, a joint stand was taken in an effort to hike the price of the "yellowcake" (extracted from the ore). The meeting set for April 18, 1974 to settle their differences with the French authorities never took place because of the timely "coup d'etat" four days earlier. Equally bothersome in Paris, was Diori's new views on regionalism in West Africa. Diori, who had played a significant role in promoting a number of francophone economic groupings, now pushed hard for a West African community to include the anglophone states. Hence, unlike December 1963 when France had "discouraged" a military uprising against Diori, she did not feel that such action was warranted this time around. Staying her hand, she permitted French-trained Lieutenant Colonel Seyni Kountche to seize the reins of power.

The Sahelian countries and Niger as a Sahelian archetype, offer "dependencia" theorists a playground that can be surpassed in few other parts of the Third and Fourth Worlds. One of the most authoritative economists to have seized this opportunity to observe the paradigm of dependency first-hand is Samir Amin. An Egyptian national who now heads a development institute in Dakar, Amin has been one of the most outspoken critics of a so-called "growth without development" phenomenon which he believes typifies the economic situation in most West African states. This result of foreign economic domination is defined by Amin as:

> Growth generated and maintained from outside without the establishment of a social structure capable of bringing about an automatic transition to the further stage of internally centered and self-regulating growth.[2]

The central dilemma shared by all the Sahelian countries is that they cannot exist at present levels of economic growth without economic dependence; it is argued in theoretical constructs such as Amin's that they cannot exist with this dependence. While there can be no denial of the fact that the economic relationship between France and her former colonies is a relationship of unequal partners, there are those like Karl Deutch who have sought to encourage a healthy skepticism about propositions alleging the all-pervasive and self-perpetrating character of foreign influence, and to establish some measure of the relative autonomy which comes from the real strength of local traditions and institutions.[3] In apiece in <u>World Politics</u> entitled "The Underdevelopment of Development Literature," Tony Smith concludes by saying: "It is the unhistorical dogmatist, a familiar fellow in dependency literature, who asserts solely on the basis of certain grand ideas that, whatever the situation, the international system is a 'trap,' and that 'self-reliance' through socialism is the only road to economic development."[4] Even the sketchiest expositions on Guinea and Mali exhibit the tremendous opportunity costs these countries have had to absorb in order to pull off their own brands of socialism. Nonetheless, there are many indicators which dowse with cold water optimism about the capabilities of Sahelian countries to modify their relationships with the former metropole and within the international system. To get a better handle on these constraints it will be useful to review Johan Galtung's structural theory of domination.

For Galtung "the world consists of Center and Periphery nations; and each nation, in turn, has its center and periphery."[5] This center-periphery pattern with its asymmetric inequality and resistence to change, is responsible for the distortion of the socioeconomic structures within the periphery nation-states. Likewise, Amin also views the center of the periphery as an alien beachhead which is instrumental in only increasing the gap between the periphery nation-state and the center nation-state. To determine whether a nation-state is in the center or the periphery Galtung proposes three major tests.

First, there is the test of partner concentration. The present world economic order, Galtung says, is "feudal" in nature. By feudal he means that there is global stratification with privileged or metropolitan countries (center states) on the high rungs and dependent countries (periphery states) on the low rungs of the world ladder. The center states with their high per capita incomes have high levels of transactions with a wide range of trade partners, particularly among themselves. On the other hand, the periphery states with little choice of their own, trade in the main with one center partner on whom they become dependent. While the center states, because of the diffuse and extensive trade ties they have established, succeed in curtailing monopoly among each other, the same clearly does not apply to the periphery states who instead, according to Galtung, become the victims of monopoly.

Secondly, there is the test of commodity concentration. Not only do the center states have a varied trade partnership but a highly diversified range of commodities with which to trade as well. This is in contrast to the limited variety of commodities that periphery states have to offer because of pressure brought to bear on them by the center states. By trapping periphery states in "monoculture" -- the production of certain crops or minerals for which the center state has particular demand -- the center state concurrently checks any threat of competition from the periphery state and ensures that its monopolistic advantage remains intact.

Lastly, there is vertical trading. Galtung argues that the center states reserve for themselves the worthwhile skilled and capital-intensive industrial occupations which have high "spin-off effects" and act as external economies. By the same token, those productive activities -- agriculture or mining -- that are backwards, intensive in labor, and require relatively little capital investment are performed by the periphery states. Klaus Knorr rejects the theory of structural domination because of its equation of domination with international inequalities. "We insist that there is no neocolonialism unless there is an effective use of power for deliberately establishing and maintaining an exploitative relationship."[6] By definition, then, France is not engaging in neocolonial activities. Indeed, the charge that France is exploiting Sahelian dependence for her own economic gain is specious. The French economy would suffer little from the dissolution of the prevailing economic relationships with the Sahel. However, where you have political preponderance on the French scale in the Sahel, it follows that economic relationships, although not necessarily exploitative, may not be optimal for the weaker party. In the following delineation of Niger's economic status in relation to France, it will become quite clear as to which state is in the periphery.

Niger, described as an "artificial colonial cut-out crippled by its failure to integrate economically with its austral neighbor, Nigeria,"[7] stradles 1,187,000 square kilometers (the size of Texas and California combined) of savannah and sahelian ecological zones. A landlocked country, with a per capita income of $160, Niger's 3,900,000 inhabitants are included in UNESCO's list of the six member countries with the lowest standards of living. With marginal natural resources except for uranium, Niger's export earnings are dependent largely on a single product: groundnuts. Whereas most of the food crops are destined for home consumption in a predominantly subsistence economy, this export crop provides the country's farmers with the necessary funds to buy other essential goods. At the same time, it brings in the government between $25 to $30 million in foreign currency annually. Introduced by the French to meet their own domestic needs, its cultivation is dependent on French artificial price supports and the French market.

Niger has inherited an economic protective framework from the colonial period which conditions much of her postindependence economic foreign policy. This framework consists of: (1) monetary arrangements with the former metropole, (By virtue of membership to the Franc zone, Niger has agreed to some explicit restrictions on her fiscal and monetary independence in return for a line of credit at the French Treasury.); (2) trade arrangements with France and her partners in the European Economic Community; and (3) French ownership and control of much of the country's modern business sector. Niger's balance of payments has never been out of the red since the country received its independence from France in 1960. Concentrating on neutralizing this deficit and on several occasions erasing Niger's debt to them, the French have done little to promote the country's infrastructural development. Instead, the Nigeriens have been frozen into a situation that leaves them little choice but to rely on the French economy for their national viability. Needless to say, there are few places in Africa where French influence has been so potent as in Niger.

Niger's foreign trade is clearly indicative of the country's peripheral status. The deficit in its balance of payments reached its highest point in 1969, with 6,324,470,000 Francs CFA compared with 635,583,000 in 1963.[8] The principal reasons for this deterioration was the increase in imports of capital goods and the fall of the price of groundnuts by almost 20 percent compared with 1963. Imports in 1969, originated from several center state suppliers: France -- 6,121,000,000 Francs CFA; Federal Republic of Germany -- 802,000,000 Francs CFA; the United States -- 639,000,000 Francs CFA; Netherlands -- 540,000,000 Francs CFA; and Great Britain-230,000,000 Francs CFA. Exports worth 3,921,100,000 Francs CFA went to France. Nigeria followed with exports of 1,005, 900,000 Francs CFA. However, Niger recorded negligible trade with its other West African neighbors, periphery states also caught in the paradigm of dependency.

In discussing the accusation of neocolonialism, the Jeanneney Report, which in 1963 established what was to become the new French policy toward her former colonies, pointed out that poor countries must trade with the rich in order to procure needed goods for development. The report then posed the question of what rich nations could do to aid the poor nations without incurring charges of neocolonialism and economic domination. The answer given by the report was "cooperation," a catch-all which subsequently became the name of the French foreign aid program.[9] "Cooperation" has figured prominently in Nigerien government perceptions. As Diori noted:"International cooperation has played a leading part in Niger's development. Without it, and left to our own meager resources, we would have to face even greater difficulties."[10] Topping the list of donor countries, France and the European Economic Community have funneled into Niger 37,525,300,000 Francs CFA between the years 1960 and 1970 alone. France continues, as statistics for the Sahel Development Program show, to be the leading donor to Niger.

The problems of dependency in Niger are exacerbated by natural conditions and forces beyond the influence of governments. Agricultural production in Niger as in other Sahelian countries is overwhelmingly rainfed; pasturage for animals and output of staple foods depend on the amount and distribution of rainfall, and irregular precipitation has wreaked havoc on Niger's fragile economy. Livestock was once a mainstay of Niger's economy. Just two years prior to the drought, officials from the ministry of agriculture were developing potentially large and profitable export markets for the country's then expanding beef output. Agreements were made with West African coastal states whose livestock is hampered by tropical disease and the tse-tse fly. As the drought worsened and rainfall dropped to a mere 48 percent of the norm, the consequent loss of livestock was staggering. While very little data has been gathered, estimates are that at least 80 percent of the country's cattle perished or were driven south across the border into Nigeria and Dahomey.

Another major development obstacle for Niger is its continental character and its vast expanses which push up transportation costs considerably. At present, all commodities going to or coming from the eastern part of the country are transported by rail for 1,150 kilometers from Lagos to Kano by Nigerian railways, and then by road to urban centers in Niger. Merchandise going or coming from the western part of Niger is sent by train from Cotonou to Parakou (438 km) and then by road to Niamey (620 km). Crowding in the ports of Lagos and Cotonou and the transfer of loads at Kano and Parakou contribute to increasing the price of Niger's imports and exports. To this we can add the high price of road transport due to the bad state of the roads, which leads transport firms to recover as soon as possible the cost of their vehicles. Soaring fuel costs are compounding the price of transportation. The French trucking firms that monopolize ground transport charged a flat rate of $100 a ton to bring goods from coastal ports. Now, after the cost of fuel skyrocketed to $2.50 a gallon, the cost is twice that. This rate is applied only on condition that a truck is returning to the coast with another full load, otherwise the cost is automatically doubled.

The Niger river, which is the third longest in Africa, was until recently considered to be unnavigable. Several French colonial studies on the subject dismissed the notion as infeasible, especially since utilization of the waterway would only reinforce ties with Nigeria. However, the Diori government requested the Canadian government to explore the possibilities offered by this river. A Canadian hydraulics expert, Jacque Cordeau, showed in 1973 that the river is navigable for seven months in the year. This discovery represents an important step forward for Niger's economy. In fact, the seven months during which the river is navigable correspond to the months following the groundnut harvest. Preliminary calculations also show that using the river for transport purposes will bring transport costs down by 60 percent for goods imported or exported through Nigeria.

To realize short-term development goals, the Niger government felt that it had only one recourse: uranium. The American Atomic Energy Commission has estimated that there are 980,000 tons of uranium reserves in the non-communist world. According to this source, 86 percent of these reserves are found in the United States, Canada, South Africa, and France, while Niger, with known reserves of 50,000 tons, comes fifth, immediately after France. In the Air massif of northern Niger, almost 2,000 kilometers from the nearest port, geologists from the French Atomic Energy Board discovered in a spot called Arlit, uranuim deposits which promise 30,000 tons of uranuim ore which can be worked by open-cast mining. Capital to exploit this site is distributed as follows:

Atomic Energy Board (France)	33.50%
Republic of Niger	16.75%
Compagnie Francaise des Mineraus d'Uranium	33.50%
Urargesellschaft (West Germany)	8.125%
A.G.T.P. Nircleare (Italy)	8.125%

Niger's uranium production, estimated at 4,000 metric tons of concentrates a year, are expected to increase to 10,000 tons by the mid-1980s, enough for half of France's uranium needs. The Arlit mining complex required total investments of 1.5 billion Francs CFA. While Diori was in office, 700 million Francs CFA were coming into the Nigerien treasury annually in taxes and dividends from the exploitation of the uranium. By 1984, this figure would rise to 1.6 billion Francs CFA or more: "Uranium has for a long time been considered as the fuel of the future, and recently it has been going up in value owing to increases in the price of crude oil and the desire of industrialized countries to extend their sources of energy supplies.[11]" This attitude, which surfaced in an interview with Hamani Diori in early 1974, is one of the principal factors that played in Diori's demise. Diori was viscerally pervious to the boost to Niger's ramshackle economy that could come from increased development of its large uranium reserves. The world price varied from six to eight dollars a pound of "yellowcake." If his regime was strong enough to drive the deal, twice that price could be asked, with demand rising as more nations, particularly France, accelerated their programs to develop nuclear power plants. As it turned out, Diori overestimated his strength.

The tactics Diori used in his attempt to secure a substantial increase in the price being paid for uranium reveal a certain naivete with regard to his conception of Franco-Nigerien relations and his own position in this matrix. Obviously influenced by the success of OPEC, Diori teamed up with President Bongo of Gabon to devise a joint strategy for negotiations with Paris. However, as Jeune Afrique noted: "It was only out of solidarity that the Gabonais head of state adopted the Nigerien position since uranium occupies an insignificant place among Gabon's natural resources after oil, wood and manganese."[12] Diori's footwork struck a sensitive nerve in Paris. This attempt by two of France's former colonies to present her, for the first time, with a united front, threatened to undermine long-standing French policies "vis-a-vis" her former territories. Had these negotiations met with success, they would have put Franco-African relations on a totally new footing, potentially more favorable to the African states. The "impasse" that followed as the French negotiating team procrastinated for 18 months -- falling back on President George Pompidou's bad health as an excuse for not being able to conclude an agreement -- proved to be lethal. The extra French revenues that would help to alleviate the disastrous economic situation prevailing in Niger were not forthcoming as Diori had hoped. It was a critical moment as the French knew well. With inflation-hit imports steadily rising, the increased cost of importing oil, the need for expensive drought relief, and falling revenue as taxes dropped by over 40 percent, something was bound to give. It is not surprising that the beleaguered regime was finally overwhelmed. The political unrest generated became very apparent, and once gauged by the military to be sufficiently supportive, this traditional outlet, in the absence of any legal channel for opposition, was used.

It is also not surprising that France, despite her interventionist record and the existence of "Operation cheval noir" (a contingency plan to take the Diori's to the safety of Niamey's Camp LeClerc, the French headquarters, in the eventuality of a coup d'etat) made no effort to help Diori. It is dubious that Jacques Foccart, the French General Secretary for African Affairs, whose intelligence network in Niger was buttressed by over 60 French officers and N.C.O.'s in the Niger army, could have been totally in the dark. The inaction of the two companies of French troops stationed in Niamey was equally uncharacteristic of normal French operating procedures in Africa. However, if the French reaction was anomalous, it was due primarily to a policy shift that Diori himself had initiated. To break out of the dependency paradigm in which he found his country entrapped, Diori had set about improving Niger's links with non-francophone states, particularly Nigeria, Canada, West Germany, and the Arab bloc. When Canadian advisers began to stream into the executive building that houses the President's office, a power struggle developed as the threatened "Corsican mafia" (the influential French advisers to the President headed by his Corsican Director of the Cabinet, Nicholas Leca) fought to retain their privileged position. In August 1972, Diori had asked France for a revision of the bilateral agreements which existed since 1961. These instruments covered all aspects of Frence's relations with Niger, ranging from cultural to military matters, as did similar "accords de cooperation" between France and most of her former Sahelian colonies. A source of resentment throughout former French Africa, these documents codify the center-periphery relationship, and have never been published in their entirety. Diori had been engaging in a kind of brinkmanship with France, whose ambassador and automatic doyen of the diplomatic community in Niamey, had indicated on several occasions the Quai d'Orsay's displeasure over Niger's rapprochement with Canada. The Nigerien leader, it can only be surmised from the policies he was pursuing, was under the impression that Niger was becoming less susceptible to French domination. In reality, the substance of relations between the two countries remained very much unchanged, as demonstrated by the "coup d'etat."

France was among the first countries to recognize the new military junta. Higgot and Fuglestad posit:

> Certainly the president of Niger had been one of France's staunchest supporters since independence, but his firm stand over the question of uranium appears to have irritated the Gaullist African policy-makers. With the overthrow of his regime, the uranium returned to square one.[13]

To be sure, shortly after the coup Gabon entered into bilateral negotiations with France and settled for a minor increase in uranium prices. When a settlement with Niger was finally reached, the military junta refused to disclose the terms.Despite Diori's popularity in Africa at large, stemming from the many years of service he had devoted to African causes, the lack of international protest was predictable; military regimes long ago established that they presented little or no threat to foreign interests. The Supreme Military Council of Niger lost no time in establishing its credentials in this respect, immediately guaranteeing all existing international agreements. The conservative and corrective nature of the coup can best be understood from Kountche's own words as quoted in _Le Monde_:

> We have no intention of passing ourselves for revolutionaries ... we do not entertain the formation of a new form of society in Niger, that which we have is in need of being purified ... the house must be put in order.[14]

In point of fact, it was Franco-Nigerien relations that had to be"purified", i.e., normalized. The military's overall prospects of increasing the economic well-being of Niger at the time of the coup were very slight. What could the junta do in the face of a global climatic shift, world inflation, and Niger's landlocked frontiers? Even with the return of the rains, less than one year after Kountche's takeover, another bloody "coup d'etat" was attempted. By dawn a dozen bodies littered the gardens of the presidential palace and, albeit Kountche managed to retain power, the "excessive confidence" for which he was criticized in Jeune Afrique all but dissipated as he imposed a strict curfew over the capital.[15] An eerie political malaise persists in Niger today.

The plight of Niger is the plight of the Sahelian countries taken as a whole. Without exception, the Sahelian governments entered the post-colonial era transfixed in a paradigm of dependency. They were more or less integrated into their respective metropoles' economies as suppliers of raw materials. However, each state was no more than a link in a long chain that would be insignificantly shortened without it but which would reduce the isolated link to helplessness. In the euphoria of independence, grappling with the political transition of power was a full-time distraction, which led to an underestimation of the economic conditions requisite for true national autonomy. Gradually the realization began to sink in that political independence meant little without a certain capacity for economic self-determination.

Colonialism in Africa introduced a process of balkanization. This resulted in a situation where at the time of independence many states had no contact with one another and,unfortunately,there has been little amelioration in this respect over the years. This situation has had a particularly debilitating effect on West Africa. Amin terminates his economic analysis of neocolonialism in the region with the "unambiguous conclusion that the fragmentation of the economic area which West Africa has undergone constitutes an irresistible pressure for the maintenance of colonial structures and policies, and that these in turn no less irresistibly produce foreign domination and underdevelopment."[16] Plainly, to effect necessary changes, the Sahelian countries must first evolve new kinds of interactions among themselves that are more fundamental than the endless gatherings of conference diplomacy. The challenge of "interdependency on real economic foundations," in the phrase of Rene Dumont, is not new but it represents one of the few avenues out of dependency.[17] Those developing countries that are most frail and vulnerable, like our archetype, Niger, will have to blaze the way. In this sense, the Sahel Development Program is a bid for collective self-reliance.

DEVELOPMENT AS A FUNCTION OF DEPENDENCE
(La crise de la cooperation)

Although each Sahelian country has its own unique problems and a distinctive resource base, they share numerous similarities. Of the francophone countries only Senegal's government remains fully civilian. Upper Volta, Niger, Mali, and most recently, Mauritania (August 1978) have experienced "coups d'etat." It would appear that of all the institutions and practices, the political ones in the Sahel have proved to be the easiest to change. Authoritarian leaders and military juntas rarely trouble themselves with cumbersome democratic processes. As the Nigeriens discovered in 1974, in a time span of 24 hours, a government that had run the country for 14 years suddenly faded away. Pounding the themes of national reconstruction and anti-corruption, the military have become a major determinant of political activity. However, it is difficult for a regime to base its claim for legitimacy on acrimony and memory of previous ineptness. Seymour M. Lipset has said: "Prolonged effectiveness over a number of generations may give legitimacy to a political system. In the modern world, such effectiveness means primarily constant economic development."[18] With a built-in tendency to resort to violence in all military-dominated governments -- after all, how else did the military gain control, an inflated, panoplistic notion of development can become an obsession for most military regimes.

The appetite for material improvement is presently of such magnitude in the Sahel -- and in most other poor countries -- that the only government with any chance of remaining in power much less adhering to parliamentary procedures is one that is determined to achieve major economic reform and expansion. Uncertainty resolution in development pivots on political tolerance for economic dependence. On occasion, fear of developmental unsuccess has led to caution bordering on ill-advised immobility. At least, this is Mamadou Diarra's contention in criticizing the opportunity costs of the monetary arrangements into which many Sahelian countries have entered with France:

> But no one, among the present leaders is unaware that this system, while it carries advantages, is nonetheless a facile solution which, in sparing them from the risks they would normally have to assume, leads in fact to irresponsibility.[19]

According to Diarra this "irresponsibility" precludes the development of the internal discipline needed to attract foreign investment. Another observer has noted that the persistence of colonial trade patterns in francophone West Africa is not a result of systematic French efforts to maintain the trade structure; rather, this structure was established prior to independence and neither France nor her former colonies has done much to modify it since 1960. By the same token, over the years France's commercial relations have shifted and the other members of the Common Market have become even more important to her as trading partners. An editorial in West Africa notes:

> In this context French policy has changed in a subtle way. Whereas in the sixties when de Gaulle advocated the unity of Francophonie, France maintained a stance strictly independent of NATO and other Western economic powers; now after the oil crisis and with the alleged threat of the Soviet Union in Africa, this independent French stand has been diluted. There also seems now to be some indecision as to where exactly they stand. French ministers have been making more frequent visits to Anglophone countries in East and West Africa; Nigeria has now become France's major trading partner in Africa south of the Sahara and north of South Africa; diplomatic relations have been established with Angola.[20]

By the same token, Sahelian and neighboring countries are not content with the status quo. Former President Moktar Ould Daddah of Mauritania withdrew his country from the West African Monetary Union in November 1972 in order to create a national currency. In December of that year, Dahomey also called for a revision of her relations with France, prompting the influential French newspaper, Le Monde, to label the situation as "La crise de la cooperation."[21] By and large, though, the Sahelian countries exhibit a kind of fatalism towards France,which is something of a leviathan next to its former colonies. E. Wesley Peterson remarks: "In general, comparisons of economic size between France and her former African colonies points up the relative unimportance of the latter in the French economy. The total foreign reserves of the UMOA, Madagascar, Mali, and the five countries of Central Africa (Chad, Congo, Central African Empire, Gabon, and Cameroon) are only 3.5percent of France's total reserves. The total value of the currency circulating in these countries represents only 3 percent of the currency circulating in France.[22]

In the future much rests on Sahelian perceptions of the trade-off between the economic benefits and the political costs of dependence. Negotiating from a position of weakness, the Sahelian countries, with most other African countries, have opted to date not to dispense with economic assistance despite the preponderant influence this aid begets and its impact on African decisions in non-economic spheres. To take the standard comparative measure adopted in official international statistics, African countries as a whole receive twice as much aid per capita as Asian and Latin American countries. They receive aid for a wider range of purposes, including budgetary support in many cases, and on relatively soft terms. The fact that they receive this favorable treatment is attributable in part to needs that are particularly large but also in at least equal part to the special relations which they have maintained with their former rulers.

The external vulnerability of the "demi-etats" of the Sahel is well documented by dependencia theorists like Amin.[23] Quite apart from dependence on a continuing inflow of external resources for development expenditure, and in some cases for the recurrent budget deficits, the Sahel relies heavily on its sources of aid for the provision of skilled personnel. In 1975, the Sahel accounted for 72 percent of all technical assistance personnel supplied by the OECD countries. A significant number of these, in the range of 15,000-20,000 out of a total of 66,561, were integrated into the civil service in ordinary operational posts -- a form of technical assistance which other developing countries regard with suspicion and which bilateral aid donors normally find politically embarassing. Equally significant is the number of expatriates teaching in Sahelian schools and universities. In 1976, 88 percent of all teachers supplied by the OECD countries under technical assistance were in the Sahel.

The private sector in the Sahelian countries exhibits the typical colonial pattern, with a heavy concentration in one or two cash crops and mining; and the miniscule size of domestic markets makes escape from this pattern difficult. In some respects, the Sahelian countries are locked at a low altitude by an automatic pilot over which they have little control. Approximately 90 percent of the Sahel's total exports go to developed countries, a higher proportion than from any other region of the world. The influence of the colonial past is seen again in the concentration on Western Europe, which takes 69 percent of the Sahel's exports. For nearly half of the Sahelian countries, more than 50 percent of exports are accounted for by a single commodity. Exports are a high proportion of gross domestic product, about 20 percent for the Sahel as a whole, rising in some countries to more than 40 percent.

The present orientation of economic relations in the Sahel is based more on historical than economic rationale. The economic arguments in favor of increased West African economic cooperation have remained essentially unchanged since the region gained its political independence. Individual markets, with the exception of Nigeria, are too small to permit a viable program of industrialization. Where per capita income is about $169, the total demand for processed goods is hardly more than 3 percent of the corresponding per capita demand in Western

Europe. The typical Sahelian country, with about four million inhabitants, has a demand for industrial products equivalent to that of a middle-sized European provincial town. Many articles that are in common use in the U.S. can be sold in a Sahelian country in quantities so limited that a machine working only a few days or weeks can produce enough for a whole year's consumption, and would have to stand idle for the rest of the time. While import substitution in many light industries was carried out in Senegal during the colonial period, since independence Senegalese industry has been deprived of its wider market in French West Africa (AOF), and the other newly independent states set up their own light industries. As a result, Senegalese industry has been operating at less than capacity since the early 1960s.

Only through cooperative efforts, therefore, on a regional basis encompassing all of West Africa, can the Sahel hope to escape continued economic dependence on export of primary commodities and move toward viable industrial enterprises, increased intraregional trade, increased investment, and higher per capita incomes. Cooperation is equally important to agricultural modernization. Exchange of information and technology; the ready access to overseas markets for the agricultural products of land-locked countries; complementary trade in the region (e.g., the Sahel's comparative advantage with respect to the large markets of the coastal countries in the sale of cereals and livestock); these necessitate closer economic cooperation among West Africans.

The pre-independence institutions of French and British Colonial Africa, particularly the francophone ones, provided considerable intraregional cooperation in West Africa, albeit then as now, the differences between French and British colonial administrations and institutions precluded much cooperation between the two groups of colonies. The division of West Africa between angolophone and francophone countries has long been a major constraint to regional cooperation but, contrary to popular belief, the importance of linguistic considerations "per se" is greatly exaggerated. Clandestine border trade has always been conducted in local dialects. The legal livestock trade is not inhibited by language differences where economic problems can be overcome. What remains different, however, is the cultural and educational outlooks of the two groupings. Some Nigerians describe their policy of closer ties with their francophone neighbors as an effort to "de-Frenchify" West Africa. And some senior Senegalese and Ivorians, taking pride in their sophisticated European lifestyles, are repelled by what they describe as "neo-Nkrumah" strong arm methods of the anglophones. Many West Africans view the lack of efficient payment arrangements among the various monetary zones in the region as the single most important constraint on regional trade. While there is no doubt that it is an obstacle, there is much evidence to indicate that, in fact, it is a relatively minor one.

Take, for example, the livestock trade between seller, Upper Volta, and buyer, Ghana. It operates something like this:

1. The Ghanaian purchaser deposits Ghanaian cedis in the Ghanaian banking system to purchase an irrevocable letter of credit, denominated in U.S. dollars.
2. The buyer then delivers the letter to the Upper Voltan seller against livestock delivery.
3. The Upper Voltan deposits the letter with his bank, which in turn transmits it to the Ouagadougou branch of the Banque Centrale des Etats de l'Afrique de l'Ouest (BCEAO).
4. The BCEAO sends it to BCEAO headquarters in Paris, which transmits it to the Bank of France.
5. The Bank of France transmits it to the designated New York correspondent of the Bank of Ghana for payment.
6. Notification of credit then must go back through the system in order to have the Upper Voltan seller paid in CFA francs.

At best,this system takes several weeks. At worst, it has extended over eleven months. During the payment process, the capital of both the exporter and the importer is completely tied up. It is not hard to see why the alternative of clandestine trade becomes so attractive. While the technical problems in this transaction lie in francophone country prohibition against dealing in foreign exchange other than French francs, the substantive problem is much greater: Ghana's recorded trade with the CFA zone is in chronic deficit. With an overvalued currency, it pays Ghanaians to import legally at the official exchange rate (and to export to CFA countries illegally at the parallel exchange rate of the depreciated cedi!). A clearing arrangement between CFA currency countries and Ghana would help reduce this problem. But it would probably also require some devaluation of the cedi. The last Ghana government, having reversed its predecessor's devaluation, was politically reluctant to consider any new devaluation. Thus, it can be argued that the real obstacle is not so much the payments arrangements as the underlying causes of imbalance among national economies.

According to recorded trade statistics, almost all West African countries receive only 5 percent or less of their imports from neighboring states. Such statistics, however, are largely meaningless. There is little correspondence between the recorded exports of one country and the recorded imports of another. The figures do not include "unofficial" intraregional trade, both traditional and clandestine. Incorporating this traditional trade, it is estimated, for example, that Nigeria actually absorbs 75 percent of Niger's total exports and provides 20 percent of Niger's imports.[24] What is more, present trade patterns are not a reliable guide for any analysis of prospects for intraregional trade under conditions of increased economic cooperation. Clandestine trade would be reduced, and traditional trade would move into official channels.

Economies of scale in West Africa today lead to industrial concentration in the coastal areas. On the other hand, stock-raising is best suited to the inland areas. The higher standard of living of the coastal areas attracts meat in areas where the tse-tse fly hampers animal production. While much can be done to improve inland meat production, there is a natural division of labor in this situation. The inland countries could also develop and export dairy products, as well as a number of other savannah crops. Major development of trade in these and other products, however, requires coordination and cooperation between coastal and land-locked countries. The former should refrain from developing and processing crops that do best in the savannah ecology, and the latter countries need to refrain from establishing industries that can be operated at less cost in the coastal areas.

Under present conditions in West Africa, the most important constraints on natural intra-regional trade movements are discriminatory tariff barriers. Within the francophone area, existing Ivory Coast levies discriminate in favor of raw agricultural imports from inland states. There is further discrimination within these constraints, which favors Entente nations, Upper Volta and Niger, over non-member, Mali. Senegalese tariffs on goods from anglophone neighbors are from 30 to 50 percent higher than from those within the franc zone. This means that it is almost prohibitive for Ghana and Nigeria to export legally to the francophone countries. It is frequently even cheaper for the francophone countries to import from Europe than from their anglophone neighbors. The reverse is also true. Consequently, Nigerian officials have stated that they cannot give binding guaranties to import from neighboring CFA countries so long as these countries maintain discriminatory tariffs against Nigerian goods.

ECONOMIC STRUCTURE AND PERFORMANCE

The Sahelian countries face a prolonged, up-hill struggle if they are to raise per capita incomes and improve living standards. Small budgets make it difficult for Sahelian governments to mount investment programs which are sufficiently large to increase literacy, raise the skill levels of the work force, and diversify the productive bases of their economies. In the face of population growth exceeding 2.5 percent per year, the task of raising per capita incomes and living standards becomes even more difficult. However, there is reason for optimism with respect to the potential for economic development in the Sahel. Revenues from mineral exports are being applied to realistic development projects and not to conspicuous consumption. National resources are being mobilized for development efforts throughout the region. Long-range planning has identified important constraints to development and focused donor attention and efforts in critical areas. Coordination among donors and Sahelians has increased the complementariness of projects and reduced the piecemeal nature of past foreign assistance. Most significantly, Sahelian governments are beginning to commit themselves to a development strategy that provides for a more equitable distribution of the benefits of economic growth.

The overwhelming majority of the population of the eight Sahelian countries lives in rural areas, a regional average of 85-90 percent in 1977. Senegal, the most "urbanized" of the eight countries reported 76 percent of its population engaged in subsistence farming in 1978. Crops such as groundnuts and cotton provide meager cash earnings with which to buy simple manufactured goods and to pay taxes. Table 2 shows the relative importance of each sector of activity with respect to gross domestic product.

From 1965 to 1975, economic growth in the Sahel was negative in real per capita income. Countries with the best economic performance were those with mineral resources such as Senegal, Niger, and Mauritania. In the latter two countries, rapid growth in iron ore and uranium production has led to high growth rates in the industrial sector and increased resources for investment. This investment, however, has yet to result in development in other sectors and consequently the rural populations of these two countries remain among the poorest in the entire region. Moreover, iron ore revenues in Mauritania were diverted from development programs in 1978 to be allocated to the military effort in Western Sahara -- a campaign Mauritania has wisely elected to give up. Senegal, as a result of its past position as the administrative and commercial center for French West Africa, is considerably more developed than its neighbors. Although the Senegalese economy has grown very slowly during the past decade, it still has a sizeable manufacturing sector and a relatively large cadre of trained manpower to work in both the private and public sectors. Per capita income in Senegal approaches $400 but it has suffered a negative average per capita rate of growth since 1960. Chad and Niger experienced similar negative rates of per capital GNP growth during the same period. Outside of Senegal and the mining sectors of Mauritania and Niger, economic activity remains largely agricultural at a very low level of productivity. Per capita incomes for Chad, Mali, and Upper Volta were all under $150 in 1976 and the latter two countries have shown virtually no growth in real terms during the previous 16 years (Table 3).

Poverty is widespread in the Sahelian countries and only a little progress has been made in improving the quality of life since 1960 when most of these countries became independent. Primary and secondary school enrollment have been doubled since independence, but only 15 to 43 percent of all children ever have the opportunity to attend school. The average

TABLE 2

GROSS DOMESTIC PRODUCT AT FACTOR COST FOR THE SAHEL*
(Current market prices in millions of $)

	1965	1975	Annual Rate of Growth of Output 1965-1975	Percent Contribution to Output 1965	1975
Agriculture	970.3	1588.2	4.9	44.3	37.2
Mining	59.1	185.0	11.4	2.7	4.3
Manufacturing	307.9	747.8	8.9	14.0	17.5
Services	854.1	1748.0	7.2	39.0	41.0
TOTAL GDP	2191.4	4269.0	6.7	100.0	100.0
Population (millions)	21.53	27.02	2.3		
Per capital GDP (dollars)	102	158	4.4		

SOURCE: USAID, Economic and Social Data Bank.
* For this table the Sahel is defined as the Gambia, Senegal, Mauritania, Mali, Upper Volta, Niger and Chad.

TABLE 3

BASIC INDICATORS FOR THE SAHELIAN COUNTRIES

	Population		GNP Per Capita		Per Capita Indices Food and Agricultural Production Average: 1975-77 (1969-1971 = 100)	
	Total 1975 (000)a/	Average % Rate of growth, b/	U.S. dollar c/	Average % Rate of growth e/		
		1970-75 (%)	1976	1960-76	Food d/	Agriculture d/
Cape Verde	290	-	260 a/	-	-	-
Chad	4,035	2.1	120	-1.1	83	88
Gambia	519	-	180 a/	-	98	98
Mali	5,697	2.5	100	0.9	83	86
Mauritania	1,322	2.7	340	3.7	70	70
Niger	4,592	2.7	160	-1.1	80	80
Senegal	5,000	2.7	390	-0.7	104	106
Upper Volta	6,032	2.3	110	0.8	96	93
Sahel Regional	27,487	2.5 e/	183 g/	0.1 e/	89	90
Low Income Countries	-	2.4	150	0.9	-	-
Middle Income Countries	-	2.7	750	2.8	-	-

Sources:
a/ Annex A, World Atlas of the Child, (IBRD, 1978).
b/ Table 13, World Development Report (IBRD, 1978).
c/ Table 1, World Development Report (IRBD, 1978).
d/ Derived from Tables 5 and 6, FAO Production Yearbook (FAO, 1977).
e/ Weighted average for six countries.
f/ Weighted average for seven countries.
g/ Weighted average for eight countries.

life span has been increased only modestly to 40 years. Electric power consumption has more than doubled since 1960. Per capita incomes have risen by 50 to 100 percent in current dollars in Niger, Chad, Upper Volta, and the Gambia. In Senegal, per capita income rose by only 27 percent, but in absolute terms, the addition to income was higher than elsewhere, except for Mauritania which tripled its per capita income between 1960 and 1974.

The incomes of small farmers range from 10-20,000 CFA (US $50-90) in most of the region, often less than two-thirds the national GNP per capita. In real terms, comparison of the consumer price index and the official millet price index using 1970 as the base year shows that in 1977, the purchasing power of the small farmer comfortably exceeded the consumer price index only in Niger and Chad although Upper Volta, Mauritania, and Senegal come very close. All the Sahelian countries have increased producer prices for food and export crops since the drought; in some, the increases have been substantial. In The Gambia where peanut production has been well established for several decades, growth in production in recent years has been low but producer prices have risen by over 200 percent since 1970, with the result that in 1976 the rural population had an average per capita cash income of $35. In the groundnut growing region of Mali, production doubled between 1968 and 1977 and producer prices rose 150 percent. During that same period cotton production in Upper Volta quadrupled. Most of the benefits from these developments occurred in the higher rainfall areas of the Sahel. However, the agricultural development that has occurred has not improved significantly either the productive capacity or economic and social well-being of the poor majority. Nonetheless, money incomes are marginally higher for small farmers who live and work in higher rainfall areas served by regional development organizations that provide greater access to current production inputs. Small farmers who own livestock are also marginally wealthier than those who do not. Such income differences as exist between small farmers do not necessarily lead to improvements in their basic human needs status as measured by nutritional status, health conditions or literacy. Most often, income differences are reflected in increased purchases of small consumer durables such as bicycles or transistor radios or of consumption items such as cloth, sugar, or tea.

It is clear that, with the exception of Senegal, significant diversification of Sahelian economic activity has not yet begun. Economic growth has been dependent on exports of a few primary commodities. Peanuts, cotton and/or livestock account for 80-90 percent of the exports of Mali, Upper Volta, Chad and The Gambia. Minerals account for a significant share of export earnings in Niger and Mauritania. Because these countries are small and disposable incomes limited, there has been very little industrialization. Consequently, these countries are almost completely dependent on imports for all of the products and commodities required for development. The economic performance of the landlocked Sahelian countries is typical of other countries under similar circumstances and simply reflects the extremely difficult problems that must be addressed and overcome if development efforts in the Sahel are to succeed.

Development expenditures for 1975 were at least 30 percent higher than in 1974 throughout the Sahel. Budgeted development expenditures for 1976 were double the 1975 levels in Niger, Upper Volta, and Senegal. Revenues collections increased throughout the Sahel in 1974 and 1975 but more slowly than development expenditures. Since the drought years, current expenditures have increased faster than revenues everywhere but in Chad. In 1975, there were current budget deficits in Mali, Chad, and Mauritania. Deficits in Mali continued to increase through 1975 principally because of growth in government wage and salary payments. However, in Upper Volta, Niger, and Senegal budget surpluses were generated which were used to increase development expenditures. Deficit countries increased their development expenditures through greater reliance on foreign loans and grants. Budget summaries are presented in Table 4.

The balance of payments structures of the Sahelian economies reflect characteristics which are typical of developing economies: there are consistent balance of trade deficits which are offset by capital inflows. The jump in the post-1973 inflation rate increased Sahelian export earnings, but the gains have not been sufficient to pay for the higher-priced imports. Thus, the trade deficit has gradually increased. The negative trade balances have been offset in large part by unrequited government transfers, a major portion of which were foreign grant assistance. The four-year average basic balance figures when compared to the most-recent-year figures indicate that two of the eight countries have consistently had to resort to short-term capital and other means to finance their deficits. Because most capital inflows tend to be on a grant basis and most of the Sahelian governments practice a conservative financial management policy, debt service ratios have remained relatively low, although the average for the Sahel has increased from 5 percent in 1969 to 6.8 percent in 1975 (Table 5).

France is the largest single trading partner for each of the Sahelian countries (Table 6). Trade with non-Sahelian Africa has declined in relative terms since 1970 but has increased in absolute terms. The trade pattern data lead to a corollary which is well known: the development of the Sahelian economies has been and will continue to be intimately linked with the economic situation and prospects of the neighboring countries, particularly the coastal states to the south. The salient characteristics of the present relationship are: the

TABLE 4

NATIONAL BUDGET SUMMARIES
(Millions of current dollars)*

	Mauritania		Mali		Niger		Chad		Upper Volta		Senegal	
	1972	1975	1972	1975	1972	1975	1972	1975	1972	1975	1972	1975
Current Revenues	48.2	86.0	52.9	76.3	55.0	105.6	53.5	65.3	48.8	75.7	201.5	341.8
Current Expenditures	46.0	93.3	58.8	90.8	52.7	85.5	61.4	71.7	41.5	66.3	187.4	309.3
Surplus/Deficit	2.2	-7.3	-5.9	-14.5	2.3	20.1	-7.9	-6.4	7.3	9.4	14.1	12.5
Development Expenditures	10.9	11.3	6.5	7.4	10.9	20.9	3.6	1.5	4.0	5.6	15.9	63.7
Overall Surplus/ Deficit	-8.1	-67.8	-12.4	-21.9	-8.6	-.8	-11.5	-7.9	3.3	3.8	-1.8	-31.2

SOURCE: I.M.F., Recent Economic Developments.

* Conversion to dollars from local currency was based on average exchange rates for the period 1972-1976: 233.74 cfa = $1; 467.48 malian francs = $1; 45.66 ouguiyas = $1.

coastal states provide transportation services for Sahelian exports and imports; the coastal states are an important market for Sahelian livestock and grains; the Sahel constitutes a market for a variety of products which can be produced at low cost in the heavier rainfall zone of the coast (wood, fruit, fish); and the coastal countries absorb a significant part of the excess labor force of at least two Sahelian countries. In 1972, workers' remittances to Upper Volta were approximately $25 million and increased to $38 million by 1976. Malian worker remittances were $14 million in 1972 and by 1975 had reached a level of $30 million. For perspective, these sums are equal to approximately one-half and one-third of government revenues for Upper Volta and Mali respectively.

The high concentration of exports in a few commodities makes the Sahelian countries particularly dependent upon external conditions and terms of trade over which they have little control. Production of primary agricultural commodities is also highly dependent on the weather. While the long-run price outlook for minerals products is promising, price instability for primary agricultural products will seriously affect the balance of payments of Senegal, Gambia, Chad , Upper Volta. STABEX, the main feature of the Lome Convention concluded among the African, Pacific, and Carribean (ACP) states and the European Community compensates signatory developing countries for unforseen shortfalls below their average value in the four preceeding years in earnings on agricultural exports to the EC. All Sahelian states are signatories to the Convention though they stand to benefit to varying degree. Six of the eight (excluding Senegal and the Cape Verde Islands) are on the ACP list of least advanced countries and are not required to repay STABEX transfers if their commodity export values rise experience an upturn in prices above the transfer payment reference values. For example, due to localized drought conditions during 1977, Senegal received a transfer of 19,000,000 European Units of Account (EUA) in 1978 (1 EUA = $1.20) to compensate for lost groundnut oil and groundnut cake earnings. As a moderately poor country, Senegal will have to repay this interest free transfer which will be used to replenish the STABEX fund. For other countries in the Sahel, STABEX transfers can be crucial: for example, transfers in a recent year accounted for 20 percent of Niger's previous four-year average earnings for skins and hides exports and 39 percent of its groundnut export earnings. Though the list of eligible exports under the scheme now cover some 19 commodities, earnings compensation favors several crops which Sahelian countries produce notably groundnuts and cotton.

In practice the Sahelian economies are relatively open: e.g., six countries (members of the West African Development Bank) have a common currency, a common central bank, and common external tariffs; between 1920 and 1970, permanent migration from the interior to the coast added approximately 4.8

TABLE 5

INTERNATIONAL PAYMENTS POSITIONS
(In Millions

Most Recent Year Country	1976 Chad	1976 Gambia	1976 Mali
Goods and Service Balance			
Most recent year	-89.3	-19.4	-118.1
Four year average	-81.9	-8.7	-129.7
Government Unrequited Transfers			
Most recent year	68.0	1.4	85.5
Four year average	55.0	3.5	79.7
Basic Balance*			
Most recent year	31.3	-14.2	-20.0
Four year average	1.2	2.3	-22.4
Debt Service Ratios (%)			
1969	5.0	--	10.7
1975	5.7	0.6	3.1

SOURCE: USAID, Economic and

* The basic balance includes
  and private unrequited trans-

OF SAHELIAN COUNTRIES
of Dollars)

1976 Mauritania	1975 Niger	1975 Senegal	1975 Upper Volta
-167.6	-72.1	-166.7	-185.9
-71.9	-58.2	-127.0	-118.9
138.0	80.0	80.3	97.1
81.6	80.1	73.8	68.0
4.0	28.1	-19.3	-22.5
15.1	20.8	-20.9	1.4
2.1	4.3	2.6	5.3
15.3	6.0	5.6	5.2

Social Data Bank.

goods and services, government
fers and long-term capital flows.

TABLE 6

DIRECTION OF RECORDED TRADE OF

	Chad		Mali	
	1970	1976	1970	1976
Total Exports ($ Mil)	29.7	80.6	35.5	70.5
Exports to:				
Industrialized countries	73.6	64.7	28.5	70.1
(Of which) France	72.8	16.1	17.1	32.3
U.S.	--	1.6	--	1.3
Percent Africa	21.6	5.7	61.2	9.2
(Of which) Sahel	--	--	18.6	1.5
Total Imports ($Mil)	65.0	96.9	44.8	216.6
Imports from:				
Industrialized countries	58.1	73.8	55.8	48.2
(Of which) France	38.9	56.7	38.4	34.3
U.S.	3.9	3.7	3.7	1.2
Percent Africa	19.3	16.6	17.6	3.3
(Of which) Sahel	1.9	2.7	7.0	4.7

SOURCE: UN Statistical Bulletin, July 1977.

SAHELIAN ECONOMIES 1970 and 1976

Mauritania		Niger		Senegal		Upper Volta	
1970	1976	1970	1976	1970	1976	1970	1976
90.1	190.4	31.7	86.4	157.5	425.6	18.8	54.7
76.8	86.1	65.0	85.9	71.8	81.3	44.6	72.3
19.4	22.8	46.7	82.6	54.6	54.4	11.9	22.4
0.7	0.2	0.2	--	0.4	1.0	--	4.3
2.5	1.0	12.6	5.7	3.5	10.5	46.6	22.3
2.3	--	1.7	1.2	8.5	5.5	2.6	1.9
55.9	217.7	58.4	173.4	190.7	730.8	47.1	139.2
61.3	76.7	69.0	79.7	71.2	68.4	65.7	77.3
33.9	43.7	45.8	39.5	51.9	39.7	44.7	50.5
13.4	9.3	5.3	5.4	4.8	6.2	4.5	8.8
7.7	9.2	12.1	10.9	3.4	4.2	24.7	16.1
6.0	6.5	5.4	1.1	--	--	6.2	2.9

million persons to the coastal population and seasonal migration is estimated to have increased from 140,000 migrants per year before the Second World War to 200,000 migrants per year by 1970. But there is substantial scope for increasing economic integration and cooperation primarily because existing commercial, communication and transportation arrangements were designed to facilitate ties between the individual countries and their former metropoles. River basin development also presents a relatively new and major opportunity for integration.

A brief review of West African economic organizations suggests that an expanding institutional base already exists for further economic integration. First, the number of organizations suggests that there is an active and widespread interest among West African countries in closer economic ties. Second, there is a history of interest, influenced by a degree of economic integration introduced by colonial powers. Consequently, the West African states tended to establish integration arrangements immediately after their independence. Now there are approximately four organizations which have economic integration as their primary "raison d'etre" and there are at least five other major regional organizations which contribute indirectly to regional integration.

The four principal organizations are the Economic Community of West African States (ECOWAS), the Economic Community of West Africa (CEAO), the Common Organization of African and Mauritanian States (OCAM) and the Entente Council. The national membership of each organization is shown in Table 6. In addition, Table 7 lists some other major regional organizations which indirectly contribute to regional economic integration. In spite of appreciable economic disparities between West African countries, the performance of these organizations has been relatively good. Albeit a high degree of economic integration has not yet been accomplished, these organizations have succeeded in maintaining integration in an active status and have kept the member states favorably disposed toward the idea. At present, groupings such as ECOWAS and CEAO constitute a promising institutional base with the potential to facilitate further economic integration as conditions gradually become more favorable.

INFRASTRUCTURE

The extensive area covered by the Sahelian rural population, long marketing distances and the high cost of an inadequate and inefficient transport system have limited the economic opportunities of the Sahel. Grain surpluses in one region cannot be moved economically into deficit areas, and the cost of transporting meat and other products to the coast is very high. Investments in adequate maintenance and management of roads, railroads, and river transport would, over time, open up markets, reduce the cost of food distribution and increase com-

TABLE 7

SELECTED WEST AFRICAN REGIONAL ECONOMIC ORGANIZATIONS

Country	Economic Integration Organizations				Organizations Which Exert an Integrating Influence				
	ECOWAS	CEAO	OCAM	ENTENTE	BOAD#	UMOA (BCEAO)	WARDA	OMVS	CILSS
Cape Verde	*								*
Chad			*						*
Gambia	*						*		*
Mali	*	*					*	*	*
Mauritania	*	*					*	*	*
Niger	*	*	*	*	*	*	*		*
Senegal	*	*	*		*	*	*	*	*
Upper Volta	*	*	*	*	*	*	*		*
Benin	*		*	*	*	*	*		
Cameroon									
Central African Empire			*						
Gabon			*						
Ghana	*						*		
Guinea	*								
Guinea-Bissau	*								
Ivory Coast	*	*	*	*	*	*	*		
Liberia	*					*			
Nigeria	*						*		
Sierra Leone	*						*		
Togo	*		*	*	*	*	*		

#BOAD The West African Development Bank.
UMOA The West African Monetary Union.
BCEAO The Central Bank of West African States.
WARDA The West African Rice Development Association.
OMVS Senegal River Development Organization.
CILSS Interstate Permanent Committee for Control of Drought in the Sahel.

munications necessary to develop all sectors of the economy.

Infrastructure in the Sahel can be divided into village-based infrastructure (such as houses, wells and feeder roads), major infrastructure works (such as dams and primary roads) and urban infrastructure. In all three categories, the Sahel is clearly less endowed than neighboring countries to the South such as the Ivory Coast or Nigeria. Indeed, infrastructure varies between Sahel countries as a result of different levels of economic development (the GDP of Chad per capita is only 22 percent of Senegal's GDP) and the nature of the colonial heritage in individual states. The relative priority of infrastructure as indicated by the percent of the total government budgets spent on the Public Works Department for construction and maintenance ranges from 34-55 percent. Several different indicators of relative development of infrastructure in four sectors are shown in Table 8. This table emphasizes the relatively low levels of existing infrastructure in the Sahel, particularly for the inland countries such as Chad, Niger, and Mali. Within the Sahel, Senegal is relatively better off with 19 percent paved roads and .01 primary schools per 1,000 population, compared with Mauritania's figures of 8 percent paved roads and .004 primary schools per 1,000 population.

Rural development is highly dependent upon transportation. The economic development process applied to agriculture involves shifting people from subsistence up the ladder into the commercial sub-sector. Increasing productivity calls for utilizing increasing quantities of purchased inputs and producing additional products for the market. While the whole transportation system in most Sahelian countries needs attention, lack of rural roads is the major infrastructure constraint for the rural poor. Few Sahelian countries have even the truck roads which are required for productive rural economies, let alone the farm-to-market roads. W. David Hopper has stressed:

> In order to unlock the potential of their soils the African nations, the poorest in the world, must therefore be prepared to make a colossal investment in land productivity, in agricultural scientific research and extension services and in the structural development of their farm economies.[25]

TABLE 8

INDICATORS OF INFRASTRUCTURE DEVELOPMENT

Country	Road Network (Total km/km)	Road Network (Percent paved)	Health (# hospitals and clinics/1000 pop.)	Education (# primary schools/ 1000/ pop.)
Cape Verde	13.0	29	.05	1.4
Chad	1.4	3	.01	.21
The Gambia	3.4	10	.01	.20
Mali	.7	12	.01	.21
Mauritania	1.4	8	.004	n/a
Niger	.5	10	n/a	.22
Senegal	.8	19	.01	.30
Upper Volta	.6	5	.03	.12
Sahel Average			.02	.38

SOURCES: # Hospitals from United Nations Statistical Yearbook, 1976, Table 206.

Primary Schools from UNESCO Statistical Yearbook, 1975, pp. 122-151.

Road Network from Louis Berger International, Road Maintenance Diagnostic Study for the Sahel, Volumes 2 and 9, 1977.

In simplest form, the present transportation network can be represented by the following diagram:

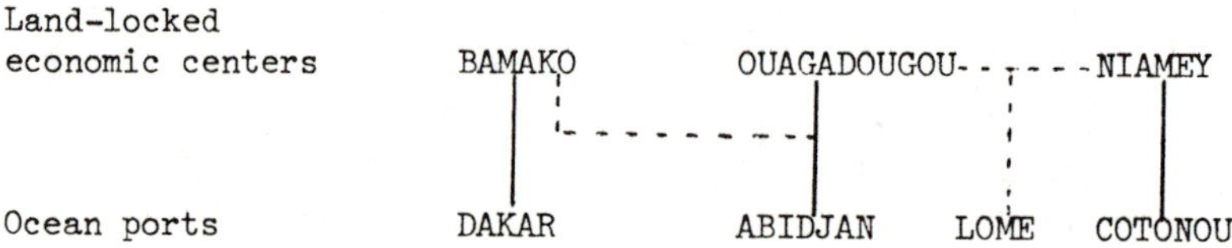

in which:

- solid lines represent rail connections or combination rail-road connections on which traffic is quite heavy and transportation costs quite low;

- dotted lines represent fairly well-equipped road connections on which traffic is light and costs are high.

There are,today, about 50,000 miles of roads and tracks. Of these, over 31,000 miles are inadequately maintained or not maintained at all, and over 6,000 miles are in a deteriorated condition. In addition, there are 1,800 miles of railroad with obsolete rolling stock and poor operating management. Of the 50,000 miles of roads in the Sahel, only 21 percent are all-weather -- 11 percent are paved, 1 percent are gravel and 9 percent are earth roads. The remaining 79 percent are either dry-weather earth roads or somply tracks.

As one illustration of the significance of these figures, we can compare the mileage of non-urban all-weather roads in the U.S. and the Sahel, as follows:

	Total All-Weather Miles	Miles/Inhabitant	Miles/Sq. Mile of Area
U.S. (continental)	3,200,000	0.01	1.1
New York State	66,361	0.004	1.4
Sahel (excluding desert area)	10,500	0.0004	0.01

Thus, the U.S. has 320 times as many miles of all-weather road as the Sahel, 50 times the miles per inhabitant and 100 times the miles per unit area of the Sahel (even excluding its desert area). New York State alone has over 6 times the miles of all-weather road of the Sahel, 10 times the miles per inhabitant and 140 times the miles per unit area. The mileage of non-urban all-weather roads in New York State, in fact, exceeds the mileage of roads of all types including tracks in the Sahel. The density of all types of roads in Africa, including feeder roads and tracks, in relation to total land area, varies between a low of one mile of road per 2,500 square miles of area in the Sudan (about 90 percent desert) to one mile per 10 square miles in Rwanda, whereas the Sahel has one mile of road per 100 square miles of land area.

With so poor a system of all-weather roads the marketing of produce from an expanded agriculture becomes difficult and uneconomical. The rapid deterioration of vehicles and their upkeep and repair raise the cost of transporting produce from the farm, reducing the profit margin and incentive. These costs also contribute to raising the price of production inputs as well as consumer goods and social services basic to improving the lot of the rural population. Even the provision of the most elementary health care and education becomes difficult and a burden on the region's limited human and financial resources. One example of the constraint on rural development resulting from the inadequate road system is the plight of the livestock sector. Although the major livestock market for Sahel cattle is in the coastal population centers, the high cost of transport and the loss of weight of animals on the long trip over bad roads can make local meat less competitive in the coastal cities with meat imported from Europe. This results in both lost income to the grower and a lost opportunity to earn foreign exchange for the economy. Of course, the growth of the livestock industry is impeded.

The Sahelian countries have identified some 3,900 km. of first-priority primary, secondary and feeder roads for new construction or rehabilitation which are essential to the general development of the region and which should be carried out in the decade of 1980-1990 at an estimated cost of $980 million. Of this total, $500 million has been committed by various donors. The relative importance to the region of all-weather roads can be judged from the breakdown of the 3,900 km. of first-priority roads. The proposals call for the expenditure of $656 million for 1,368 km. of primary all-weather roads and $288 million for 2,135 km. of secondary all-weather roads, as opposed to only $30 million for the construction of 397 km. of dry-weather feeder roads.

The sparseness of major rural infrastructure is further indicated by the fact that there are only three large irrigation areas in the Sahel, despite the existence of over 3,000 km. of major rivers flowing through the Sahel zone. The Sahel contains some 60 million hectares (150 million acres) of arable land. Of this total, about 12.6 million hectares (31.5 million acres) are under rainfed cultivation, primarily in areas where rainfall varies between 12 and 32 inches per year. Only 600,000 hectares (1.5 million acres) are under irigated or flood recession cultivation. The balance, or four-fifths of the arable land of the Sahel, is unused. The one-fifth of arable land that is under cultivation is farmed by traditional methods subject to the vagaries of scarce annual rainfall and recurring droughts. All this despite (a) the existence of plentiful water in the large river basins of the Senegal, Niger, Gambia, Casamance, Chari-Logone and Volta Rivers which together could provide irrigation for four million hectares (10 million acres), and (b) other sources of water which could irrigate another 10 million hectares (25 million acres). Thus, the 13 million hectares presently under cultivation in the Sahel could be increased by an additional 14 million hectares with controlled irrigation.

At present only one major dam exists in the Sahel -- the Markala, a low dam upstream of the interior delta of the Niger River, in Mali. Another dam in Mali, the Selingue, is now under construction on the Sankarani, a Niger tributary, upstream from Bamako. The cost of the remaining major dam construction for the four basins of the Senegal, Gambia, Niger and Volta Rivers is estimated at $1,130 million at 1977 prices. To fully utilize the water made available from the structures for irrigation in the Sahel would require an investment of an additional $4,000 million at 1977 prices over the next two decades for land preparation and the construction of accessory irrigation structures (canals, dikes, pumping installations).

The Sahelian countries estimate that in the next 20 years, if funds are made available, 940,000 hectares could be placed under controlled (all-year) irrigation which would yield two crops per year. About one-fourth of this area could be irrigated within the next two-three years for double cropping without the need for new dams to be built. By constructing water control projects, another one-fourth of this area could be in operation between 1983-1990 and the remaining half brought under cultivation between 1991 and 2000. Estimates of the cost of this work are not presently available. However, even if the necessary sums were available, it would be unrealistic to expect controlled irrigation agriculture to expand to the areas envisaged in the next 20 years without the technical personnel both to manage and operate the water control systems and, just as importantly, to extend the new farming methods to the rural population who will be the main beneficiaries. This will require setting up the necessary institutional framework for training, credit and marketing. An estimated $1.5 billion would be required in the 1980-85 period for this purpose alone, of which something less than $1 billion has been committed by various donors.

INDUSTRY AND MINING

Sahelian elites recognize the critical role that agriculture must play in their development in the next few decades. Yet, they also believe that ultimately industrialization must assume greater relative importance. While some industry may effectively complement agricultural development during the next 15 to 20 years, the more important contribution during this period will be in laying the basis for industrialization in the twenty-first century. This will occur through the skills created in existing industry, through the expansion of markets for manufactured goods associated with agricultural development, and through laying the groundwork for hydroelectric power development.

The industrial sector in the Sahel is small in terms of its share of GDP but it is important because it conserves or produces foreign exchange and because the industrial sector is and will continue to be the principal user of excess labor from the agricultural sector. Industrial activity is also an important stabilizing force because it is somewhat less sensitive to the vagaries of Sahelian climates. After mining, the industrial sector was the only other sector to have achieved a positive rate of growth during the 1965-1975 period. The industrial sector also increased its share of Sahelian GDP from approximately 14 to 18 percent during 1965-1975.

Industry in the Sahel is mostly engaged in producing relatively basic import substitutes and in processing agricultural commodities for export. Foreign capital and expertise are involved in most industrial activity in partnership with host governments. Senegal has the largest and most diversified industrial base, deriving about one-fifth of its GDP from the industrial sector.

Mineral exploitation in the Sahel employs modern, capital intensive techniques and is therefore not a significant employer. Its share of GDP is also small, accounting for only four percent of GDP in 1975. Mineral production is becoming increasingly important as a foreign exchange earner for Senegal (phosphates), and Niger (uranium). Iron and copper exports have been a mainstay for Mauritania for several years where mining accounts for about 27 percent of GDP and 70 percent of export earnings. Upper Volta is expected to start exploiting a manganeese deposit and some minor gold deposits. The impending exploitation of oil in Chad and coal in Niger will substantially decrease the energy import requirements for these countries and generate new domestic economic activities. Besides earning or saving foreign exchange, mineral exploitation in the Sahel is important because it provides a stabilizing influence on revenue flows. Mining is the only major activity which is not linked to agricultural production and can thus help maintain the continuity of development efforts even during dry periods. Over the 1965-1975 period mining recorded a real growth rate of about three percent annually while other sectors, except industry, had negative real rates.

Mineral exploitation could ramify to the direct benefit of Sahelian agriculture. The low level of phosphate in the soil of the Sahel is one major restriction on the increase of agricultural production. Yet, phosphate is mined commercially in Senegal and Togo. In Senegal the raw material is made into fertilizer mixtures and a superphosphating installation is planned for Togo. Beds of coprolitic (fossil) phosphate have been found in Mali and Niger suitable for crop production. The deposits are low enough in fluorine to be used additionally as a component in mineral supplements for livestock. Substantial deposits of phosphate rock have been discovered in the area of the junction of Niger, Upper Volta, and the Republic of Benin with portions of the deposit in each country. The material is suitable for crop fertilizer, but may have too high a fluorine concentration to allow its use in livestock food supplements without further processing. Increased crop production will also require the addition of nitrogen and subsequently potash to Sahelian soils. After a few years of adding phosphate and nitrogen, a need develops for the application of potash. There are no presently identified sources of potash and nitrates in the region. There is, however, a possibility that they would exist in fossil saline lake beds. Prospecting for potash and nitrates should, therefore, be given a high priority in any general mineral survey being contemplated. Since nitrogen also can be obtained from LP gas, Nigeria could become a supplier of ammonia to the region.

Most of the identified mineral deposits in the Sahel other than uranium are of low concentration. Their distance from evacuation points (ports, railheads, roads), the lack of electric power for exploitation, and low concentration, hinder more extensive mining. In the case of transport of Nigerien uranium, there are political complications too. Algeria's trans-Saharan highway reaches the Niger border, but the Niger government, under pressure from France, has balked at having the highway extended to the Arlit uranium works in northern Niger. The French prefer to truck the uranium southward and ship it from the port of Cotonou, a route nearly twice as long.

With satellite and magnetometer techniques now available, preliminary surveys can be made at relatively low cost to locate possible areas of commercially exploitable deposits. Donor assistance to Sahelian governments for a regionwide survey would be justified within the framework of a long-range development program. As programs of road construction, railway improvement and expansion, and development of river transport progress, those sites identified in preliminary surveys close to access arteries could become attractive enough to encourage the expenditure of private funds for more detailed exploration.

AGRICULTURAL RESOURCES

The Sahelian economies are agricultural economies. Agriculture, including livestock production, employs most of the population and it is a major component of GDP. Agricultural products are a major source of foreign exchange earnings and they constitute the raw material for much of domestic industry.

Despite the large proportion of population working in the agricultural sector usually less than 50 percent of GDP is derived from that sector. This relatively modest share of GDP reflects the low (and declining) productivity of agriculture and, for certain countries -- Senegal, Niger and Mauritania -- increase in mining and industrial activity.

Agricultural production can be divided into two major categories, crops and livestock. Agriculture, as it pertains to crop production includes crops which are grown primarily for cash and ultimate export, and food crops grown primarily for consumption by the producers with local sale of any residual amounts. Groundnuts and cotton are the major cash crops with small portions of both commodities going to local consumption. Millet, sorghum and legumes are the principal food crops. Relatively small amounts of rice, wheat, corn and sugar cane are also cultivated mostly for sale on domestic markets.

Albeit donor resources are primarily directed to increasing food crop production, it is essential to be aware of the importance of cash crop production. First, the cultivation of cash crops and food crops is inextricably linked through the production process in which both types of crops compete for the same land and labor resources. Second, cash crop production is a crucial component of rural incomes, a factor of prime concern to the donor community. Third, cash crop production constitutes the main source of foreign exchange for most of the Sahelian economies.

The share of cash crops in total agricultural activity is relatively modest, contributing perhaps 10 to 15 percent of gross value added in agriculture. In 1973 and 1974 approximately 2 tons of millet and sorghum were produced for every ton of groundnuts and cotton. A yearly average of 2.9 million metric tons of millet and sorghum were produced in 1973 and 1974. Based on 1975-1975 production figures, Niger, Upper Volta, and Mali are the largest millet and sorghum producers. Senegal and Mali rank first and second in groundnut production, with Chad and Mali being the largest Sahelian producers of cotton.

In contrast to the modest share of cash crops in total agricultural production, earnings from exports of groundnuts and cotton (and cowpeas in the case of Niger) comprise about 50 percent of total export earnings for Senegal, Mali, Upper Volta, and Niger. Cotton exports provide Chad with 85 percent of its export earnings. The international prices for groundnuts and cotton have remained at relatively high levels.

Sahelians dependent upon livestock for a major portion of family subsistence and cash incomes are estimated at roughly 5.2 million persons. Family income of livestock-dependent households is estimated to be between $70-$150 per person. The sale of live animals is the main source of cash income in areas with less than 20 inches of rainfall. Thus 70 percent of the population is engaged in raising livestock in Mauritania with the figure ranging around 20 percent in Niger, Chad and Mali and 6 percent in Upper Volta. Livestock production averages about 11 to 15 percent of GDP in each of the Sahelian economies except Mauritania where it constitutes one-fourth of GDP. Exports of livestock and livestock products vary from 40 percent of total exports in Upper Volta to 20 and 28 percent respectively for Niger and Chad and near zero for Senegal.

Cattle exports fell drastically in 1974 and 1975. Livestock production is potentially an important source of income and improved nutrition for both herders and small farmers because of the growing domestic and export demand for livestock products. Productivity as measured by calving rates or herd off-take is low. The opportunity and desire of Sahelian countries to develop the livestock sector is constrained principally by the state of the natural resource base and the institutional setting of the livestock enterprise. Moreover, the latter impacts on the farmer since the deterioration of the range is a consequence of inefficiencies in its use. The principal institutional constraints are: the herder-owner relationship in which the herder's compensation is derived principally from milk for subsistance and sale (as a consequence, overmilking results in high calf mortality and low rates of reproduction); the limited access of the livestock-owning population to consumer commodities and, hence, limited need for cash together with the absence of savings/investment alternatives, resulting in maintainence of large unproductive herds (an off-take rate of about 8 percent is the general rule); the limited availability of credit for either production or marketing activities; and government policies which regulate marketing of animals within and across national boundaries.

The Sahelian countries have fish producing waters totaling 9,500,000 ha of marine coastal waters over the continental shelf and 8,300,000 ha of lakes, rivers, and flood plains. The coastal waters are chiefly along the Senegal and Mauritania coasts and 90 percent of the inland waters are found in Mali and Chad. The annual value of the fish catch to Sahelian countries is $147,000,000 or roughly 4 percent of the regional gross product. Fishery products exported are valued at $96,000,000 or about 16 percent of the value of the export trade for the entire Sahel. While 4 percent of the gross product of the region was generated by fisheries only 1.5-2 percent of the total labor force is involved with fisheries. Full time fishermen in the Sahel region number 160,000 of which 75 percent fish in the inland lakes and rivers.

In 1978 animal fish production from coastal waters was 1.7 million tons of which 1.3 million tons were taken by foreign vessels and 400,000 tons caught by Sahelian countries. It is estimated that the potential sustained annual harvest from the coastal waters probably will not exceed 2.1 million tons. Freshwater production is presently estimated to be 220,000 tons per year. One study indicates that sustained freshwater harvest could be increased to 390,000 tons per year by the year 2000.[26]

In Mauritania, the fishing and processing operations use foreign capital and labor and the output is exported. Fishing produces over 5 percent of GDP and is expected to reach 10 percent by 1980. In Senegal, offshore fishing is a high growth industry three-quarters of which is based on traditional methods. Including the 17 fish processing plants, this industry in Senegal employs over 40,000 workers.

The contribution of fish to the animal protein needs of Sahelians is high. Per capita consumption of fish averages 14.8 kg per person. Subsistence fishing is common during periods of food shortage and, since statistics on this fishing activity are not available, the importance of fish in the diet of poor people is probably underestimated. This supplement to Sahelian diets is critical in view of the fact that fish protein contains a broad spectrum of amino acids which supply sources of essential nutrients lacking in the diet of people consuming, in the main, cereal grains. Like mining, offshore fishing is significant as an economic stabilizer because it is independent of rainfall variations. The foreign demand for fish is expanding and unlike mining, offshore fishing and fish processing provide considerable scope for employment.

CONCLUSION

A review of the Sahel's economy and resources reveals considerable potential for development. The natural resources of the Sahel consist of large expanses of semi-arid land suitable for the production of cereals and livestock, major river basins that can be developed for irrigation, and minerals in largely unknown quantities. These resources provide a sound basis for development, particularly as national development becomes increasingly integrated with West African regional development. The agricultural area under rainfed conditions is estimated to be on the order of 60 million hectares with only 20 percent currently under cultivation. It is reasonable to project a 2-3 fold increase in the rainfed agriculture sector over the next 20-25 years -- if a sufficient level of effort is spent on research for improving production technology, on expanding and improving services to farmers; and on improving the health environment in the higher rainfall areas. The water resources of the Sahelian countries are estimated to be sufficient to irrigate about 14 million hectares -- with only about 600,000 ha. currently under irrigation. With improved management and marketing, livestock production could be improved 50-100 percent as herd structures are brought into balance with increasingly higher rates of off-take. The Sahel's potential for serving as a principal food supplier to the coastal countries is being reaffirmed as the Sahel recovers from the effects of the great drought.

There are a number of interrelated constraints to improving rural welfare in the Sahel. The natural resource endowment is difficult to manage and is subject to environmental deterioration. A low level of technology keeps both human and resource productivity low. The region lacks all-weather secondary roads and feeder roads to link rural and urban areas. Transport linkages with coastal states are inadequate, especially for the landlocked countries. Highly centralized political and administrative institutions constrain independent local action. Human resource constraints include poor health, the prevalence of endemic diseases, and limited numbers of people trained in needed development skills. Government policies are evolving but still tend to favor urban over rural interests. Finally, the Sahelian countries depend on the export of a few primary commodities for foreign exchange earnings.

These natural resource and technological constraints are surmountable and there is considerable potential for creating productive employment opportunities in agriculture in the higher rainfall areas and river basins and in livestock in the semi-arid zones. At the same time, social structure, institutions, and policies are beginning to evolve in directions that are more compatible with an equity-tinged development philosophy. Moreover, the Sahel has attracted substantial interest and investment on the part of donors who have joined together with Sahelians for the purpose of rationally developing the region.

3
A Strategy for Drought Proofing the Sahel

As the international relief operation moved slowly into gear during the spring of 1973, there was little coordination between either recipients or donors. While Sahelian governments made occasional joint appeals for more assistance, self-interest understandably dictated national positions when conflicts of interest arose. Governments would permit diversion of grain initially intended for them to meet critical needs in other states, but not when the original recipient felt its need also was urgent. Late in 1974, Mali and Upper Volta became embroiled in a border conflict which diverted substantial resources for arms purchases. Niger and Senegal were among the four African states which succeeded in mediating the dispute.

Donors were no less divided. The French made it clear that they preferred to dispatch aid to their former colonies bilaterally. Inquiries by U.S. embassies in other donor capitals met with sketchy responses. The pattern of donor coordination in the Sahel remained uneven until FAO sponsored multinational teams to assess grain needs before the 1974 harvest. This approach heightened cooperation and secured the vast quantities of grain needed to avert starvation. This is not to say that there were no complications. The perennial problem of coordination of deliveries was only slightly alleviated. The Soviets and Chinese provided FAO with no delivery dates and, Sahelian governments, fearing a reduction in donated grain, refused to reveal the extent of their commercial imports. The prepositioning of grain in the Sahel well in advance of rainy season flooding, although risking depredations of insects and other pests, made for much more effective outreach and confirmed the necessity of cooperation among donors.

Coordination between recipients and donors varied substantially and not surprisingly usually was a function of the efficiency of the local government. Problems were most acute with the Tombalbaye regime in Chad, which was preoccupied with insurrection and an authenticity campaign. Food aid from both West Germany and the United States was rebuffed in response to an alleged violation of Chad's national sovereignty during negotiation for release of a German hostage in the first instance and to U.S. press criticism of drought relief administration in the second. In several countries the local drought coordinator was an official already overburdened with responsibilities, and it was difficult to attract and hold his attention.

Inept and corrupt administration of emergency assistance were among the justifications the military cited while ousting civil governments in Chad and Niger. In Upper Volta a planned return to civilian government was postponed on the grounds that political activity was interfering with drought relief. In areas adjacent to the Sahel, several governments sought to exploit the drought situation with claims of local crop failures. Other area nations were found actually to be suffering from the drought, and U.S. assistance was given to Cameroon, Guinea, and Ghana. Nigeria chose to look after its own drought victims and provided funds for drought relief elsewhere.

Even before the true proportions of the drought were recognized, senior State and AID officials were calling attention to the deterioration of the region's economy and the consequent need for a long-term and financially intensive program to develop the Sahel. In 1972 a working group composed of representatives of State, AID, and the National Academy of Sciences was established to study ecological implications as well as development options. Discussions were held with the French late in 1972 and early the following year. They indicated a willingness to cooperate, as long as a long term program would not appear to be a uniquely American initiative. The French subsequently agreed to inventory and to make available to the U.S. studies undertaken by French experts which might relate to a long term development effort. The European Development Fund (FED) responded positively to an American inquiry, suggesting the possible applicability of advanced technology, including that of the ERTS satellite system. At a donors meeting convoked by FAO in May 1973, the U.S. delegation called attention to the long term needs of the Sahel. The following month U.N. Deputy Secretary General Brad Morse announced formation of a special unit, the Special Sahel Office (SSO), which would focus on medium and long term relief, while FAO concentrated on the emergency.

By early 1975, there was consensus among members of the donor community that an opportunity was present for mobilizing substantial long-term development resources and that a truly global approach to development in the Sahel might be considered. With this opportunity came the realization that a new order of development could be sought; that the difficulties in the Sahel which cause continual decline and periodic cataclysms during drought must be viewed from a perspective that is explicitly comprehensive. Underlying this international consensus was the conviction that the agricultural production framework in the

Sahel, which operates effectively, but inefficiently, during average years and displays extreme fragility when rainfall is short, can be brought to much higher levels of productivity, that it can display very meaningful characteristics of resilience during bad times and that these improvements can be achieved without destroying either the agricultural basis of production or the rural culture of the Sahelian people. Corollary conclusions from these analyses are that short-term aid flows will not stem the historic decline in agricultural production, that current medium-term development projects will not prevent occurrence of another disaster, and that continuation of current aid patterns implies the specter of a drought disaster whose relief will entail costs beyond the capacity of donor resources. The development goal which formed in response to this analysis was regional self-sufficiency in food production and, in the longer term, sustained economic growth. Viewing regional "performance" as the goal of development assistance is a fundamental departure from previous planning. Its consequences with respect to program design, programming methods and justification, management and evaluation of program implementation,and coordination of the aid resources and diplomatic interests of both donor and recipient countries are enormous.

To achieve a synthesis of social justice and economic growth, the choice of economic development strategy is critical. Alternative development strategies conceal explicit and implicit assumptions that have substantial implications for national direction, institutional capacities, political stability, and social organization. There are both significant transactions costs and opportunity costs for any development strategy. Moreover, as the Sahel amply demonstrates, exogenous factors can be decisive in the selection of strategy. However, the key question is not whether the Sahelian countries are exploited in a neocolonial bind but how to maximize benefits that come along with encroachment upon national sovereignty?

Recipient governments often desire projects with short-term results for immediate demonstration of results to their constituents. This congeniality to a crash modernization strategy is shared by donor governments because they do not like to commit funding for long periods. A dual development strategy or "development as usual" is the common outcome of the traditional project-by-project approach. Let us briefly consider these strategies as contrasted with a progressive integrated development strategy.

The crash modernization strategy takes the view that front end technology and organization are synonymous with economic development. This strategy seeks to equip the labor force, or at least part of it, with the most up-to-date tools as quickly as possible. Its philosophy has been expressed in the following terms:

> . . . the objective of economic development must be clarified or, if necessary, redefined. Let the objective be a society in which all are employed in activities in which the most productive methods known to man are used.[1]

This objective may be achieved, it is argued, by concentrating on the establishment of an advanced sector and expanding it rapidly to absorb and integrate those presently engaged in the traditional sector. This advanced sector would be composed of large complex organizations run by a "techno-structure" -- professional managers and technicians -- contrasting with "the last remnant of the atomistic society of nineteenth-century liberals -- the family-run and operator-owned farmes."[2]

In the model for the dual development strategy the main emphasis is placed on modern technology. But this is confined as far as possible to areas that are complementary to existing traditional activity (for example complementary relationships between small and large firms are encouraged), or where quality and price considerations are paramount (for example in the export markets), or for the exploitation of natural resources when little technological flexibility exists (for instance oil). Nor are the most capital-intensive complexes necessarily selected. Some capital saving might be realized by modernising only the basic production processes, leaving ancillary operations to be performed by labor-intensive methods.

Neither of these strategies will do for the Sahel. To begin with a technical critique, in the crash modernization strategy the elimination of unemployment is a very long-term goal indeed. The over-all effect of the dual development strategy does not represent much of an improvement. While the advanced sector achieves significant expansion in output and productivity, the dualism of the economy is accentuated. The great majority of the population is left outside the development process and does not benefit directly, or for that matter indirectly, from economic progress. Cognitive exposure is not a tenable polarity on a wide scale in either strategy. Santanya's maxim, "those who do not remember the past are condemned to repeat it" is germane. Over exposure or double exposure are the most likely polarities to hold under either of these strategies (see discussion in Chapter 5).

The third strategy takes the same starting point as the dual development strategy, that is, it recognizes the presence in the developing countries of an advanced sector widely separated in technological, productivity, and income levels from the residual sector that employs the majority of the labor force. In the progressive integrated development strategy, however, a primary aim is to close the gap by promoting growth from the base upwards. This is to be achieved by targeting the bulk of investment funds to the residual sector, thus allowing a progressive increase in the capital/labor proportions and, hence, in productivity, while maintaining capital stock and employment levels in the modern sector constant.

Given the assumptions of constant investment/income and capital/output ratios, the three strategies considered here are very similar in their effect on the growth rate of GDP and the average labor productivity. But the progressive strategy is significantly superior when measured against social welfare and conceptual tectonics criteria. Not only is there reduced inequality in the distribution of income and improvement in the material well-being of the poor, together with an increase in productive employment, but the chances for wide-scale cognitive exposure are multiplied exponentially in an incrementalist framework. Unfortunately, the organic growth process that characterizes the integrated development strategy has not proved to be attractive to policy makers, involving as it does a "cooling of the heels" by elites, while the rest of the economy attempts to catch up. Progressive, evolutionary change is believed to offer a slower over-all rate of growth than can be anticipated from a more radical transformation of the economy. as a result of the transfer of advanced technology and large-scale organizational structures from the industrial countries. These emotive and "a priori" judgments have tended to obscure the fact that most successful long-term integrated development has taken the form of progressive modernization in the past. Indeed, the gradualist approach typifies capitalist growth. Montesquieu captures the process as follows:

> One commerce leads to another: the small to the medium the medium to the large; and the person who was so anxious to make a little money places himself in a situation in which he is no less anxious to make a lot.[3]

As Hirschman notes in a remarkable history of the intellectual ascent of capitalism, the doctrine benefitted from a long buried vein of thought among seventeenth and eighteenth century scholars; the world of the "full human personality," replete with diverse passions, appeared to these individuals as a menace that needed to be exorcized to the greatest possible extent. Money-making and commerce together made for a calm passion that could introduce such assets of an interest-governed world as predictability and constancy. Capitalism, according to Montesquieu in his De l'esprit des lois contributed to a felicitous condition for man: "Et il est heureux pour les hommes d'être dans une situation où, pendant que leurs passions leur inspirent la pensée d'être méchants, ils ont pourtant intérêt de ne pas l'être."[4] Unfortunately, even where men have espoused capitalism, the desire for a fast buck has rigidified rather than undermined the passion known as impatience.

The upshot of this digression is that interest in long-term development is not common. This interest will not grow unless such developments can be shown convincingly to be directly related to human needs. Long-term developments must have clear, unambiguous goals. But donor organizations and nations need a measure of achievement in the short run. Thus, any long-term program must have intermediate objectives which have meaning for the lives of the people in the region in question. To go beyond important but short-term humanitarian relief implies major changes over periods of at least 10 to 20 years. A problem in long-term development projections is estimating the kinds and magnitudes of investments that are needed to have an appreciable effect on the lives and opportunities of the target group. The nature of various governmental and national interests over a long period of time must be clarified and consolidated as opposed to taking a piecemeal approach. Following a clearer definition of the program and its goals, the essential ingredients of the program must be ranked in terms of a logical time sequence. This kind of critical path projection is key to Sahelian development efforts.

Near Term (1976-1980). A pace-setting view of a balanced development program for the Sahel is presented in considerable detail in AID's Development Assistance Program for the Central-West African Region (revised November 1975). In this document, AID recommends that emphasis be placed during the initial five-year period on food crops and livestock, on rural health, and on training related to key tasks. The agency also strongly recommends that the U.S. program in the Sahel maintain a balance between projects with short-term results and those with long-term payoffs, between national and regional project orientation, and between projects with an extensive impact (e.g., assistance in dry land farming) and those with an intensive effect (e.g., irrigated farming).

The composition of the projects undertaken in this near-term period, regardless of funding source, has been determined by needs evidenced by the drought and by the requirements of the long-term program. In the 1976-1980 period, several tracks of the regional development program run concurrently.

First, there are those activities designed to improve directly the lot of rural families in the near-term by applying the resources and technology now available to crop production, protection, and storage and other immediately beneficial ends. Examples of this approach are found in the small-scale, local activities not exceeding $500,000 and of 12-24 months duration which AID proposed in its FY 1977 presentation to the Congress as the Accelerated Impact Program. Other examples are the projects initiated since the spring of 1974, with three to five year objectives, including such activities as the sorghum and millet production program in central Senegal. While these activities have a direct impact on the lives of those involved, the number of people affected is limited, and the projects represent a learning experience for African governments and donors on new approaches which can later be broadened.

The second important track of projects in the 1976-1980 period are the initiation of medium-term programs which also employ available technology but over a somewhat wider geographic area. These are: integrated rural development schemes, broader approaches to dryland farming, regional range management and livestock production programs, infrastructure studies and construction activities, area-specific health care and training programs. Although significantly expanded, these projects still largely represent area-specific programs affecting only a portion of total national and regional populations.

The third track of undertakings active in this period are those studies and pilot schemes required to bring into play the entire potential of the area. This includes studies in developing new technologies for dryland farming and planning for the development of the river basins and other water resources of the area. Some development of irrigation is initiated to gain experience that could result in better utilization of the river basins. Studies of potential minerals exploitation and industrial development in conjunction with river basin development are conducted.

A final track entails the initiation of training programs and building of institutions which subsequent, broader development programs will require. This involves training managers, technicians, research scientists, and others who will be needed to manage and design modernized dryland farming, develop river basin facilities, organize and manage health programs, carry on broader educational and training programs, undertake improved transport maintenance, and plan for a new transport development.

Medium Term (1980-1990). A major push will be undertaken in this period to extend the productive capacity of dryland farmers throughout the region and to provide the people of the Sahel with a more adequate and equitable distribution of life-support services. It will be essential to continue to expand training programs and institutions which were initiated in the initial period. Development will continue to be concentrated primarily on dryland farming. This will be achieved by introducing improved dryland farming techniques and by extending and replicating smaller projects and pilot programs undertaken in the earlier phase. Dryland farming will also be made more effective in the medium term by extensive development of storage systems both at the farm and district levels, of crop protection services, and of information and marketing systems. The accent will be on strengthening commercial links between rural areas and urban centers. Programs to improve the commercial off-take of livestock and to improve the management of range resources will go forward.

These efforts in the directly productive sector will be complemented by programs to extend preventive health care, nutrition, and mother/child care programs to all but the most thinly populated areas of the region. At the same time, the trial work which commenced in the near-term period to develop production-oriented literacy programs and community-oriented school programs will be extended to adults and to primary school-aged children throughout the Sahel. Simultaneously, planning will be accelerated for the exploitation of river basins and other water resources. A broad range of sizeable irrigation experiments will be undertaken, and diseases which have prevented development in some areas of the river basins will be eradicated. The effort in this period will be directed towards development of the river basins on the broadest possible basis during the last decade of the century.

Long-Term and Onwards. Drawing upon studies, pilot projects, training programs, and institution-building activities undertaken in the two earlier periods, a regional development program in its long-term phase will seek to tap the larger resources of the region, particularly the major river basins. By phasing in basin development beginning with the Senegal River Basin, the development program will move from food self-sufficiency towards self-sustaining economic growth in the Sahel and permanent improvement in the quality of life of its peoples. These conditions will be founded not only on greater yields derived from irrigated agriculture, but from industry (principally agro-industry) and mineral exploitation which hydroelectric power networks could make possible. Health services will be expanded to monitor and offset the greater hazard of waterborne diseases introduced by extensive irrigation systems. As the long-term phase advances, the balanced development of modernized agriculture, both in dryland systems and in the river basins, complemented by a modern, functional system of livestock production would be realized. With incentives of improved production and marketing systems and with reduced health hazards, population growth will have slowed. As a consequence of these and other factors, the Sahelian environment will be better protected for the future.

FROM DESERT FRINGE TO DEVELOPMENT FRONTIER

Agreement on the urgent need for a long-term regional development program in the Sahel has given rise to two important institutions. They are the Permanent Interstate Committee for Drought Control in the Sahel (CILSS), responsible for coordination among Sahelian countries of long-term assistance, and the Club des Amis du Sahel, a consultative group of donors and recipients concerned with Sahelian long-term development interests.

The CILSS was originally formed by five Sahelian countries in March 1973. It attempted from the beginning to represent the needs of the member states for donor financing of specific project proposals. In September 1973, CILSS, representing six Sahelian countries, called the first important international conference at Ouagadougou, Upper Volta to address the post-drought period. At the meeting, in an action which has influenced the post-drought development agenda, CILSS presented for donor consideration a list of 300 projects, totalling an estimated $3 billion, of which CILSS identified $850 million as "priority" activities. The following March in Bamako, Mali, the CILSS states set forth their principal objectives for a post-drought program in the Sahel. These included: 1) reducing the consequences of emergency situations in the future; 2) insuring self-sufficiency in staple foods; and 3) accelerating economic and social development in the region's least developed countries.

Coordinating Sahelian (Mali, Chad, Upper Volta, Mauritania, Niger, Senegal, Cape Verde and The Gambia) activity toward regional long-term development has become the primary role of CILSS. The Committee has evolved from an initial role of donor resources solicitation for drought relief to leadership in regionwide integrated planning. The CILSS Secretariate is accountable to the Sahelian Chiefs of State, who periodically meet to review issues of policy or to resolve special problems, and to the CILSS Council of Ministers (at least one minister from each member state) which meets at least twice a year to examine and approve the CILSS program of work (plans and progress). The senior policy maker in the administration of CILSS is the President of the Council of Ministers, who is "ex officio" designated as the Minister-Coordinator. At the December 1977 meeting of the CILSS Chiefs of State and Council of Ministers in The Gambia, the Presidency of CILSS passed from Mauritania to the President of The Gambia, Sir Dawda Jawara, and the Senegal Minister of Rural Development, Adrien Senghor, assumed the duties as Minister-Coordinator from Minister Boulama Manga of Niger. The CILSS Secretariate, located in Ouagadougou, Upper Volta, is headed by an Executive Secretary (Ali Cisse from Mali). The staff is largely expatriate, on secundment from donor governments. The CILSS Heads of State meeting in December 1977, also provided for national CILSS committees whose task will be to integrate the results of CILSS' planning and programming work into the national development plans of each of the Sahelian countries. The working groups and CILSS Secretariate also report to the Heads of States meetings which take place every two years, and to the CILSS Council of Ministers which meets biannually to examine and approve CILSS programs.

With the end of the severe drought and the resumption of the rains in the Sahel in June-September 1974, CILSS and the international donor community continued to search out additional ways to bring about a basic transformation of the region. CILSS, AID, and the Rockefeller Foundation arranged for a conference of select experts on the Sahel, which was convened under the auspices of the National Academy of Sciences in Bellagio, Italy, October 24-29, 1974. By 1975 the donor agencies had completed initial studies which determined the long-term development needs of the region. Among the first of these studies was the Massachusetts Institute of Technology's "Framework for Evaluating Long-Term Strategies for the Development of the Sahel- Sudan Region," funded by AID. Other important studies for a post-drought program were conducted by the World Bank, FAO, the UNDP, various Franch agencies, and by AID. An analysis and synthesis of these studies were subsequently made under the auspices of the Organization for Economic Cooperation and Development (OECD).[5]

While not constituting a strategy for the development of the region, something which only the Sahelians themselves can conceive, these surveys share various assumptions which together appear to form an indispensable foundation for the development of such a strategy. These studies all suggest the necessity of planning for the Sahel as a single economic entity, including the Sahel's vital ties to contiguous territories. Furthermore, the major studies all support, subject to more precise definition, the declared long-term objective of the CILSS: food self-sufficiency in the context of accelerated economic and social development. The major studies are also unanimous in respecting the long-term nature of the task (20-30 years). These studies assume that the comprehensive character of the Sahel program will necessitate an integrated development in which agronomists, river basin engineers, educators, health specialists, and other specialists must work together.

As to the Club du Sahel, it has been noted that, "The creation of multilateral institutions has become a standard response of statesmen and peoples, for purposes both intensely realistic and highly idealistic, to the challenging problems of international life in an era of increasing interdependence.[6]" As the conclusion of the emergency relief effort mounted following the 1968-1974 drought, it became evident that it was not enough to return to the "status quo ante" in the Sahel. A mechanism was needed that could bring donors and recipients together to transform the region so that it could attain its full economic potential.

The United States, in furtherance of the Foreign Assistance Act of 1974, authorizing AID to contribute to "the development and support of a comprehensive long-term African Sahel development program," asked the Chairman of the OECD's Development Assistance Committee (DAC), Maurice Williams, to take the initiative in trying to create an institution which could coordinate a long-term development program in the Sahel. A number of donors met at Williams' suggestion to discuss this concept and to exchange information on plans for bilateral assistance to the Sahel. There was substantial, but not unanimous, agreement on the desirability of forming a coordinating institution, which was christened -- prior to its birth -- Le Club des Amis du Sahel. Williams subsequently attended a CILSS meeting where he outlined the proposal to Sahelian ministers. Their initial reactions were noncommittal, but more enthusiasm for the proposal developed when, following another donors' meeting and more thorough briefings in Sahel capitals, it was made clear that the Sahelian governments would have an important voice in the decisions of the Club. An organization reminiscent of the Aid-to-India Club during the early 1960s was established. Since the United States, France, and other principal donors began working with DAC to develop a forum for international consideration of long-range development objectives, the concept has won general acceptance among Sahelian states and donor organizations. The Club Secretariate is located in Paris, where its primary function is coordination with DAC donors.

The Club held its inaugural meeting on March 29-31, 1976, in Dakar, Senegal. Reflecting the collaborative nature of the effort, the meeting was hosted by President Senghor of Senegal and was co-chaired by both President Ould Daddah of Mauritania (as Chairman *pro tem* of CILSS) and Maurice Williams. Representatives of the CILSS states including two of its most recent members, The Gambia and Cape Verde Islands, and all major donors and funding organizations attended the Dakar meeting. Major sectoral studies by the IBRD (on transport), by FAO (on agriculture), and by the French (on water resources), inter alia,were presented. At this first plenary session, it was concluded that the Club should not become another international development organization, but rather should serve as the forum to coordinate and design an international development program for the Sahel. Maurice Williams has described in detail the Club's central role in the evolution of "a unique process of concertation which constitutes a new approach to cooperation with the Third World countries."[7] The Club has filled the requirement for an international forum for open discussion of needs, priorities, and resources, and complements well the CILSS, which has acted as the nexus for Sahelian decision and participation in development efforts.

The Club/CILSS, as an innovative multi-donor, multi-recipient organization, relies strongly on bilateral programs. It is a mechanism designed to undertake a planning process, not to establish a definitive plan. Results to date have provided broad guidelines for program development. CILSS particularly is seen as a unique mechanism for regional planning to address problems of development common throughout the Sahel. The Club is seen as a useful forum for mobilizing resources and for discussing issues such as pricing and marketing which are difficult to address in other contexts. The Club/CILSS provides a mechanism for regionwide planning and for mobilizing resources in support of national development efforts which grow out of planning. What makes this mechanism unique is the recognition by all participants that achieving significant development in the Sahel is a long-term process, requiring the coordinated efforts of the Sahelian countries and donors. This is a process that cannot and is not prescribed in a detailed set of neatly bound plans but provides for:

- Continuous planning and evaluation so that new information based on research findings and actual field experience can be factored into emerging plans;
- Open and frank dialogue between and among Sahelians and donors. This continuing dialogue engenders understanding and recognition of special priorities of others. Specifically, this dialogue is essential in promoting basic human rights, an increased role for women in development, and family planning.

The complexity of the planning mechanism which has evolved since the first meeting of the Club in March, 1976 is reflective of the complexity of both the development and the coordination problems facing the Sahel. Concrete work originates from two forums, the working group teams and the two secretariates. Currently there are working groups to develop strategies and projects for six sectors: crop production, livestock, fisheries, ecology and forestry, human resources, and transportation. Despite this organizational complexity, which has produced a mountain of paper, most development projects are still contracted for and implemented on a bilateral, donor-institution-to-individual-recipient basis. To date the Club/CLISS has launched four specific projects: Agrhymet, the Institute du Sahel, Crop Protection, and Reforestation.

In the wake of the drought, the CILSS agreed that one of the most urgent needs was to improve weather prediction and reporting. In 1973 it established the Agrhymet project in cooperation with the World Meteorological Organization (WMO) and FAO. This project is designed to upgrade national meteorological and hydrological services and establish a regional center for training and the application of agrometeorology and operational hydrology to Sahelian problems. The resulting network of weather stations made it possible to predict the 1977 drought far enough in advance to facilitate the delivery of emergency food supplies. The regional center in Niamey is in place and has begun both training and research. By November 1977, $15 million of the total $18 million budgeted for the first stage of the project (1975-1980) had been committed.

The establishemnt of the Institute du Sahel in Bamakao, Mali was formally agreed to by the Council of Ministers in December 1977. The most important task of the Institute will be to reinforce the efforts of national institutes by coordinating research by and for CILSS countries. It will also provide training for some researchers and specialized technicians but will not duplicate training already available in member countries. AID plans to implement a demographic program for the Sahel through the Institute. The projected budget for the Institute du Sahel is $90 million. It will start on a small scale, and expansion will depend on its demonstrated capacity.

The Crop and Harvest Project serves as an example of how the unique features of the Club/CILSS have been used to plan, design, and fund a project. In a study undertaken by a Club team of experts, it was stressed that protecting basic food crops, while growing and in storage, would significantly contribute to food self-sufficiency. Analysis indicated that to accomplish this, it would be necessary to strengthen the national crop protection services of the Sahel countries, undertake integrated research activities against the main food crop pests and post-harvest crop loss, and create a regional training and information center. Once general agreement had been reached on the importance of the project and its essential components, the Club proceeded to form teams, composed of Sahelian and donor experts to design the project. All the Sahelian countries and experts from over ten assistance agencies participated in the actual design of the project. As a project of this magnitude is beyond the means of any one donor to finance, or more accurately, not palatable for a single donor (it is estimated the project will cost $78 million), multi-donor funding was necessary. This has been achieved. Commitments totaling the $78 million necessary for the project have been received from the United States, West Germany, France, Canada, the United Kingdom, Denmark, Norway, the Arab Bank for African Development and the UNDP.

The reforestation program will provide another model for implementing multi-donor, multi-recipient development programs. It includes about $100 million worth of projects which will be implemented on a bilateral basis. FAO developed the overall design and AID, France, and Belgium have agreed to a memo of understanding about coordination mechanisms and environment criteria (see Chapter 7).

Like so many mosaic chips, the Club/CILSS-inspired projects and dozens of others come together in a dramatic tableau. The Sahel Development Program (SDP) is unique in its scope, its magnitude, and its ambition. It integrates the efforts of more than 20 donors and international development organizations. Current estimates are that $10 billion from all sources will be required over 10 years and the planning for the entire program spans 30 years. SDP's now familiar-sounding goal is an upgrading of the region's agricultural production framework to permit food self-sufficiency, strong resilience in droughts, and accelerated socioeconomic growth.

Conventional aid has not had a substantial effect on the fundamental weaknesses of the Sahel. Projects have been administered more often than not within a narrowly defined political relationship. Evaluations of these projects were made in standard cost-benefit terms which considered only isolated effects at the local level. Coordination among projects and potential for a regional mesh were tertiary concerns. The project-by-project efforts could not attack the interrelated core problems of the region because the necessary inter-project linkages were not built in. However, SDP is not now, and probably will not become, a "development program" such as those implemented by multilateral donors like the World Bank, or by bilateral donors, or even like the economic plans put forward by individual developing countries. Rather, it is intended to be a large scale, long-range planning and coordination process to equip the region to combat the effects of future droughts. This process attempts to ensure that both regional and individual country development projects have the maximum positive impact upon individual countries and the overall region. Actual project implementation can occur in a variety of ways: individual donor to individual recipient, multi-donor to individual recipient, several donors and recipients together or regional projects which are monitored by the CILSS/Club mechanism. The SDP springs from the Club's work to draw up a plan for the development of the Sahel over the period 1978-2000 and a first program of action for the period 1978-1982 that can enable the Sahel to overcome, progressively, its state of dependence and poverty. Of paramount importance is the process by which the joint planning and agreed program has been achieved. All the partners, Sahelian and non-Sahelian, have been able to meet informally within the Club framework on an equal footing to share ideas, air differences, and to turn their experience to account in searching for new ways of achieving the objectives chosen by the CILSS member governments.

To initiate the planning process necessary for Sahelian development, the Club established an International Working Group. The Working Group adopted a new approach. It established sector teams in which Sahelian, European, and American experts worked in close cooperation. Each of its teams was headed by a Sahelian assisted by a rapporteur from a bilateral or multilateral aid agency. Four of these teams were asked to plan action programs for food production, including rainfed crops, irrigated crops, livestock, and fisheries. Five other teams addressed the problems common to all sectors: human resources, ecology, marketing, pricing and storage, technology, and transport. Finally, a synthesis group, composed of the leaders and rapporteurs of the nine teams, attempted to give coherence to the whole. Each subject was therefore examined from a number of different points of view with the aim of building a program which would not be a collection of isolated activities. This matrix approach, albeit confronted with a formidable time constraint, has proved to be invaluable.

The end product of this extensive programming effort is the Club's "Strategy and Program for Drought Control and Development in the Sahel." With disciplined aim maintenance, the primary, long-term goals in this strategy are consistent with CILSS wishes: food self-sufficiency and sustained socioeconomic growth. The goal of food self-sufficiency is not meant to be absolute autonomy in food production at a national level. Rather the goal is defined as regional food self-sufficiency in staple foods. The strategy also recognizes that food self-sufficiency can not be the sole objective of a long-term program. Consequently, the goal of sustained socioeconomic growth is given equal priority. While the strategy represents a substantial first step to integrated long-term planning, it is clearly stated in the document that "...under no circumstances should the proposed program be considered final. It is suggestive, especially since it relates to a distant time frame and it should be reviewed periodically."[8] The plan was drawn up by a Working Group, placed under the chairmanship of the former Minister-Coordinator of CILSS, Boulama Manga, Minister for Rural Development in Niger. The latter has emphasized that the proposal submitted by the Working Group was the outcome of a concerted effort:

> Foreign and Sahelian experts worked side by side for months to jointly draw up and propose the development strategy and programs ...

submitted to the Sahelians and adopted by them;

> ... it is evident, and our work has just proved this, that solutions arrived at jointly have much more chance of being accepted and applied by the parties concerned than solutions presented as veritable prescriptions ... Sahelian and non-Sahelian experts were able to have a particularly rewarding exchange of experience which enabled all concerned to be more open to dialogue and to have a new conception of international cooperation. This is an example which all countries and institutions concerned over the effectiveness of aid to developing countries could usefully learn from.[9]

The plan of development for the Sahel proposes options which start with the priority consideration of meeting basic needs. This is an approach consistent with the concerns of most of the international community. It assumes that meeting human needs is the first sequential step in expanding absorptive capacity, and programs with social objectives can and should be designed accordingly. This aim of the strategy was spelled out in the terms of reference given to the Working Group: "The strategy proposed by the Working Group should enable the Sahel States to achieve food self-sufficiency, whatever the climatic hazards, and should lead to self-sustaining development of those States."[10] In other words, no development is possible unless above all else the Sahelians are able to meet essential food needs.

The Sahelian decision to opt for food self-sufficiency was

questioned by some of the members of the Working Group on the grounds that this flouted elementary economics: namely that it is more advantageous to turn to account one's comparative advantage (in the Sahel's case, its facilities for producing and exporting cotton and groundnuts) in order to obtain the products for which this advantage does not exist or exists to a lesser degree (a large proportion of the cereals which the Sahel needs). The Sahelians agreed with their critics that food self-sufficiency can, for the time being, be achieved only at the regional level and that it would be absurd to seek autarky in cereals. However, they rejected excessive reliance on imported grains because of the vulnerability to which they would be exposed in any future drought; nor do they want to be permanently dependent on international aid, either as due or dole. Even in the period prior to the drought, several Sahelian countries had to import annually a larger share of their total cereal needs (between 20 and 40 percent) which left very little room for other purchases abroad.

The objective of food self-sufficiency is for the Sahelians a choice that is political, economic, and social. It is a political choice because of the traumatic experience of the drought, and the fears felt by all Third World countries during the world grain shortage of 1972-1973 (fears that in the event of a recurrence the poorest would be the most vulnerable). It is an economic choice because it represents a correct assessment of the potential of the Sahel to produce appreciable quantities of cereals and foodstuffs. It is a social choice because it is based on recognition of the severe limitations of job creation outside agriculture and the observation of the day-to-day ravages of malnutrition.

AMENDING DONOR-RECIPIENT POSTURES

Unlike political platforms that transform reality by influencing popular perceptions, economic policies often have concrete as well as perceptual ramifications in the real world. While political ideologies can be arrived at independently, economic policies are often constrained by the temptation and, at times, overwhelming need for external expertise -- with rare cases like China in the exception. It is not easy to put one's finger on how this intrusion by donor economists -- invited or uninvited -- manifests itself in the economic doctrines of recipient governments. To be sure, development strategies are often pushed on recipient governments via interventions euphamized as policy and performance conditioning. Depending on the recipient's persuasibility, strategies can also be packaged attractively so as to be voluntarily accepted. Perhaps, the best strategy for selling a development strategy is to pass it off as a new trend in the usually vogue-conscious development circles. Often, however, even the most subtle "modus operandi" for introducing a new strategy is promptly branded as interventionist, stimulating heated debate as to what precisely constitutes intervention. In a world that has seen its technological space shrink many times over, making national jurisdictions a scarce item in the process, the painfulness of coming to grips with interventionism stems largely from the bitter struggle between nationalism, with its fixation on national sovereignty, and transnationalism, with its ideologizing of interdependence.

An early attempt at a development activism, which offers a number of caveats, is the sad experience with engineering socioeconomic change in Latin America that received the misnomer,"Alliance for Progress." In contrast to the Alliance, the Organization for European Economic Cooperation (OEEC) organized and directed by Europeans, had far more input in the disposition of Marshall Plan funds. To the United States, the Marshall Plan was a more flexible framework for carrying out development objectives than the Alliance, for two reasons. The first was that unlike Latin America, Europe was equipped with all the requisites for reconstruction except capital. The second was more delicate. The United States felt greater confidence in the commitments of European governments than in those of Latin America. Purse strings in the Alliance were fully controlled by the United States and, in the first two years, no formal Latin American organization comparable to the OEEC existed. There was constant pressure in Congress to withhold aid from Latin America until definite commitments were made concerning agrarian reform, stabilization, development plans, and the like, and to suspend aid at any point when it appeared that these commitments were not being carried out. Few attempts were made to be even cynically cosmetic in the ubiquitous interventions. As a result, the Alliance became a powder keg, alienating recopient countries, as they rejected the impingement on their political structures, and donor, as it became obvious that the overture was backfiring.

Both the Marshall Plan and the Alliance for Progress are monuments to unswerving confidence in capital. In Europe, after World War II, economic organization or the capacity for such organization, industrial skills, technical competence, highly developed public administration, and services already existed. The only missing ingredient was capital. When it was supplied by the United States, miracles predictably followed. This was not the case with the Alliance for Progress. Where the pre-existing European ingredients of success were missing, the power to work miracles was, not surprisingly, nonexistent. Where organizational, administrative, and technical capacity and skills are lacking -- where, in short, there is no industrial infrastructure or experience -- the economy does not respond to an infusion of capital. This concern with capital was transfered to the developing countries. Mahbubul Haq states: "We were confidently told that if you take care of your GNP, poverty will take care of itself. We were often reminded to keep our eyes focused on a high GNP growth target, as it was the best guarantee for eliminating unemployment and for redistributing incomes later through fiscal means. Then what really happened? Where did the development process go astray?"[11]

Until the present trend, the eradication of the worst forms of poverty was not accorded great importance by Third World development planners. Trained in the West, they were preoccupied with the tradeoff between unemployment and growth, whose gauge was high growth rates in GNP. In the interim, this neglect of the low-end poor had a snowballing effect on poverty, eventuating in the tragic circumstances of this substantial segment of the world's population. The lesson to be learned is that even with a high growth rate in GNP, poverty is not automatically alleviated. Brazil is a good example. Having attained a growth rate close to 7 percent, it is still plagued with maldistribution of income, a problem threatening the fabric of its society. The ideas immanent in growth theory and the ontology underlying the GNP approach to human welfare betray the insensitivity of development strategies introduced in countries where delicate societal and ecological balances must be reckoned with. In part, it was this approach to modernization that gave rise to structures of domination and violence in many parts of the Third World, where traditional defenses against monolithic state power were eroded, and increased militarization resulted as a side effect of advanced techno-economic packages. Thus, the belated reversal in development approaches. This time around, the immediate target is poverty --GNP having lost much of its earlier luster.

Whether targeting aid to the low-end poor is a cyclical response with antecedents recorded in the most elementary history textbooks or whether it is a secular trend is a moot question for the recipient government policy maker. The "problematique," rather, is how to adapt proven policies to new and, therefore, indeterminate contexts. Only naive and gullible governments fail to discriminate for themselves between the various approaches to development -- no matter whose advice they may be discarding. For instance, one can go so far as to say that a judicious selection of the features of both outward- and inward-looking strategies is at the core of the progressive integrated development strategy. The lessons of industrializing France, Germany, Japan, and Russia, which used and adapted foreign ways, blending new institutions with old traditions, are instructive. Even these countries in their early stages of development did not gear themselves to the established markets of England but at new opportunities and the growing markets of other newcomers; the main point being that there is a choice of different styles of integrated development, depending on which blends of indigenous and foreign impulses are made to congeal.

In many respects, the Club du Sahel is a kind of alliance between the industrialized world and the developing world. In the past, Sahelian leaders repeatedly called for a Marshall

Plan to see the region through a full recovery from the great drought. However, to replicate either the Marshall Plan or the Alliance for Progress would be counterproductive and, fortunately, this awareness is reflected in macro planning for the Sahel to date.

An original feature of the Sahel Development Program is that it makes clear the conditions for its success, particularly the willingness of both Sahelians and donors to consider policy changes. There is a growing recognition that sound domestic policies, which Sahelian governments alone are in a position to implement, are central to the success of the development strategy. Even "sans" procrustean rigidity, these may be difficult to adapt and enforce: governments are under pressure to meet urgent daily needs and to respond to the economic and social changes resulting from population growth, rapid urbanization, improved communications and information, not to mention the many claims of the international agenda. Moreover, Sahelians are not immune to gobs of foreign advice -- often contradictory, at times useful -- which they are left to sort out for themselves.

Some of the difficult choices to be made hinge on the relative emphasis in overall economic and social policies toward urban and rural constituencies. They relate to the distribution of income among the various social groups as more income is generated over time. National leaders must strive toward a careful policy mix between the preservation and improvement of traditional life patterns -- which have made survival possible in a dangerous ecological zone -- and the modern economy. Complex policy options have to be made as regards favoring the better watered areas of the south or the more marginal Sahelian parts of the country, opening new lands, and helping populations to settle. Trade, price, and storage policies must be designed to improve the farmers' incomes from cereals without discouraging cash crops which produce monetary incomes and foreign exchange. Training policies have a great influence on economic and social change. All these choices and many others make a considerable difference in the effectiveness of aid and in shaping a better future for the Sahel.

An important constraint on agricultural development derives from government influence on commodity prices received by farmers and herdsmen. For a variety of reasons, including the desire on the part of government for export tax revenue and political pressures to keep food prices low for urban consumers, the prices received by farmers in the past have been generally low in relation both to their levels on world markets and to prices of manufactured goods. One consequence has been lower real income of rural producers, discouraging investment in agriculture and slowing the expansion of production. Another has been to encourage the consumption of imported foods, especially rice and wheat in Senegal and Mauritania. Although producer prices were raised quite substantially during

1973-1975, the effects of these price increases have been eroded somewhat by inflation, and the danger of maintaining too low levels of producer prices remains. At the same time, manufacturing activity is usually protected from competing imports and granted direct incentives such as tax holidays and subsidized credit. In the case of public enterprises, direct subsidies are often substantial. All this enables industrial activities to exist despite frequently high economic cost and a natural tendency to draw resources away from agriculture.

One of the effects of low incomes in rural areas is to encourage migration to the cities and to other countries where wages are higher. This has several adverse consequences. First, migrants are apt to be those who are most skilled, in their most productive years, leaving behind people who are least able to undertake rural development. Second, there frequently are not enough jobs available in the formal sector to employ all of these migrants, so they often move into the small scale, informal sector, where productivity may be very low and where they increase the demand for public services. On the other hand, migrants who find useful employment are a source of income and capital. These earnings also help to stabilize family consumption during poor agricultural years. This is an area in which relatively little research has been done in these countries and, thus, the relative magnitude of these effects is not known. It seems likely that government policies concerning wage legislation, agricultural prices, etc., are critical variables.

There are a number of important constraints closely related to government policies. One of these is the limited capacity of the public sector to generate the tax revenue needed to finance even the recurrent operating expenditures required for the provision of essential government services.[12] This is due in part to the weak tax base which results from a poor resource endowment and a low level of economic development. It also stems from the difficulty of collecting taxes in an area where administrative services in general are stretched thinly over vast areas of low population density and where national frontiers are long and difficult to patrol.

Past experience indicates a very weak Sahelian capacity to finance a major portion of the investment needed for development. The Sahelians already contribute to project expenses by paying local personnel and operating cost, but their ability to expand this contribution or to purchase capital equipment and otherwise pay for investment is extremely limited. As an indication of this, the combined current budget surplus of all Sahelian countries averaged only $19 million per year from 1969 through 1972, of which $16 million was accounted for by Senegal. Revenue in the Sahelian countries is inadequate, in fact, to finance at sufficient levels even recurrent expenditures for essential government services. This has a detrimental effect on development and, especially, on the ability of these countries to operate on a sustained basis programs initiated by various investment projects. However, ultimately, development projects will contribute to increased production, which will broaden the tax base and result in greater public revenues. Gestation periods may be relatively long, since there is much information to be acquired, many projects are pilot in nature, and the benefits of improved technology will not be achieved for some time to come. The timing of project-related current and capital expenditures is such, therefore, that these expenditures cannot be financed directly out of general revenue derived from the increments of income they create. This is especially true because budgetary pressures faced by the different governments cause them to direct any additional revenue they acquire toward their most pressing immediate needs. As mentioned before, however, there may be some scope for establishing systems of payments which are related closely to services provided and which therefore channel newly created resources back into productive activities. This is already done in most of the agricultural development programs which involve export crops.

Although these payment systems help to cover recurrent operating expenditures in the programs concerned and even permit some repayment of capital, they cannot provide the initial financing for capital investment. It is here that the almost complete absence of financial intermediaries poses severe problems for the accumulation of private savings and their investment in productive activities. There is private investment, of course, but it is generally limited to the occasional purchase of cattle or a few farm implements, or to the investment of some working capital in commercial activities. There are few individuals or families in these countries wealthy enough to invest in substantial productive enterprises, and the absence of financial intermediaries prevents them from combining their capital for this prupose.

As a result of all these factors, it seems clear that the financing of most investment and even a substantial part of initial recurrent expenditures must come from external sources. Foreign private investment is important to most Sahelian countries as we have seen earlier, but it is confined almost entirely to commerce and industry. There are also several international sources upon which the Sahelian countries may draw.

One of these is the International Monetary Fund (IMF), where Sahelian countries have, in addition to their regular drawing rights, access to the Compensatory Financing Facility to meet balance of payments difficulties arising from temporary export shortfalls and to the Oil Facility Special Account which was established to lend to members faced with balance of payments problems resulting from increased oil import costs. Each of these has disadvantages, however, because of restrictions placed on the recipient country's policy-making authority or, as in the case of the oil facility, because rates of interest charged are relatively high. Combined resources available from the IMF in 1975 for the Sahelian countries were $74 million compared with an overall basic balance of payments deficit in that year of $110 million. Sahelian countries can borrow from a Third Window of the World Bank, albeit at an interest rate of 4.5 percent, and on more liberal terms from a special trust fund established by the IMF, using its profits from gold sales. All Sahelian countries except Mauritania also have access to the franc zone Compte d'Operation, and Mali has made considerable use of this over the past few years. Finally, as associate members of the European Economic Community, the Sahelian countries can participate in STABEX, the export earnings maintenance scheme adopted by the Lome Convention. All of these facilities could at best, however, contribute only marginally to the overall capital requirements of Sahelian countries and, because of interest which must be paid or restrictions which may be imposed, they are probably best reserved for short-term emergency situations.

As a result, Sahelian countries must look to long-term loans or grants from foreign donors to finance the bulk of their investment needs. The question remains as to the terms upon which this assistance should be given. At first glance, it appears that these countries are not excessively burdened with external debt. Except for Mali, the debt service ratio (ratio of debt service to exports) is not generally high, varying from 1.5 percent in Mauritania to 9 percent in Upper Volta. The ratio is very high for Mali largely because of debts accumulated during the socialist period of the 1960s, but in fact few, if any, of these debts are actually being repaid. Because the ratio is relatively low for most of these countries does not mean, however, that they have the ability to service large amounts of debt. Export earnings are very limited and are likely to remain so for some time, though they should start to expand as rural development programs gather momentum. To the extent that a development strategy succeeds, the ability to repay debt should increase. Therefore, the Sahelian countries ought to be in a position by the early part of the next century to begin to pay interest on their borrowings, albeit initially at relatively low rates. It is evident, then, that economic assistance should be highly concessional for the first few decades or so, but that as production increases as a result of these development efforts, the terms of aid can be made increasingly stronger.

A big and, one could say, suspicious fuss has been made in donor circles about the Sahel's capacity to absorb increasing amounts of aid or, simply put, its "absorptive capacity." Work on the long-term plan for the Sahel has demonstrated that if donors really wish to design basic human needs programs for the poor countries, they may have to alter their ideas about absorptive capacity. The obstacles to absorptive capacity are, for example, the absence of memory systems of well-designed, successful projects and of personnel able to direct projects; thinly spread, uncertain or deferred returns on most projects; insufficiency of public funds to maintain these projects and make them operational; inadequacy of road and rail links; and so on.

There are two ways of tackling the problem of aid absorption capacity. The more usual is to adjust downward the financial resources to their apparent use potential. The effect of this is to ration assistance to the poor as opposed to the rich. The poor are caught in a vicious circle: because they are poor they are entitled only to meager assistance. The more original way to tackle the problem is to identify the inhibiting factors and try to remove them. These factors are numerous and interwoven: illiteracy, poor health, short life expectancy, isolation, remoteness, etc. Developed countries have difficulty in identifying ways and means of overcoming them; they are often handicapped by their impatience and that of their legislative bodies and by the demands of public opinion for quick results that are practical, visible, and immediate. Such instantaneous results are even more unrealistic in removing the factors which restrict absorptive capacity in the poorest countries. Sustained and concerted efforts are required.

One of the best ways of increasing absorptive capacity is to finance a high proportion of the local costs of projects rather than just the foreign exchange costs, as is the rule at present. More flexibility in this type of financing would simplify project management, reduce the financial burden on the recipient and in some cases encourage local entrepreneurs to produce the goods and services required by the projects. Donors must increase the volume of their aid considerably. Too often it is no more than a "shot in the arm" which gets the recipient through the year. This approach runs counter to real effectiveness. Without a critical mass there can be no chain reaction and efforts become diluted through dispersion. Yet, nothing is less certain in aid policy than constancy of effort, and experience has shown that external assistance may be reduced for reasons which have nothing to do with aid requirements.

Harmonization of aid procedures is the favorite topic of aid discussions and the most overlooked in practice. One of the conditions for the Sahel plan's success is simplification and standardization of aid procedures in order to lighten the tasks of the governments of the CILSS countries. The diversity of practices in regard to project formulation and appraisal, contract procedures, human and financial counterparts, tendering, calculation of costs and benefits, and so on, is such that it places considerable burdens on governments. Similarly, the "studies" requirement is often the chief curb to timely project action. Although it would be wrong to underestimate the importance of studies when their aim is evident and they serve to clarify options, there is no denying the excesses they often entail (duplication, repetition, cost).

Experience shows that it is sometimes easier to obtain appropriations for studies (disbursed in the donor country) than appropriations for projects, whereas the reverse ought to be the rule.

Project design and appraisal is essential in order to ensure that scarce resources, both domestic and external, are correctly used, but new thinking is required on project appraisal criteria. Inadequate criteria in the sense of being too restrictive or short-sighted would maintain the Sahel in a state of underdevelopment prejudicial to Sahelians. Excessively lax criteria would lead to a wastage of resources. The Working Group did some preliminary work on the subject and developed a proposal for a multi-criteria method that would take account of the many different development goals and the specific economic, social, and ecological characteristics of the Sahel. Since this method is a departure from current practices, it is undergoing a trial period in connection with on-going project studies.

TRANSFER OF RESOURCES

A first outline strategy for the development of the Sahel was submitted to the Ministerial Council of the CILSS at its meeting at N'Djamena in December 1976. The Ministers assured the Working Group, by way of a resolution, that they approved of the work begun and mandated it to pursue that work to its conclusion. A more complete proposal for a development strategy which synthesized the work of the nine teams was presented to the Ministerial Council of CILSS at its meeting in Ouagadougou in April 1977. The Ministers thoroughly reviewed the strategy options and amended the synthesis plan on several points. They approved it officially. With this ratification the plan took on the recognized status of a formal policy framework within which the efforts of the Sahelian countries and of the international community could be deployed and concerted. The action program also was drawn up by the various teams in consultation with the Sahelian governments. Its total cost over five years will amount to over $3 billion, not including the cost of developing the major river basins. This first generation program (1978-1982) in some cases lacks the consistency that might be desired, but it nevertheless constitutes a guide for the selection of projects to be financed (see Table 9).

The preparation of the various sector plans and the "Strategy and Program for Drought Control and Development in the Sahel" was keyed to the second meeting of the Club du Sahel held in Ottawa in the spring of 1977. The meeting was attended by representatives of all Sahelian countries. Bilateral participants included the United Kingdom, Switzerland, Denmark, Germany, Norway, Belgium, France, Sweden, Japan, The Netherlands, Austria, Saudi Arabia, the United States, Canada and Italy. International organizations participating included all of the

TABLE 9
FIRST GENERATION PROJECTS AND PROGRAMS
Recapitulatory Schedule by Country and by Sector ($000.000)

Country / Sector	Cape Verde	Gam-bia	Upper Volta	Mali	Mauritania	Niger	Senegal	Chad	Region	Total by Sector
Rainfed Agri.	$3.0	$32.1	$87.4	$36.3	$99.3	$90.0	$175.7	$25.5	$.6	$549.9
Irrigated Agri.	1.2	27.0	16.4	120.1	534.5	70.5	229.4	30.5	--	1,029.6
Water Resources	2.7	.5	5.6	14.9	17.6	3.2	18.9	2.5	4.5	70.4
Livestock	13.1	12.4	26.2	40.0	67.7	126.6	38.8	3.9	--	328.7
Fisheries	6.1	4.5	6.6	4.9	14.4	4.1	11.9	10.9	9.5	71.9
Crop Protection	.6	1.1	2.8	4.0	1.5	2.5	2.8	1.6	53.5	70.4
Trade	--	--	--	3.3	6.0	--	--	--	--	9.3
Ecology	15.7	.7	19.2	30.7	25.3	13.6	48.8	9.5	9.4	172.9
Transportation	12.3	50.3	113.2	109.8	80.9	109.9	80.8	52.9	.7	610.8
Human Resources	9.5	3.6	119.4	117.8	7.0	63.3	9.0	28.0	10.0	367.6
Total By Country	$64.2	$132.2	$396.8	$481.8	$854.2	$483.7	$615.1	$165.3	$88.2	
Grand Total of First Generation Projects and Programs in the Sahel Region										$3,281.5

Source: Club du Sahel

principal UN organizations, the World Bank, the FED, and a large number of African regional organizations.

Two major accomplishments resulted from the second meeting of the Club: 1) Unanimous acceptance by the donor community of the strategy approved by the Council of Ministers of the CILSS at the April 1977 meeting in Ouagadougou; and 2) Donor pledges of close to $1 billion in annual assistance to the Sahel along with messages of support for and commitment to the Club from the Presidents of France and the United States and the Prime Minister of Canada. Numerous donor governments and organizations indicated that they will be increasing their financial contributions (see Table 10) and should therefore be able to take part in the execution of projects in all sectors of the strategy's application. France announced that it intends to allocate about $1.2 billion to the development of the Sahel over the period from 1978 to 1982. Canada pledged assistance amounting to $560 million between 1977 and 1985. Assistance from the EDF under the Lome Convention would amount to roughly $150 million a year. West Germany's 1977 commitments of $115 million would remain at that level. The World Bank doubled its IDA lending in the Sahel to approximately $200 million annually. The OPEC countries, currently contributing in excess of $100 million annually, stated that they expected to increase this amount. The Netherlands, having increased their aid several fold from $214 million in 1974 to $35 million in 1976, promised to continue this trend. Even Switzerland scaled up its aid commitment from $3 million in 1976 to $10 million in 1979. The programs of the UNDP, the Arab Bank for Economic Development in Africa and the Islamic Development Bank are to be stepped up.

Since the great drought, the international community has committed over $3.7 billion in assistance to the Sahel -- $754.9 million in 1974; $763.3 million in 1975; and beginning in 1976, parallel to the Club/CILSS effort to mobilize donor resources around food self-sufficiency, aid levels have averaged over $1 billion per year, and increasing amounts -- up to 24 percent of the total -- have been in support of agriculture development. The DAC countries provide the largest percentage of assistance to the Sahel, with France, Germany and the United States leading as the top three DAC donor countries. France is not only the top donor country but, with an average yearly flow of $192 million, it is also the leader in comparison with all multilateral and bilateral agencies. Among the top five bilateral OECD/DAC donors, the Federal Republic of Germany and Canada have shown the most significant increases since 1975; commitments from Germany rose $10 million (from $86 million) and Canada increased its flows by $26 million (from $57 million) over the 1975-1977 period.

American assistance to the Sahel during and immediately following the great drought was primarily emergency food assistance under Public Law 480, Title II. By 1974, the United

TABLE 10

COMMITMENTS OF DEVELOPMENT ASSISTANCE TO THE SAHEL

	1974	1975	1976	1977	1978	1979
Belgium	6.5	6.1	6.0	6.5	7.0	8.0
Canada	29.0	65.3	50.0	60.0	75.0	75.0
France	185.0	222.5	236.8	238.0	240.0	240.0
Germany	76.0	76.7	72.0	90.0	110.o	118.0
Netherlands	2.5	8.4	35.0	36.0	38.0	40.0
Switzerland	2.4	3.2	3.1	6.0	8.0	10.0
United Kingdom	7.3	5.1	12.7	13.0	14.0	15.0
European Economic Community	157.4	48.4	176.9	140.0	145.0	150.0
IBRD	42.3	107.9	110.3	150.0	180.0	200.0
U.N.	40.0	52.8	22.6	40.0	50.0	50.0
ADB	16.5	46.7	44.4	45.0	50.0	55.0
OPEC	83.7	91.2	75.9	90.0	100.0	120.0
Other DAC Member Countries*	12.3	10.3	3.3	18.0	16.0	20.0
United States**	2.9	5.7	11.5	36.0	67.4	97.1
TOTAL	663.8	750.3	860.5	968.5	1100.41	198.1
U.S. as Percent of Total	0.4	0.8	1.3	3.7	6.1	8.1

* Austria, Australia, Denmark, Finland, Italy, Japan, Norway and Sweden.
** Does not include emergency or drought related assistance.

States was the largest food donor to the Sahel. However, the United States has provided assistance to Sahelian countries since 1961. The majority, $306 million of the total $475 million allocated by the end of FY 1976, was provided following the drought. Most of this assistance consisted of emergency food supplies, although $54.5 million was expended on small scale development projects funded out of a special drought relief appropriation. Since 1974, $70 million has been obligated for projects funded under the regular functional accounts. For FY 1980, AID's Africa Bureau requested a total of $422 million. This amount consists of $322 million in Development Assistance, which includes the Sahel Development Program ($105 million) and $100 million in Security Supporting Assistance for southern Africa. This compares with $329 million in FY 1978, which included $50 million for SDP; and in FY 1979, $320 million was requested with $75 million allocated to SDP (see Table 12). FY 1980 represents the third year of American funding for SDP.

AID has testified that it envisions the United States contributing $1-1.5 billion over the next 10-15 years to the Sahel program with other donors contributing approximately 10 times that amount over the same period. AID is presently restricted by legislation from providing more than 10 percent of the total donor commitment to the Sahel. To date, AID annual levels have averaged approximately 8 percent. The legislative restriction raises two points-of-concern: How to interpret the restriction? If it is assumed that Congress intended the 10 percent limitation to apply on an annual basis, AID backs itself into an annual exercise of trying to determine its appropriate contribution well before other donor funding data becomes available. A more reasonable approach is to assume that the restriction applies to the 10-15 year initial financing period for SDP. This interpretation allows for more flexibility in the early years of the SDP timeframe and permits adjustment of contribution percentage later in the period when data for the early years has been tabulated. Whether 10 percent is an appropriate contribution level for the United States? While AID concurs that a ceiling should be set in order to assure full involvement of other principal donors, it would seem that a figure of 15 percent would better reflect the U.S. GNP position.

The basic investments needed to realize the full potential of the Sahel require a long-term commitment by donors to the development of the region. The alternative is a series of rescue operations over the next 25 years that may salve the consciences of developed countries, but will be vastly more expensive than the development program needed to place the Sahel on a sound footing for the future. The insulation of the Sahel from future droughts requires what Paul-Marc Henry calls a "contract for a generation."[13] One of the most basic assumptions now underpinning the development process underway is the commitment to a sizeable transfer of resources over the long-term by

TABLE 11 - PROFILE OF DONOR ACTIVITY

Table 11A - Profile of Donor Countries (excluding the U.S.)

Country	Average 1975-1977 $	Increase From 1975 to 1977	Focus of Present Assistance Including Contributions to Club/CILSS
FRANCE	$192 million	$7 million	Budget support and technical assistance in agriculture, education health, industry transport, cultural affairs to all eight countries. Projects in agricultural, rural development, transport, harbors and telecommunications. Budget support, personnel and financial assistance to Club and CILSS Secretariats.
FRG	$83 million	$10 million	Assistance to all CILSS countries; agriculture, infrastructure technical assistance water supply, livestock, and credit· Selingue Dam, Mali; financial and technical assistance to CILSS
CANADA	$60 million	$26 million	infrastructure, forestry, integrated rural development, and crop protection. Direct cash grants to Club, CILSS Secretariats, Sahel Institute.

TABLE 11A (continued)

Country	1975-1977 $ Average	Increase From 1975 to 1977	Focus of Present Assistance Including Contributions to Club/CILSS
NETHERLANDS	$29 million	$33 million	agriculture, infrastructure, mostly in small projects; cash grants to Club Secretariat.
JAPAN	$9 million	$16 million	fishing, transportation mining (uranium-Niger) and technical assistance
SWITZERLAND	$6 million	$12 million	diverse activities in health, humanitarian aid, agriculture and technical assistance; mostly to Upper Volta, Mali and Senegal. Technical assistance to CILSS
SCANDINAVIAN COUNTRIES	$14.1 million	varies from country to country	Sweden - transportation, commodity assistance and food aid in Cape Verde. Denmark, Norway and Finland - fishing, helath, technical assistance in CILSS countries
BELGIUM	$13.6	none	technical assistance (scholarships, experts, studies, research). $100,000 per year to CILSS activities.

UK	$9 million	none	mostly The Gambia for infrastructure, transportation and technical assistance; food aid, technical assistance, and rural development for other CILSS countries.
OPEC	$194 million	$78 million	Saudi Arabia, Kuwait largest donors, mostly to Mauritania.

TABLE 11B - Profile of Multilateral Agencies

Agency	1975-1977	Focus
EDF (EEC)*	$380 million	agriculture, transport/infrastructure, balance-of-payments and budget support
World Bank	$277 million	mostly agriculture and transport/infrastructure; loans to all countries except Cape Verde.
ADB**	$95 million	agriculture, rural infrastructure and health.
U.N.	$154 million	technical assistance, training, planning, health, food assistance, rural infrastructure.

* European Development Fund - European Economic Community

** African Development BAnk/African Development Fund

TABLE 12

ALLOCATION OF AID FUNDS TO THE SAHEL - FY 78-80 ($000)

Sector	FY 78 (SDP)	FY 78 (functional)	FY 79 (SDP)	FY 80 (SDP)
Agriculture	28,745	10,947	33,885	48,206
Livestock	1,006	1,300	8,718	9,738
Fisheries	-	-	-	255
Ecology/ Reforestation	4,645	7,375	6,749	8,533
Human Resources Development	6,044	4,166	9,238	12,980
Health	1,117	4,946	9,714	12,910
Transport	3,915	1,373	3,161	8,684
Club/CILSS Support	2.136	-	2,137	2,156
Design	2,238	-	1,552	1,538
TOTAL	49,846	30,107	75,154	105,000

the international donor community to the Sahelian countries.

An important issue for long-term development assistance is the level of costs to which governments implicitly commit themselves in maintaining infrastructure or continuing to employ the resources put in place through development projects with long-term payoffs. Investments in health, education, and basic infrastructure typically do not yield positive returns for 10 to 20 years. Prior to the payoff, governments must maintain the health and education systems put into place with foreign assistance. For this reason, Sahelian governments will encounter frequent budget deficits at least for the rest of this century if they are to maximize the benefits from a long-term investment program.

Aid to the Sahel tends to be extended on a grant or soft loan basis. Thus, the increasing levels of foreign assistance have not greatly increased current or projected debt service. In 1975, payments of principal and interest on foreign debts amounted to only two or three percent of government revenues. However, Mali and Mauritania are expected to incur increasingly large external debt service burdens. Consequently, it is imperative that assistance be given on the most favorable terms. At the Ottawa meeting, donors agreed to the idea of participating in a joint commission to study the terms and conditions of aid (financial terms, financing of local costs and recurrent expenditure, allocation procedures and quality of aid). More problematic has been the business of securing funds for infrastructure. Not only is the construction of infrastructure necessary to increase absorptive capacity, but infrastructure projects themselves are easier to absorb because they require less management than many other development efforts. The infrastructure question is a difficult one for the United States. Since the advent of the Congressionally mandated New Directions policy in 1973, the use of development assistance for the construction of infrastructure has either been forbidden or severely limited. This limitation was a response to the perception that many large infrastructure projects have not contributed much to economic development in the past and the benefits of these projects have not "trickled down" to the poor. In the case of the Sahel, however, there is a broad consensus that the lack of adequate infrastructure is a key impediment to economic development. A GAO report states: "In our opinion, for effective development in the Sahel, the major infrastructure problems must be remedied."[14]

The modality of U.S. participation in the Sahel Development Program is pivotal because of the leadership role the United States has played "ab initio" in efforts to ameliorate the living standards of Sahelians. AID, acting under explicit Congressional directives, has been a prime mover in the formation of the Club du Sahel. For some time, the United States has been uncertain about the best way to help the poorest countries with basic needs without evolving unnecessarily paternalistic relations. The Sahel Development Program seeks to address basic needs in a manner which sequentially expands absorptive capacity, establishes food and health security and establishes a foundation for rural-based self-sustaining growth. The Club-CILSS mechanism appears to be an effective conduit for extending a helping hand to a group of countries who, by any standard, are among the poorest of the poor.

Club du Sahel representatives feel that it has made significant progress and has even more substantial potential. The progress of the Club du Sahel was discussed at a plenary meeting of participating nations and organizations in November 1978 in Amsterdam, The Netherlands. Accomplishments reported included the (1) increase in annual donor assistance from $750 million in 1974 and 1975 to over $1 billion annually for 1976 and 1977, (2) the increased participation by nontraditional donors in the Sahel development process, (3) sponsoring numerous multidonor conferences to review complicated development proposals, such as human resource development, livestock and crop protection, and (4) the usefulness of the Club process to discuss complex and sensitive issues.

Many issues, however, were still unresolved. For example:

--Dissatisfaction was still expressed over the shopping-list nature of the first generation projects and the need to prune the list.

--Significant questions, such as the need for a cereals-pricing and marketing policy were still being reviewed and analyzed.

--National CILSS committees, an essential element of the program strategy, were still not fully functioning.

Because it has been less than two years since the initial Club du Sahel development plan was adopted, it would be premature to judge its performance. The Club is not only effectively monitoring donor flows, but actively attracting new donors to the Sahel, making special efforts to bring non-traditional donors into the funding arena. During FY 1978 the Club Secretariat sent two missions to the Middle East to provide OPEC donors with background documents and project files; in turn, several OPEC countries (all of whom, taken together, provided 18 percent of the total ODA going into the Sahel in 1977) took a more active role in Club activities.[15] Talks were also held with Japan and Denmark. At the Amsterdam meeting, Denmark attended for the first time as an active participant in the Club and will be contributing to the functioning of the Club Secretariat beginning this year. And, the Club Secretariat made a special effort to bring the recently-created, billion-dollar International Food and Agriculture Fund (IFAD) into the Sahel. The consensus expressed at the Amsterdam meeting was that the Club/CILSS process has been vital in mobilizing resources for the Sahel and in improving the dialogue on critical problems. The desirability of continuing international cooperation within the framework of the Club/CILSS was also endorsed. What is manifestly evident is that this process is essential if the 28 countries and organizations actively participating as of January 1978 are to interact in a way that maximizes benefits to the Sahel. With understatement, AID's annual report concludes: "All members of the Club enjoy an egalitarian status that is not always found in donor-recipient relationships."[16]

A PRELIMINARY APPRAISAL

During the forthcoming legislative cycles, decisions about the future of the Sahel Development Program will be made, either directly or indirectly. These decisions concern not only U.S. participation in the program but the scale and character of that participation. Congress will be asked to decide whether the development of the Sahel is sufficiently important to merit extensive U.S. investment and effort, or whether these resources should be channeled to other foreign policy arenas where they could impact on larger populations or futher more immediate short-term foreign policy goals.

The Sahel Development Program raises questions about four general aspects of U.S. foreign assistance policy. The first is the length of time which the United States is willing to commit itself to involvement and participation in development programs in other parts of the world. Current firm commitments are based on annual appropriations and forward project planning is largely limited to five years. Plans for the Sahel, proponents argue, must of necessity extend to the end of the century. Can or should the United States participate in this program without making a long range commitment? The second issue concerns the scope and scale of U.S. involvement in the Sahel both in terms of absolute monetary amounts and specific programs. In percentage terms, the U.S. contributions to economic development have decreased significantly in the past few years and current readings of the political climate make a change in this trend seem unlikely. A program to effectively insulate the Sahel from the consequences of future droughts will, as we have seen, cost billions of dollars, some of which will need to be contributed by the United States. It will also require the construction of large-scale infrastructure, yet current U.S. policy limits the use of development assistance for infrastructure. Should U.S. policy be changed, an exception made for the Sahel, or can the United States limit its participation to the non-infrastructural aspects of the Sahel program? A third issue relates to cooperation with donors and with recipients. As a multi-donor, multi-recipient development effort, the Sahel Development Program represents a concrete effort to develop the kind of cooperative mechanisms which Congress has frequently called for. The planning involved has been time-consuming and the inter-relationships will continue to be complex if not awkward. Are the potential rewards from cooperation enough to justify these delays and complications or would a continuation of more traditional bilateral assistance make better sense?

U.S. involvement in the Sahel Development Program affords an opportunity to explore the political implications of development assistance. All assistance relates to political concerns in one fashion or another. The issue is whether development assistance should be targeted toward the long range U.S. political interest in development as a building block for future peaceful coexistence in a North-South as well as East-West sense, or should development assistance concentrate on areas of immediate political concern. Only recently has the United States considered the continent of Africa an area of immediate political concern. The Sahel presents fewer opportunities for short-term political gains than southern Africa, Zaire or the Horn. Yet, precisely because the U.S. has little short-term political interest in the Sahel, assistance to this area would demonstrate to Africans that the United States is genuinely interested in their own primary concern: development.

Since 1974, AID has expanded the size of its field mission in the Sahel, increasing the overall workforce from 46 in 1974 to 191 in 1978. It has also designated five of the eight AID area development offices in the Sahel as full-fledged U.S. missions. Yet, there is a very real limitation on the part of AID and other donors to support and sustain large numbers of development activities. French-speaking technical personnel have been difficult to find and recruit to live under hardship rural circumstances. Of over 100 technical positions established by AID in 1978, 40 percent remained unfilled by the end of the year. While social scientists in AID field posts are now readily accepted, the problem is in finding properly trained sociologists and anthropologists who are prepared to work in the area on a full time basis. For them this usually means taking up residency in the Sahel for a minimum of two years. Contrary to popular beliefs, this is not necessarily a life-style which is amenable to most American academics. This is especially so since many of them feel that two or four years outside of their academic system will work to the detriment of their future career opportunities. One way of countering this problem is a recent attempt by AID to bring into its foreign development service a number of young social scientists who are prepared to consider AID on a career basis so that they will apply their training to development problems of the Third World on a long-term basis.

In contrast to some AID initiatives in other parts of the world, AID performance in dealing with sociological encrustations in the Sahel has been quite good. There has been a minimum of fumbling with the propaedeutics of Sahelian social life. In large measure, this is due to a continuing awareness of the importance, in the words of Goler T. Butcher, AID's Assistant Administrator for Africa, "to adapt to Sahelian society since we know less about Sahelians than other peoples with whom we work intimately and our experience is rather thin."[17] Consequently, AID has pioneered in social soundness analysis within the foreign aid community. However, it has been observed that in many instances the introduction of such analysis into the project planning cycle is delayed until it is already too late for the results to have a major impact on the selection of development strategies. The question now is how best to broaden the utility of such analysis in the earliest stages of program and project formulation.

An equally significant recommendation posited in a GAO report to the Congress is the need for AID to emphasize the implementation phase of development assistance to the Sahel. The report alleges that AID "lacks a current regional development strategy identifying what it wants to accomplish in the Sahel and outlining clearly how to achieve its objectives."[18] In fact, AID has prepared a cogent document known as the "Regional Development Strategy for the Sahel" (RDSS) which was finalized in April 1979. It is expected that Sahel field posts will use the RDSS as a resource document. In general, AID officials recognize the importance of a regional policy thrust to resource transfer to the Sahel, and have worked closely with CILSS and the Club du Sahel. However, out of the regionally coordinated planning process flow specific projects normally developed by each donor individually pursuant to bilateral agreements between donors and national authorities of the individual Sahelian states. Accordingly, most of AID's assistance to the Sahel follows the normal programming practice of designing and implementing specific bilateral country projects. In an internal memorandum, Jim Kelly, Director of AID's Office of Sahel and Francophone West African Affairs states:

> There has been a tendency within the USG to equate our participation in the Sahel Development Program with a presumed portfolio of AID regional projects in the Sahel. This has occurred because we have dealt with the Sahel as a region through our authorization and appropriation process and through our involvement with the CILSS/Club machinery. People thus assume the existence of a "regional blueprint" for the entire Sahel which encompasses a number of "regional" projects, each operating in several Sahelian states and supported by several donors acting jointly.[19]

A more legitimate GAO criticism of AID's performance in the Sahel is the lengthy design time for individual projects -- a problem I have flagged elsewhere (Foreign Service Journal, December 1977). The AID design system is critical to the success of U.S. development projects in the Sahel. However, the lengthy review process produces advocacy documents which are often too theoretical to be operationally useful. The present design process is overly complex, requiring between 2 and 4 years for each project. To increase its effectiveness, AID needs to (1) reform its design process, including its procedures for reviewing and approving projects and (2) improve the management of its design effort. The GAO's indepth review of 10 projects in Senegal, Mauritania, and Niger showed that it took an average of 24 months to develop project proposals into approved project plans. An additional 2.5 months was required to finalize project agreements with host governments. For most projects in this group over 18 months was required to design, review, and approve them. Design times ranged from 15 months to 40 months.

Another area that could benefit from greater synergy both in Washington and in the field is the state of Peace Corps/AID collaboration. Peace Corps has volunteers in 7 of the 8 Sahelian countries but is infrequently tapped by the AID programs in these countries. Joint collaboration is estimated to be as high as from 25 to 30 percent of Peace Corps projects in some countries such as Chad -- as little as 10 percent of total AID projects. No evidence exists of an established joint programing process. Generally, joint projects are developed simultaneously. AID support is usually in the form of materials (shovels, trucks, seedlings, etc.) or monies for this purpose, and has concentrated in noneducational programs, such as water resource development in Chad or sending trucks to Niger.

AID is responding to the need for greater coordination within the U.S. Government and in the context of its own operations by creating a number of organizational units. In 1976, the AID Administrator approved the establishment of a Washington-based Sahel Development Planning Team(SDPT) to be responsible for AID's SDP strategy formulation, sector design, and evaluation of the entire Club/CILSS program. By April 1979 Assistant Administrator Butcher, in an action memorandum for the Acting Administrator recommended that the SDPT be moved to the field to bring AID's Sahel program planning closer to AID project activities:

> Since the start-up of the SDPT in 1976, the Sahel Program has now progressed to the point where the requirements of the program necessitate on-site planning and evaluation. Accordingly, it is now proposed that the SDPT be moved to a Sahelian country to bring the overall planning function for the Sahel region in closer association with AID programs in the field. Out of a total $1 billion assistance program for Sahel Development from all donors, the U.S. has appropriated $75 million for FY 1979 and projects a $105 million program level for FY 1980 and $130 million for FY 1981. Given continued Congressional interest in the Sahel

> program and the need for continued long-range coordinative planning, I support this as an important step toward integrating our planning and operations thereby helping to improve the over-all effectiveness of our Sahel program.[30]

A Sahel Development Planning Regional Office (SDPRO) was approved and is presently located in Bamako, Mali. SDPRO operates independently of the AID mission to Mali and has a staff of eight AID officers. This initial staffing for SDPRO includes a regional development officer as the Director of SDPRO, a macro-economist, an agroeconomist, a rural sociologist, a health planning officer, a human resources development officer, a transport economist, a livestock economist (contractor) and a general services officer.

The Director of SDPRO reports directly to AID/Washington, where he is backstopped by the recently established Sahel Regional Desk. This office coordinates the development of AID policy and planning for the Sahel with other AID and U.S. Government offices. It has a staff of three officers. To assure full complementarity of regional and bilateral programming, SDPRO is beginning to coordinate directly with the AID Mission Directors in the Sahel through the recently established Sahel Mission Directors Council (SMDC). This advisory council on U.S. input into the Sahel Development Program meets quarterly and is composed of all the principal AID officers in the Sahel. Representatives of AID/Washington and U.S. ambassadors to Sahelian countries are welcome to attend. A standing invitation should also be extended to Peace Corps Directors in the Sahel.

CONCLUSION: THE SAHEL IN THE FUNCTIONALIST PARADIGM

The problems of development and modernization are rooted, according to Lucian Pye, in "the need to create more effective, more adaptive, more complex, and more rationalized organizations ...The ultimate test of development is the capacity of a people to establish and maintain large, complex, but flexible organizational forms."[21] The intricate Club/CILSS structure is to be credited for a bold, multifaceted design that looks far ahead and on a grand scale. It has been suggested that the Sahel Development Program is quixotic. In fact, it is viscerally pragmatic. The Club/CILSS have sought to show that, in the Sahel, development is not possible without continuity and collectivity of effort.

The emphasis on informal cooperation and coordination is a frequent theme in the rhetoric about the Sahel Development Program. Indeed, the problems encountered in establishing and maintaining the existing mechanism have been cited to explain why the initial planning stage has taken several years. Even the surface complexity of getting 20 donors and 8 recipients to agree to anything without an acknowledged source of authority is difficult at best -- especially since each actor has its own process and agenda. Nevertheless, the Sahel Development Program is a genuine effort to respond to the frequent plea, especially from donors, to coordinate development efforts as a means to maximize effectiveness. In this sense, the Club/CILSS process has played an essential oversight role and seems ideally suited to the business of systematically planning the overall development effort. In addition to the Club/CILSS structure, there is a plethora of other regional and local development organizations. These include the various river basin commissions for the Senegal River, Niger River and Lake Chad Basin; a Joint Organization for Control of Locusts and Birds; a West African Rice Development Association; and numerous others. All of these organizations compete for leadership and management time, membership dues, and relative status.

Despite some confusion, an uneasy balance has been struck between the need for cooperation, coordination, and some ultimate authority; and the demands of national sovereignty on the part of donors and recipients alike. Significantly, Sahelians are increasingly in control of the program, and this helps to dampen their fears and increase their enthusiasm for a cooperative effort. Nevertheless, the cost has been high in terms of the amount of time it has taken to strike this balance. It would clearly have been easier and perhaps more efficient in the short run to concentrate on bilateral projects. Nevertheless, given the high priority accorded cooperation and coordination and the region-wide nature of development problems, it would be short-sighted to become too impatient with the Sahel development process just as the outlines of its informal planning mechanism are being clarified. Like so many other aspects of this program, the multi-donor, multi-recipient regional planning process is experimental.

The Sahelian development effort is as much a political phenomenon as an economic one. It is a "functionalist" experiment with tremendous implications for international development synergy. The theory of "functionalism," which is essentially an assertion and defense of the proposition that the development of international economic and social cooperation is a prerequisite for geopolitical harmony, has the great merit of appealing both to humanitarian idealism and to national self-interest. "Functionalism proposes not to squelch but to utilize national selfishness; it asks governments not to give up the sovereignty which belongs to their peoples but to acquire benefits for their peoples which were hitherto unavailable, not to reduce their power to defend their citizens but to expand their competence to serve them."[22] Functionalist structures such as the multinational Club des Amis du Sahel may, by focusing attention upon areas of common interest, help ease tensions and fuse the energies of protagonists in a common enterprise. Functionalist theory ultimately envisages the evolution of a world capable of sustaining peaceful relationships.

Paul S. Reinsch adumbrated a "concentric circles" concept of international organization, according to which the idea of multilateral assaults upon world problems would be analagous to a pebble dropped into the international pond, giving rise to a series of circles of cooperation ramifying out into many spheres.[23] Functionalism assumes that political unity must be built, pearl-wise, around a central irritant; it offers a new type of common enemy -- poverty, malnutrition, illiteracy -- to serve as the focal point around which men can unite. Albeit the record to date indicates that functionalist activity is, at least in the short run, more dependent upon than determinative of political climate, experiments as the one currently being conducted in the Sahel indicate that, in the long haul, this approach can contribute to a system whereby man can put the passions and the interests in international life in perspective.

4 The Human Factor in the Development Equation: The Physical Quality of Life

If there is one important lesson which development planners have learned in the past two decades, it is the importance of human resource development to complement capital and to bring about technological change. Low levels of education and dependence on expatriate skilled manpower are important constraints to economic development in the Sahel. Studies of the sources of income growth in Europe and the United States have attributed one-fifth to one-third of that growth to improved education and training.[1] Despite the concentration of populations in the southern areas of Sahelian countries, population densities are low and the population is widely dispersed by comparison with many Asian countries. This dispersion reduces the size of markets and increases the costs of many services, but unlike densely populated Asian countries, it also makes it easier to bring about changes in land use, agricultural techniques, and resettlement of populations on underexploited land.

While there is room for some growth, the momentum of population growth makes it a certainty (barring unprecedented catastrophic events) that the population of the Sahel will quadruple by the year 2050. The rapidity of population growth in the Sahel is a serious problem (see Table 13). For the region as a whole, population is growing at the rate of 2.5 percent a year. While it may be possible for the Sahelian countries to accommodate such rapid growth, the quality of economic development may be seriously compromised as a consequence. The problems of adjustment to rapid growth stand out clearly in the context of long-term planning. For example, health systems must be doubled in size in less than 35 years merely to maintain the present levels of service.[2] Providing larger proportions of the population with more and better health services requires doubling the delivery of this system in much shorter periods .

Disease and malnutrition reduce the amount of work that can be performed by Sahelians and also reduce the productivity of the work that is accomplished. The cost in terms of lost output is high but the resources available for attacking health and nutrition problems are limited. Annual per capita national expenditures in the health sector average $2.00 and only a small minority of the population receives health services. Rural health services providing basic preventive and curative care -- especially immunization, nutrition, and family planning reach only about 20 percent of rural Sahelians. Ratios of medical personnel to populations are way below WHO standards, and rank among the lowest in the world.

Health problems are exacerbated by malnutrition and lack of drinking water. It has been estimated that total food consumption in the Sahel meets only 85-95 percent of the FAO minimum daily caloric requirements.[3] Potable water is available to only about 15 percent of the population.[4] The current nutritional status is very slightly improved over the 1968-1974 drought period. No Sahelian country attains an average of 2500 daily calories per capita. The more severe forms of protein-calories malnutrition such as kwashiorkor and moragmus are less prevalent since the drought, although debilitating forms of malnutrition such as goiter, anemia, and vitamin deficiency are widespread. Indeed the Physical Quality of Life Index (PQLI) developed by the Overseas Development Council to measure the degree to which basic human needs are being met starkly sketches the contours of vital social services in the Sahel. While the United States and France reach the mid-90s, only Senegal of the Sahelian countries surpasses 20 and the Sahelian regional PQLI averaged 17 in 1978 (see Table 14).

POPULATION AND HEALTH

The poor health and nutritional status of the people of the Sahel is a significant determinant of its limited capacity to engage fully in activities designed to achieve overall development of the region. Over the past several decades, the health profile of the Sahelian population has changed very little: infant mortality is higher than in any other area of the world (averaging 177 per 1,000 live births); life expectancy at birth averages under 40 for the region; crude birth and death rates are extremely high. Although accurate data are generally unavailable, it is known that bacterial and viral infections, in combination with poor nutrition, are the major causes of morbidity and mortality. There are high rates of malaria, measles, meningitis, and other communicable diseases, tuberculosis and other broncho-pulmonary ailments; onchocerciasis; trypanosomiasis; schistosomiasis.

As the Sahel Development Program unfolds, the sectoral importance of health will be magnified. Roadbuilding, like most other development projects pursued in the Sahel has the capacity to spread vector-borne diseases (diseases passed from infected to uninfected individuals through other organisms, or "vectors," such as flies, mosquitoes, snails, etc.). Large borrow pits, one or two hectares in area and one to three me-

Table 13: DEMOGRAPHIC TRENDS IN THE SAHEL

	Life Expectancy at Birth [a]		Mortality Rate Per Thousand [a] Infants Aged 0-1		Infants Aged 1-4		Crude Birth Rate Per Thousand Population [a]		Crude Death Rate Per Thousand Population [b]	
	1960	1975	1960	1975	1960	1975	1955-60	1970-75	1960	1975
Cape Verde	43	50	95	79	-	-	47	33	-	-
Chad	34	39	160	-	-	-	46	44	26	24
Gambia	36	40	67	-	-	-	42	43	-	-
Mali	35	38	123	-	-	-	50	50	30	25
Mauritania	36	39	187	169	34	-	45	45	26	24
Niger	36	39	200	162	-	-	52	52	27	25
Senegal	36	40	193	158	-	-	48	48	25	22
Upper Volta	32	38	182	-	-	-	50	49	31	25
Regional	35	39	168	159[c]	-	-	48	48.3	28[d]	24[d]
Low Income Countries [e]	36	44	142	122	-	-	48	47	26	20
Middle Income Countries [e]	49	58	72	46	10	5	45	40	17	12

Sources: a <u>World Atlas of the Child, 1978 (IBRD, 1978).</u>

b Table 15, <u>World Development Report, 1978</u> (IBRD, 1978).

c Weighted average (for years) for four countries.

d Weighted average (for years) for six countries

e Table I, <u>World Development Report, 1978</u>, (IBRD, 1978). Figures are for the years 1960 and 1975, respectively.

Table 13 (continued)

Percentage Change: Crude Birth Rate	Crude Death Rate	Total Fertility Rate [b]	Mid Year Population (000's)
1955-60/1970-75	1960-75	1975	1975
-42.4	-	-	294
- 4.5	-8.3	5.3	4035
+ 2.4	-	-	519
0.0	-20.0	6.7	5677
0.0	- 8.3	5.9	1322
0.0	- 8.0	7.1	4562
- 0.0	-13.6	6.3	5000
- 2.0	-24.0	6.5	5900
- 1.9[d]	-11.0[d]	6.4[d]	27309
- 2.1	-21.1	6.2	-
- 9.2	-27.3	6.1	-

TABLE 14 Physical Quality of Life Index (PQLI[a])

	Life Expectancy at Birth (years)	Infant Mortality Per 1000 live Births	Adult (15 years +) Literacy Rate (percent)	PQLI
Cape Verde	50	105	37	45
Chad	38	160	6	18
Gambia	40	165	10	21
Mali	38	188	5	14
Mauritania	39	187	11	18
Niger	39	200	5	14
Senegal	40	159	5-10	21
Upper Volta	38	182	5-10	16
Sahel Regional	38	177	7	17
France	73	13	97	95
United States	73	15	99	95

Source: Overseas Development Council, Agenda 1979, p.132:

The PQLI combines three indicators - infant mortality, life expectancy at age one, and literacy - into a single composite index. Each of the components is indexed on a scale of 0 (the most unfavorable performance in 1950) to 100 (the best performance expected by the end of the century). The composite index, the PQLI, is calculated by averaging the three indices (life expectancy, infant mortality, and literacy), giving equal weight to each of them.

a) The United States and World Development: Agenda 1979 (Overseas Development Council, pp. 156-159, 1979).

b) Weighted average by population, using literacy rates of 10 percent for Senegal and 7.5 percent for Upper Volta.

ters deep, are dug along the routes of roadways throughout the Sahel. When these pits fill up with rainwater they may be used by the local population as a source of drinking water, and, if unattended, may facilitate the spread of vector-borne and water-borne infections. By increasing human contact with standing water, projects involving transport, agriculture, livestock, and fisheries all tend to contribute to the transmission of such diseases as malaria, schistosomiasis, and guinea worm. Yet, with simple precautions, development projects need not be hazardous to one's health. A family health care report submitted to the CILSS, suggests that these pits could be stocked with "Gambusia," a fish that feeds on the larvae of the malaria-bearing mosquito (genus Gambusia). Properly managed, the pits could be an asset, improving health status by serving as a source of clean drinking water for people, as watering-holes for livestock, and/or as sources of irrigation water for nearby fields.[5]

Vector-borne disease, which is probably the most widespread and universal health problem associated with development, could snowball into one of the Sahel's principal development stumbling blocks. Although a significant effort to free higher rainfall areas from riverblindness is underway in Upper Volta, few disease control programs have been initiated in other parts of the region. Vector-borne diseases associated with water, such as malaria, schistosomiasis, onchocerciasis, and dracontiasis (guinea worm) occur today primarily in the southern portions of the Sahel. If, however, water-related development projects such as irrigation systems, dams, and reservoirs are implemented in the semiarid North, breeding habitats may be created, facilitating the northward spread of vector-borne diseases. This can be particularly serious if the exposed population has little or no acquired immunity to a disease such as malaria. Moreover, as more and more people congregate at major project sites, it becomes increasingly likely that air-borne, water-borne and vector-borne diseases will spread.

Protein-calorie malnutrition contributes to the severity of these diseases, especially among young children. In turn, malnutrition is made more severe due to lowered efficiency in the use of nutrients by a population already weakened by infections. Within the family, adult males may have first claim on available foods, while mothers and children are residual claimants. An Economic Commission for Africa document gives a descriptive account of food consumption patterns:

> Unfortunately, in many areas, men of the household get the lion's share of available food and in particular the soups, stews, and relishes (which women produced). In some African cultures, it is still considered ill manners for a woman to eat much of the

> more nutritious foods, in spite of her higher physiological needs. Within households, women are likely to consume a lower proportion of their requirements than men, not to mention among children, girls as opposed to boys.[6]

At present, women have virtually no access to family planning information or services in the Sahelian countries; a combination of indigenous traditions and government policy continues to reinforce this situation. Some Sahelian governments are beginning to accept family spacing if not family planning as a means of limiting population growth. The benefits that can be derived by the spacing of births has long been recognized in the Sahel and accomplished by traditional methods of abstinence, contraception, and prolonged breast-feeding. There is evidence that urbanization and other modernizing forces are eroding these traditions. The lengthening of birth intervals by modern child spacing measures (combined with improved child and maternal nutrition) markedly increases the survival chances of infants and young children, and also improves maternal health. In The Gambia, Niger, and Senegal maternal-child health programs are being broadened. Despite this progress, population growth will probably not abate until families perceive that there are social and economic benefits to be derived from fewer children.

Life expectancy has gone up slightly since 1960 but infant mortality rates have changed only marginally during the last 15 years. By comparison, infant mortality for all the "low income" countries of the world dropped from 142 per thousand in 1960 to 122 in 1975. Only Cape Verde in the Sahel was well below both sets of averages. Given the lack of significant change in the patterns of disease, it is apparent that the health services and infrastructure in the region have been ineffective in addressing the major health and nutrition problems of the people of the Sahel in the context of limited resources. Development has been concentrated on high-cost, urban, and hospital-based health services which serve only a small segment of the population. Basic preventive and curative health services to the rural majority are minimal or nonexistent except for traditional medical practices whose value is little understood or recognized. Along with the development of high-cost services there is a strong emphasis on expensive education of high-level health professionals.

The demand for unmet medical or educational services in urban areas is high and there are powerful incentives that encourage health workers to choose urban as opposed to rural jobs. Broadening access to health facilities can be accomplished with more extensive use of para-medical staff trained in preventive medicine but the provision of such services requires a high level of technical and administrative supervision

Table 15: NUTRITION AND HEALTH STATUS IN THE SAHEL

	Percent of Minimum Daily Caloric Requirement [a]		Daily Protein Intake in Grams[b]	Population Per Physician		Population Per Nursing Person [c]		Percent With Access to Potable Water [c]
	1961-65	1973-77	1976	1960	1974	1960	1974	
Cape Verde	-	-	-	-	-	-	-	-
Chad	98.8	76.7	60	70,000	44,370	-	6,990	26
Gambia	92.7	96.8	58	-	-	-	-	-
Mali	86.3	75.1	64	39,000	33,000	1,490	2,480	-
Mauritania	86.5	79.2	62	30,000	17,770	7,130	3,790	-
Niger	91.1	80.6	62	71,000	41,060	8,800	4,840	27
Senegal	90.4	95.0	67	35,000	15,360	4,410	1,920	-
Upper Volta	82.0	76.4	59	100,000	59,570	4,370	4,520	25
Regional	88.9	80.9	62.3	62,092[d]	38,048[d]	4,602[e]	3,989[d]	25.9[f]
Low Income Countries	-	-	-	37,000	21,185	4,515	6,710	25
Middle Income Countries	-	-	-	3,050	2,430	2,235	1,570	52

Sources: a Figures derived from FAO-established minimum daily requirements in 1978 Global Assessment Report to Congress (U.S. Department of Agriculture, 1978).
b Table III, World Military and Social Expenditures 1978.
c World Development Report, 1978 (IBRD 1978).
d Weighted average (for year) for six countries.
e Weighted average (for year) for five countries.
f Weighted average (for year) for three countries.

which is not often available. This does not deter advocates of a village-based health system that is organized by and for local residents. David Shear posits that such a system can be "supported by a back-up health infrastructure which provides those services which are not possible at the local level. However, by basing the principal systems at the local level it offers the most effective and efficient way to promote and to protect community health for the majority of the people dispersed in rural areas."[7] The cost factor makes the Shear proposal appealing. The percentages of the total national budgets of the Sahelian countries which are allocated to health are usually under 10 percent, and reach levels as low as 5 percent in Chad. These allocations reflect health investments of about $1.00 per capita for the rural population, and, operationally, of only 30 cents per capita in Chad. With such scant financial resources, it seems clear that only minimal kinds of services of a very rudimentary nature can be provided, and/or that only a few people can be served. Reflecting on these figures for a moment, one can imagine what must be the enormous dimension of the health problems.

It is instructive to examine how these limited funds are spent. Certain patterns in allocating funds repeat themselves. For example, a large share of the Sahelian health budgets is allocated to supporting hospitals, resulting in an unbalanced support of therapeutic services. In Mali, for example, three-fourths of the health budget goes to support 10 hospitals, while the division of sociopreventive medicine receives only 16 percent. The same is true elsewhere. Also, a large share of the budgets goes towards recurrent personnel costs, and this leaves only limited funds for drugs, equipment, and supplies. Therefore, even basic curative services that might be provided by a system weighted in that direction are hampered by inadequate resources in providing these services. As an example of how serious this problem can become, an astounding estimate of 85 percent has been made for the amount of the health budget devoted to personnel costs in Upper Volta.[8]

Since hospitals and personnel receive most of the available funds, and since these are located almost exclusively in the largest population centers, it is not surprising that there is great disparity in the services provided to urban and rural residents. If measured in terms of per capita health expenditures in Mali, it is estimated that Bamako city residents receive $8.40 per capita compared to only $1.10 for rural residents.[9] These observations concerning the inadequacies of total resources available for health, and of the unbalanced nature of even the few resources that are available in favor of therapeutic services among urban residents, have clear-cut implications for policy recommendations. There are a number of perspectives which should be adopted. First, there is the perspective which emphasizes the importance of preventive public health services. Second, we have the perspective of seeking to help populations which evidence the greatest need. Lastly, there is the perspective of seeking to help populations targeted to participate in economic development schemes. Since rural populations appear to have the greatest needs, as well as the largest roles in agricultural development, approaches to improving their health levels must receive the highest priority. From the magnitude of the inadequacies in total resources, large infusions of funds will have to be invested. The knowledge and technology needed for effective action in the health sector is available, Thus, the potential for effective action is very great. Furthermore, a carefully planned package based to the largest extent possible on local or community resources (including community health workers) need not be extravagantly expensive. James Grant of the Overseas Development Council has pointed out that the current health care/nutrition package in Sri Lanka has produced a life expectancy at birth greater than that in Washington, D.C., at a cost of less than $15 per person per year.[10]

EDUCATION

Throughout the Sahel, trained manpower is a limiting factor in every sector and at both administrative and technical levels. Trained scientists, technicians, and administrators are in short supply and the continuance of the colonial education system in the region has contributed to the excessive growth of public employment rather than to the preparation of skilled manpower for agricultural and rural development. Educational institutions are ill-equipped -- in terms of facilities, teaching staff, curricula, practical orientation -- to produce the appropriate mix of skills needed for rural development.

Differences in enrollment in secondary schools between the low- and middle-income countries in the Sahel is quite large, indicating that the latter are better able to afford secondary education but also that increasingly complex economic and social activities go hand in hand with development (see Table 16). Although data is not available on the numbers of trained personnel in various skill categories in the Sahel, we do know that their numbers are increasing rapidly. During the 10 years ending in 1974 the number of Sahelian university students approximately quadrupled and the rate of increase has probably quickened since then.

A comparison between the growth of the education systems in 14 francophone states of sub-Saharan Africa, which have an aggregate population of 45 to 50 million, and the growth of the mother system in France, which has a population of the same magnitude, reveals a dizzying growth trend in the African states. The latter registered a trebling of primary school population during the period 1956-1966, rising from one million to three million, with an annual growth rate of 12 percent. France took 75 years to do as much, with an annual growth rate

TABLE 16: Primary and Secondary Education in the Sahel

	Numbers Enrolled in Primary School as Percentage of Age Group (6-11 years) [a]		Numbers enrolled in Secondary School as Percentage of Age Group (11-20 years) [a]	
	1960	1975	1960	1975
Cape Verde	56	-	6	-
Chad	16	37	neg.	2
Gambia	12	31	3	9
Mali	7	22	2	3
Mauritania	8	17	neg.	3
Niger	5	17	neg.	2
Senegal	27	53	3	11
Upper Volta	8	14	1	2
Senegal Region	12[b]	27[c]	2[d]	4[c]
Low Income Countries[a]	30	52	2	8
Middle Income Countries[a]	79	97	12	35

Sources: a <u>World Atlas of the Child</u> (IBRD, 1978).

b Weighted average for eight countries.

c Weighted average for seven countries.

d Weighted average for five countries.

of about 1 to 2 percent. The African secondary school population has increased over the last decade from 60,000 to 300,000 thus increasing fivefold in 9 years, with an annual increase of nearly 20 percent; it represents, on average, 10 percent of the primary school population (the ratio achieved in France in 1930). In France, it took over 100 years for the secondary school population to rise from 30,000 to 250,000, with an annual growth of 2 percent. The number of secondary students accelerated only after 1950, when it quadrupled in 20 years, and even so, the annual growth rate was only 7 percent. In 15 years, from 1951 to 1966, the number of Africans seeking higher education went up from less than 1000 to more than 12,000, of whom more than 50 percent were being educated locally; this represents a mamouth undertaking since the annual growth rate in enrollments has been in the order of 20 percent. In France, the present growth rate of 14 percent is regarded as "explosive," though it is true that the numbers concerned are wholly incommensurate -- nearly 40 times as great as the African figure.[11] If massive "brain drain" is to be averted, plainly, the growth of the education system must be more closely aligned with that of the economy. Otherwise, it will be necessary to find sufficient financial resources to create adequate job opportunities for the new waves of educated Sahelians. In the face of the exceptional importance attached to education in our technetronic age, and the upheaval that can result from an education system progressing faster than the economy, the brain drain as a palliative to unemployment, may not be all bad. However, for the Sahel to export human resources would suggest a gross waste of human capital that cannot be rationalized.

The existing Sahelian education systems are elitist and urban, i.e., they are geared to the needs of those few who will rise through the entire system to take professional positions, rather than to the vast majority who will receive only a few years of schooling. The disparity of education levels is most pronounced between the urban poor and the rural poor. For the latter there are sharp gradients between farmers, herders, and nomads. The education system is fundamentally open to those in the cities and especially the national capitals, but closed to those in rural areas. Furthermore, enrollments are drastically unequal between males and females. Access to primary schools as a percentage of age group still favors enrollment of boys over girls by margins of 6 percent to 34 percent. Dropout levels from rural primary school are extraordinarily high before completion of fourth grade, the educational level necessary for students to maintain literacy. The relatively few in rural areas with a primary education must generally move away to larger cities if they wish to continue with secondary education.

In terms of cost, education consumes an average of 26 percent of annual national budgets and, of this amount, approximately 65 percent is devoted to primary education. While the total amounts devoted to education grew substantially during the first 10-12 years of post-independence, it now appears that budgetary allocations to education have begun to reach a plateau because expenditures and rates of growth experienced earlier could not be maintained. Yet, in spite of these tremendous efforts, the results have been discouraging. None of the Sahelian countries has achieved more than an estimated 10 percent literacy rate (the estimated rate for Africa is 17 percent) and, while Senegal has managed to enroll 23 percent of its students, the other Sahelian countries average out at an enrollment rate closer to 10 percent (for all of Africa the rate is 27 percent).

Budgetary expenditures indicate that education and human resources development, certainly a "quid pro quo" for development, is recognized as a priority area by the Sahelian countries and this commitment is even more profound in view of the meager resource base in each of these countries. Although Sahelian governments are committed to providing schooling for their populations, they have been emulating dysfunctional educational models. The heavy demand for highly trained leadership during the first decade of independence generally meant that an inordinate allocation of resources was directed toward secondary and post-secondary institutions. This did address a need. Now, however, most countries have surpluses of graduates in the liberal arts field while there are substantial manpower requirements unsatisfied in those areas which are essential to national viability -- agriculture, livestock, health, water resources management, etc. Thus, the education system is suffering from both internal and external inefficiencies.

Internal inefficiencies in the primary education system relate to high drop-out and repeater rates. The external inefficiency of the shcool system relates both to the exodus of school graduates and drop-outs away from the rural areas (and even from their own countries) and to their subsequent failure to find employment related to even their minimal levels of schooling. The magnitude of the human resources drain from rural areas has been estimated in Senegal: of 100 rural students obtaining Certificates of Primary Studies, only two remain in the village. For David Shear and Roy Stacy, the prescription is re-education of Sahelians on the value of education:

> To make education more "relevant" will require changes in popular perceptions regarding the rewards of education. A shift is required away from expectations of employment and upward job mobility to expanding the ability of people to make meaningful decisions about their lives; to expand their options and to supplement their abilities in multiple resource exploitation.[12]

Besides the conceptual re-orientation and, perhaps, the only way to bring it about, the process which, in successive steps, divorces children and, subsequently, adults from the rural sectors and urbanizes them must be reversed. Education must be taken to the target group rather than "vice versa." Moreover, its contents must be geared for Sahelian consumption.

With roughly 37 distinct ethnic/linguist groups in the Sahel, the question of choice of language is a controversial one, and has relevance to national goals, the function of education, availability of basic and technical material, social custom, and so on. Clearly, this is a matter for national deliberation and choice. Many educators do feel, however, that more attention could be focused on the advantages of the local languages than heretofore.[13] While in most Sahelian countries this would mean teaching in as many as three or four languages, this could be accomplished in each country by sharing materials where vehicular languages cross national boundaries. Materials could be produced cheaply and distributed to schools where such materials in French are now lacking or are in short supply.[14] At present, an inordinate amount of time in primary schools is spent learning French. Yet, there is increasing evidence that once a child becomes literate in his indigenous language he is more proficient in learning a second language.[15] Teaching French at the secondary school level might, therefore, be accomplished faster and better as a result of having learned an indigenous language first. However, the argument that by not learning French it will be impossible to communicate across tribal and national boundaries appears to be somewhat of a "strawman." For hundreds of years prior to the French presence, the peoples of the Sahel criss-crossed the area communicating, trading, and founding sophisticated economic and political systems. At present only 1 percent of the rural population in Senegal (the most developed of the Sahelian states and the one with the longest association with France) is literate in French, although all official communications are in the French language. That means that 99 percent of the rural population is effectively barred from official communications and from sources of information related to improvements in their styles of living and economic productivity.

Given the general average of over 90 percent illiteracy in Sahelian countries, a functional literacy program is essential in order to promote development programs and to improve the prospects and possibilities for communication and information flows directed toward improved life styles of the rural and female populations. Curricula reforms in the primary school to further indigenous languages could help to prevent revertible illiteracy after leaving a primary school program prematurely. Availability of local language training and appropriate adult education materials available through the schools, and having teachers trained to teach adults as well as children could contribute much to the school system's outreach. However, it is also recommended that these formal school programs be closely integrated with non-formal and agricultural production programs aimed at increasing food crops as well as cash crops, livestock production projects, fishing, and handicraft programs. At curriculum development centers, materials could be produced with inputs from relevant ministries to prepare inexpensive and practical printed materials to assist adults to become literate and to maintain their literacy.

Non-formal education can with and without the formal school system, make a major contribution to the education outreach of Sahelian governments. Functional non-formal education programs should be promoted in conjunction with literacy programs. As a principal education goal, functional literacy has important ramifications for future generations. An impressive array of psychologists have come to the conclusion that the period from birth to about age six is critical to the individual's future cognitive development. Benjamin Bloom, for instance, estimates that half of mature intelligence is developed between birth and four years, and another 30 percent by eight years.[16] One-third of future school achievement is determined before the child enters school. O.K. Moore contends that the early years of life are the most creative and intellectually productive.[17] The implications of these findings are straightforward. The "pre-school" years merit greater attention by development-minded good-doers. Education of parents, in this context, acquires special importance because of its multiplier effect. In this context, village day-care center proposals do not have an extraneous quality to them. By providing a more stimulating and creative environment in a formative period, such facilities could upgrade the whole educational enterprise.

At present the most cost-effective and efficient means of conducting non-formal educational programs is by radio. Limited radio education programs are already operating in Senegal, Upper Volta, and Niger, but their scope is far too limited and their resource and personnel bases restricted. Nevertheless, experimentation underway in the Niger program has indicated that radio and television education programs have been effective in reaching herding populations in the desert regions. This model should be evaluated and expanded not only more generally over Niger but throughout the Sahel. Funds should be allocated for systematic utilization of modern technology in expediting education. Frederick Harbison observed that the need for new technologies of pedogogy is greater in the developing countries than in those with more fully developed education systems. He recommended that African countries in particular give serious thought to the establishment of centers for research in educational technology. "In this area, they may have to lead rather than to follow the more advanced nations of the world."[18] Donors can make greater contributions in assisting the Sahelian countries in pioneering new methods of teaching. Foreign assistance agencies need to be more fully attuned to the requirements of educational reform in the Sahel and they must not be deterred by the inhibition posed by French cultural dominance.

EMPLOYMENT: THE URBAN CONNECTION

Sahelian employment opportunities, whether in towns or rural areas, are very meager even for those few who are literate or for those who have received a full primary education. PECTA, a regional office of the ILO, issued a special report in February 1977 for the Club du Sahel's Human Resources Team on the employment situation in the Sahel. The report confirms that four-fifths of those employed in the Sahel, with the exception of Senegal (69 percent) and Mauritania (51 percent) are farmers or herders. Employment in the modern secondary sector (manufacturing, construction) is weak, between 9 percent and 13 percent of the urban employed. By contrast, about 30 percent of urban employed find work in commerce, transport, and related services. By far the most important of these is the civil service, which has often served in the Sahel as the employer "par excellence" for those with secondary school credentials and above.[19] Visible unemployment, according to the PECTA report, which does not attempt to assess the extent of disguised unemployment, is particularly serious in Cape Verde (59 percent of the population over 15 years of age), Senegal (20 percent), and Chad (17 percent). By other calculations, however, rates may be just as high elsewhere. Mauritanian officials, for example, estimate unemployment in that country at roughly 50 percent of the work force.

Current rates of population and labor force growth in the Sahel are approximately twice those experienced in Europe during its rapid expansion in the nineteenth century.[20] Government policies which have concentrated investments in urban areas, coupled with skewed resource holding patterns in the rural areas, have created a pull and push effect which has accelerated rural-to-urban migration. The absence of adequate capacity in the non-agricultural sectors to absorb this influx of labor has resulted in a change in the form in which the unemployment problem appears "... from disguised unemployment in the rural area, to open unemployment in the urban, the latter posing more of a social threat."[21]

Rapid growth is a relatively recent phenomenon in the Sahel's major cities. Smaller cities and towns have witnessed a similar period of expansion. The influx to urban areas of persons displaced by the drought and famine in more recent years has exacerbated the already heavy demand on essential urban services, particularly housing and sanitation, and strained the ability of local governments to respond. For many newcomers unable to find work, this move simply exchanges the tenuous life of the countryside for the insecurity of the town.

TABLE 17: URBAN POPULATION AND URBAN POPULATION GROWTH RATES

	Sahel	Chad	Mali	Mauritania	Niger	Senegal	Upper Volta
Urban Population 1975 (in thousands)	3,700	558	760	200	430	1,250	500
Urban Population Growth Rates 1970-75	5.0	6.1	4.5	5.5	5.3	4.0	5.1

Source: United Nations, Population Projection, 1950-2000, Medium Variant, December 1974.

In the last 10 years, urban areas have almost doubled in population, with rural migrants accounting for the greatest part of this increase. Thus, a very sizeable portion of the urban population consists of recent arrivals from rural areas, equipped with essentially untransferrable rural skills and possessing a world view shaped by a rural setting. More often than not, the urban poor are recently arrived poor. By occupation, the urban poor include a) self-employed persons in the services sector: hawkers, shoeshine boys, barbers, repair and maintenance workers; b) unskilled workers employed in manufacturing, construction, or services -- some in the modern sector sometimes irregularly; c) recent migrants who take on casual work while looking for better jobs; d) skilled artisans usually self-employed whose skills such as pottery or spinning are relatively obsolete and whose products have low demand and others such as carpenters and tailors, who operate on a small scale; and e) aged and disabled persons who are live-in dependents of other urban poor.

Some urban poor are only temporary migrants from rural areas during the dry season when demand for farm labor is nonexistent. A significant portion of rural incomes in the Sahel derives from remittances sent home by these migrants who return to their villages for spring planting. However, as migrant urban workers find higher paying or steadier jobs, they extend their stay and ultimately become permanent residents of the cities. This increases the effective demand for social services and heightens the competition between rural and urban areas for scarce development resources.

TABLE 18: SHARE OF URBAN POPULATION GROWTH ATTRIBUTABLE TO MIGRATION AND NATURAL INCREASE, 1975

	Sahel	Chad	Mali	Mauritania	Niger	Senegal	Upper Volta
Annual Urban Growth (in thousands)	176	34	34	7	25	51	25
Percent of Growth Attributable to Migration	49.5	65.5	46.2	64.0	49.4	40.7	55.5
Absolute Growth by Migration	87.5	22	15	4.5	12	20	14
Percent of Growth by Natural Increase	50.5	34.5	53.8	36.0	50.6	59.3	44.5
Absolute Growth by Natural Increase	88.5	12	19	2.5	13	31	11

Source: United Nations, op.cit, 1974.

According to the World Bank, the urban population of the Sahel is expected to triple between 1975 and 2000. Given the extremely high wages of the public sector compared to rural incomes in the Sahelian countries, urban centers have attracted rural migrants who, depending on their qualifications, often seek public sector jobs or employment in service activities geared toward public sector employees. Urban investment in the Sahel represents roughly between 20 and 30 percent of total investment in each country. This range is significant because it is considerably higher than the percentage of urban population found in each country (averaged regionally, 14 percent in 1975), confirming past charges of "urban bias" in the world's most rural countries. This bias has been characterized by Michael Lipton as a bias in the process, structure, and consequences of decisions affecting the use of national resources in developing countries.[22] Manifestations of this bias include the transfer of agricultural surpluses from the rural to the urban sector, where they are converted into urban consumption without fair exchange in manufactures or services needed for economic growth. Too literal a definition of urban bias obscures the distribution of absolute poverty within the Sahelian countries. The "poorest of the poor" are found in urban centers as well as in the remote rural areas. To be sure, even with an obviously inefficient and inequitable transfer of surpluses, given the scarcity of resources and low incomes in rural areas, the Sahelian urban condition is not to be envied; indeed, levels of public services are among the lowest in the world.

TABLE 19: URBAN POPULATION DISTRIBUTION, MID 1970s

	Sahel	Chad	Mali	Mauritania	Niger	Senegal	Upper Volta
Capital city (thousands)	1,787	193[a]	350[b]	150[c]	122[c]	800	172
Percent of Urban Population in Capital	38.0	34.0	34.6	75.0	28.4	49.0	34.0
Other Urban (percent)	62.0	66.0	65.4	25.0	71.7	51.0	66.0
Percent of Urban 10,000 in Capital	47	45	44	85	50	52	40

a World Bank estimate for 1974.
b World Bank estimate for 1975.
c World Bank estimate for 1976.

A major constraint to improving the welfare of the rural poor has been agricultural and food policies that have increased the real incomes of urban consumers at the expense of small farmers and herders. Official prices for domestically produced staple grains have been kept low both in relation to world market prices and to prices of manufactured goods. The prices urban consumers pay for imported rice and wheat have been subsidized in time of world shortages and high prices, thus reducing the demand for cheaper, less preferred domestically produced staples such as millet and sorghum which are somewhat more nutritious. Low producer prices for food, food imports, and subsidized urban consumption have all combined to keep producers real incomes low, discourage investment in agriculture and slow the expansion of domestic production. On the other hand, manufacturing activity, which accounts for only a small fraction of GDP in the Sahelian countries except for Senegal, is protected from import competition and granted direct incentives such as tax holidays and subsidized credit. State enterprises which receive substantial direct subsidies engage in the manufacture of import substitutes. High levels of protection for industry generate little industrial employment and the domestic resource costs of import substitution remain high. A number of factors, in addition to infant industry problems account for the inefficiencies encountered during attempts to industrialize. Protectionist policies eliminate competitive pressures that might encourage efficiencies. Employment practices of the state industrial and trading enterprises further remove the pressures of competition. The lack of infrastructure and high transport costs especially in the interior countries add to the costs of industrial activity.

In his classic Quiet Crisis in India, John P. Lewis states in a particularly seminal chapter of his work: "Any development plan has a spatial dimension in the sense that each newly established installation or activity requires a locational decision."[23] He observes that the attempt to bring the development effort into correct spatial focus is seriously obscured by a dichotomizing of development issues along rural-urban lines. By seeing the rural and urban problems as mutually exclusive, a false polarization ensues that conveys no sense of the continuum of "centering" alternatives, stretching from the smallest villages to the largest metropolis. In admonishing against metropolitan-centering, Lewis stresses its propensity towards a dual society, whereby the progressive elements in the society, in terms of income and ideas are winnowed out and pulled farther and farther away from the traditional rural mass. In contrast, town-centering (towns in the 20,000 to 300,000 range) would be conducive to a synthesis between the traditional-rural and the Western-urban strands of an indigenous culture. Lewis speculates that town-centered industrialization's requirements for many social overheads might, in total, be less than would be posed by unrestrained metropolitan agglomeration. The town-centered alternative has its greatest selling point on the employment front. As Lewis notes, town-centering would, at the very least, yield a less feverish problem of urban unemployment and make it easier for frustrated migrants to retreat to the relative congeniality of village unemployment. He states: "To a degree that would be quite impossible in large cities, for example, town-centering could marshal many of the rural unemployed -- part-time as well as full-time -- to the tasks of urban reconstruction without dislodging them from their villages.[24] This direction in spatial planning applies "a fortiori" to the Sahel. A World Bank study on urban growth and economic development in the Sahel concludes: "More equitable allocation of national resources between rural and urban areas is essential if the Sahel countries are to improve their incomes. ... Urban sector analysis, within macroeconomic planning, needs to identify and encourage activities in secondary towns which will support rural development."[25]

The analysis of public investment patterns presented in the World Bank study flags the fact that towns other than national capitals receive relatively small shares of total allocations to the urban sector. When compared to the distribution of urban population, despite the importance of the capital cities, it was evident that secondary towns do not receive an equitable share on a per capita basis. While it could be argued that the administrative overhead costs of national capitals necessarily lead to disproportionate expenditures in the capitals, this imbalance is interpreted as a persistent phenomenon which is growing more acute with each subsequent investment program. Whether this trend stems from the greater absorptive capacity of new investment as a result of previous investment or whether the capital cities have greater needs, the resulting bias towards the capital cities reinforces economic and spatial patterns. As showplaces for young countries trying to carve out national identities, capital cities will continue to receive a disproportionate share of urban investment. Genuflections to the imperative of rural development notwithstanding, Sahelian leaders continue to be motivated by not a little sense of intra-regional competition in which impressive capitals figure prominently. Moreover, we would be deluding ourselves if we thought that measures to reverse the rural exodus will meet with much immediate success. The cities of the Sahel will continue to hold an otherworldly sway for residents of the hinterland, who have been known to gather around traffic lights, gawking at these paragons of automation. However, town-centered policies could alleviate the present strain that capital cities are experiencing. A sizeable research agenda dating back to when Lewis first proposed this approach must be tackled. These include such items as identification of the relationship between marketing and settlement patterns; studies of the industrial-scale and market-size implications of technological choice; studies of competitive structure in the context of dispersed industrial location; and studies of the "company town" problem.

Given the sheer size of the agricultural sector "vis a vis" the other sectors of the economy, as well as the rapid rate of population growth, in the short run, agriculture must somehow absorb a significant portion of the annual increase in labor supply. At the present time, a great disparity exists in the absorptive capacity for labor in agriculture as evidence by numbers of workers employed per arable hectare in various West African countries. The Ivory Coast, for example, employs two agricultural workers per hectare whereas Upper Volta averages

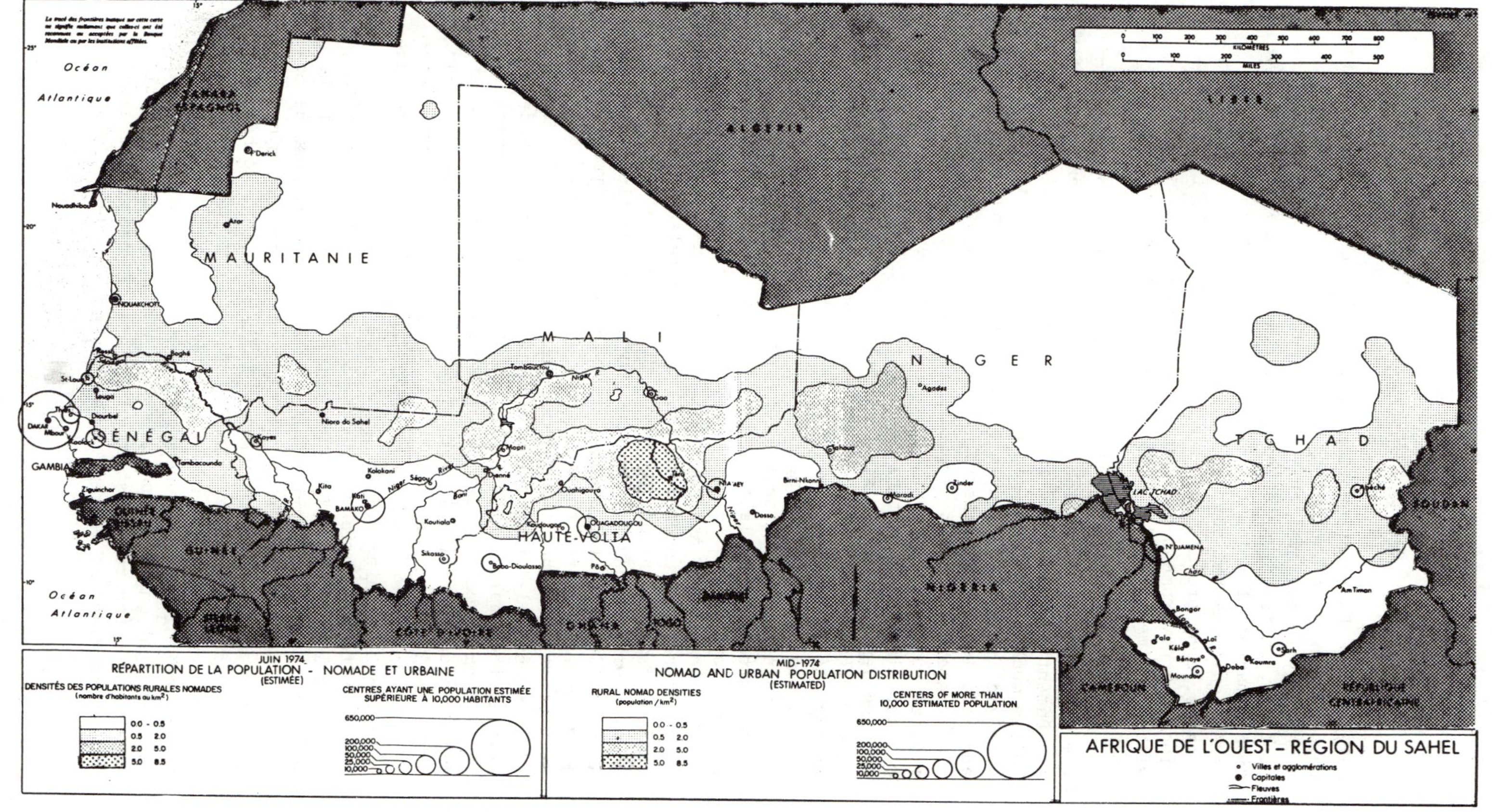

AFRIQUE DE L'OUEST – RÉGION DU SAHEL
Villes et agglomérations
Capitales
Fleuves
Frontières
JUIN 1974
RÉPARTITION DE LA POPULATION – NOMADE ET URBAINE
(ESTIMÉE)
DENSITÉS DES POPULATIONS RURALES NOMADES
(nombre d'habitants au km²)
0.0 - 0.5
0.5 2.0
2.0 5.0
5.0 8.5
CENTRES AYANT UNE POPULATION ESTIMÉE SUPÉRIEURE À 10,000 HABITANTS
650,000
200,000
100,000
50,000
25,000
10,000
MID-1974
NOMAD AND URBAN POPULATION DISTRIBUTION
(ESTIMATED)
RURAL NOMAD DENSITIES
(population / km²)
0.0 - 0.5
0.5 2.0
2.0 5.0
5.0 8.5
CENTERS OF MORE THAN 10,000 ESTIMATED POPULATION
650,000
200,000
100,000
50,000
25,000
10,000
KILOMÈTRES
MILES
Océan Atlantique
MAURITANIE
MALI
NIGER
TCHAD
SÉNÉGAL
HAUTE-VOLTA
GAMBIA
NIGERIA
CAMEROUN
LAC TCHAD
Derick
Nouadhibou
Atar
NOUAKCHOTT
St-Louis
Dakar
Tambacounda
Ziguinchor
Kayes
Nioro du Sahel
Kita
BAMAKO
Kolokani
Ségou
Sikasso
Koutiala
Bobo-Dioulasso
OUAGADOUGOU
Ouahigouya
Mopti
Djenné
Tombouctou
Gao
Agadez
Tahoua
Maradi
Zinder
Birni-Nkonni
Dosso
Niger
N'DJAMENA
Am Timan
Bongor
Moundou
Sarh
Doba
Koumra
Pala
Kélo
Bénoye
Laï

only one.[26] Labor absorption capacity in agriculture appears to be strongly influenced by a number of factors, including technology (e.g., availability or irrigation, commercial fertilizers, improved varieties, extent and nature of mechanization), markets for labor intensive crops, land-holding patterns, cultural patterns and traditions (e.g., livestock grazing vs. crop production), soil types and rainfall distribution, and government policies -- particularly those dealing with investment, credit, import and export controls, and exchange control.

An ILO mission to the Sahel observed that a redressing of the unemployment situation requires a basic reorientation of government policies, and in the process these policies must become much more "rural-minded."[27] Similar messages are being received from other study missions, international agencies, and individual researchers. An Organization of African Unity (OAU) paper urges that development strategies for Africa emphasize rural development, focusing on increasing not only output but also job opportunities and rural incomes, and on improving general rural living conditions.[28] Another ILO paper stresses government policies which are designed to create employment in rural areas and develop the traditional sector. This would constitute a major attack on poverty rather than considering the rural sector as a mere "residual" which can accommodate surplus labor unable to secure employment in the modern sector.[29]

The complexity and constantly changing nature of the various sub-sets of underemployment has made reliable quantification of the magnitude of the problem practically impossible, even in urban areas of the Sahel. The difficulties are greatly magnified in rural areas. Nevertheless, employment specialists generally agree that the less visible forms of unemployment constitute the most serious manpower waste. The ILO mission concluded that three generalizations can be made regarding the employment situation in Sahelian rural areas: (1) the employment situation varies sharply from area to area within a country; (2) it varies considerably during the year (seasonality); (3) the nature of rural life makes overly-precise urban concepts such as "active labor force" or even "unemployment" meaningless.[30]

Despite the obvious conceptual and measurement problems, from a policy formulation standpoint, a better grasp of the existing situation, particularly in rural areas, must be obtained. As M. Dantwala has pointed out, "For economic analysis as well as policy purposes, it is necessary to have information, not only on the overall average level of unemployment, but also on the nature of unemployment and the distinctive characteristics of the unemployed."[31] He and others stress the need not only for quantitative, but also for qualitative information (characteristics of age, sex, educational level, status or class of worker, race, family size, etc.) regarding who the unemployed are and where they are located. In-depth rural studies in smaller geographic areas may prove vastly more valuable than the current national estimates, both in terms of obtaining reliable qualitative information and in providing guidance for remedial action. It may also be that provisions need to be made for viewing employment in terms of earnings rather than just hours or days worked. Various country missions and other research groups have experimented with the feasibility of using some form of "inadequate income" measure of underemployment.[32] In those studies where income level has been used as a major proxy for an underemployment measure, the estimates of the number of underemployed are invariably substantially greater than when reliance is placed only on an hours or days worked concept.

Whatever the modifications adopted, it is imperative that an expanded data collection effort be mounted, and that increased attention be devoted to developing a meaningful grasp of the true situation in rural areas -- where information on employment, income, and standards of living is least reliable. Existing manpower projections should be reviewed carefully for each Sahelian state and a revised compilation of needs, indicating the problems (e.g., the statisitcal unknowns and soft data), should be prepared as a guide for nampower planning. In establishing the existing manpower base, an attempt should be made to determine the extent to which trained manpower are being employed in areas corresponding to their training and education.

In considering future manpower needs, both for the presently projected levels of development and for the levels which might result, careful consideration should be given to Sahelians presently undergoing training and post-secondary education abroad. The importance of this component is indicated by the fact that Chadian officials now estimate that there are approximately 1,500 persons outside of the country (most of whom are in university level programs in France), while in Niger it was estimated that at least 400 were presently abroad. In Mauritania some officials thought that as many as 100 might be studying abroad. Obviously this potential reservoir of trained personnel will not fit into all the skill categories which Sahelian countries require, but a substantial number of them will and others may, with additional training, fit identified manpower needs.

In conjunction with the manpower surveys, a special effort should be made to determine how many Sahelians have remained abroad following the completion of their training and education programs. A repeated observation heard in the Sahel is that the number is substantial. In part this is attributed to difficulties they experienced, after completing their degrees and training programs, in obtaining positions in their own countries relevant to their studies. Within the context of projected development plans, efforts should be made to identify these people to determine how they might fit into national and regional development schemes, either with or without additional preparation, and their recruitment, placement, and repatriation should be attempted on a priority basis.

The most widely discussed and controversial question concerning dual economies is undoubtedly that of whether the backward sector of such an economy sustains surplus labor in disguised unemployment. A complete discussion of the debate would fill volumes by itself and clarify little. Many of the questions raised and answers, where they exist, are much better understood in light of the workings and results of the rival theories, which by and large arrive at the general conclusion that the marginal productivity of labor in the traditional sector is a far less important parameter compared to some others, especially the elasticity of supply of food to the modern sector.[33] While much remains to be known about the nature and dimensions of the unemployment problem in the Sahel, it is clear that employment is often a secondary, not a primary, objective of development. Mahbub ul Haq's candid account of attention to employment in Pakistan's five year plans is equally applicable to the Sahel:

> ... the chapter on employment strategy was always added at the end, to round off the plans and make them look complete and respectable, and was hardly an integral part of the growth strategy or policy framework. In fact, most of the developments which affected the employment situation favourably, such as the rural works programme and the green revolution, were planned primarily for higher output, and their employment-generating potential was accidental and not planned.[34]

A promising approach to economic development, as articulated by John Mellor, is a strategy of employment-oriented growth.[35] Mellor stresses the pivotal place of agriculture in an employment-oriented strategy. Agriculture performs two key related functions in this approach. First, because foodgrains make up the bulk of marginal expenditures among the poorer classes, agriculture provides the physical goods to support increased employment and higher wage earnings. Second, it provides much of the increase in employment, directly through raising agricultural production, indirectly through the stimulus of increased income to the cultivator class and the demand effects of the consequent expenditure. Increased agricultural production, based on cost-decreasing technological change can make large net additions to national income, and place the income in the hands of the cultivator classes, who characteristically spend a substantial portion of it on nonagricultural commodities. Agriculture is looked to as a demand drive for development similar to that often depicted for foreign markets in export-led growth. While accelerated growth of agriculture may be an important condition for a high-employment policy, a high-employment policy is an important condition for continued rapid growth rates in the agricultural sector. This important inter-relationship requires astute government policy if it is to work smoothly and effectively.

CONCLUSION: THE CLUB AND HUMAN RESOURCES

"Man is at once the means and ends of development."[36] This has served as the organizing principal for the Human Resources Sector Team since its formation in July 1976 as part of the Club Working Group. From this broad perspective, the Human Resources Team has been concerned with three aspects of human resources development in the Sahel: with the improvement of productive and adaptive skills, through education and training systems at all levels; with more effective means for people in the community at local levels to plan and manage their own development -- through cooperatives, credit societies, and other means; and with improved health, nutrition, and planned family growth.

The Human Resources Team, representing the above concerns, may yet assume the central, unifying role to which it seems eminently suited in the Sahel planning process. Problems of organization, however, have thus far restricted the team's effectiveness. The perspective and first generation program of the Human Resources Team are delineated in the report adopted at Dakar March 29-31, 1977, and accepted two months later at Ottawa by the Club.[37] According to this report, there are three limiting conditions of particular importance to the development of human resources in the Sahel. These are: unemployment, lack of communications, and the inappropriateness of local education/training institutions.

A major corollary problem to unemployment, in the view of the Human Resources Team report, is the rural-urban migration rate. While for the moment, at least, the rate of emigration from Mali and Upper Volta to coastal countries appears to have slowed, internal migration from rural areas to the towns continues apace. In Mali, where towns are small, PECTA estimates urban growth at between 20 percent and 25 percent each year. This is perhaps the highest rate in West Africa today. Elsewhere in the Sahel, urban growth is officially estimated between 5 percent and 10 percent annually, Seasoned observers, however, stress that the rural to urban migration is a more pronounced phenomenon in the Sahel than in other areas of the world at a comparable time in their development.

Taken together, the lack of productive employment and the high rural-urban migration rates reduce appreciably the impact of the established education/training institutions in the Sahel.

These conditions underline the need to search for means of educating people in the context of rural programs launched under the Sahel Development Program. Reaching people directly, however, will require deliberate measures to strengthen communications. The diversity of population in the Sahel, low population densities, and the striking lack of communications facilities within the region impede human resource development in ways which are difficult to measure. Including city dwellers, sea fishermen, dryland and river basin populations, and several nomadic herders, life styles vary sharply across the Sahel. Settlements are small and scattered. Roads are often impassable in the rains, while in the dry months, waterways are closed to volume traffic.

Not surprisingly, modern communications networks -- telephones, radio, and the press -- are not yet adequate in the region. Information does not circulate rapidly or reliably. Radio and telephone systems are particularly thin in Upper Volta, Mali, Niger, and Chad (see Table 20). A public sense of participation, or developmental empathy, is difficult to engender and sustain under these conditions. Education and training activities, as the Human Resources report points out, are in no significant sense buoyed by a rising level of public dialogue, or by growing possibilities for Sahelians to learn and talk with each other more widely about their development concerns.[38]

Sahelian education/training institutions are particularly inadequate, both in size and content, to forming man as an end and means of development. Still primarily geared to producing civil service "fonctionaires" and "law and order" administrators, schools and training colleges alike are in need of reform. Even at local levels, the language of instruction remains French. The distribution of schools still favors the urban areas. Reform programs, which are on the books in every Sahel country, are stalled, partly for lack of funds. In part, too, public sentiment still supports the schools as they are, representing "the best way out of the village" and into secure jobs in the civil service. Although primary schools in the Sahel enroll less than 25 percent of the primary school age population (fewer still graduate), the Sahelian countries generally cannot afford to expand the systems. School and training establishments already absorb about 25 percent of recurrent national budgets.

Taken together, the employment, communications, and institutional constraints of human resources development in the Sahel are manifestations of the low level of productivity, accented by drought. As the Team report acknowledges, the development of human resources in the region will depend upon simultaneous action on all three fronts: action to promote productive employment, to develop information and communications networks, and to transform the education/training institutions which serve the Sahelian countries.[39] The Human Resources Team

TABLE 20

SAHEL COMMUNICATIONS SYSTEM (JULY 1977)

Country	Radios (per 1,000 pop)	Telephones (per 1,000)
Cape Verde	105	8
Chad	17	1
Gambia	110	5
Mali	14	1
Mauritania	59	1
Niger	21	0.8
Senegal	55	7
Upper Volta	16	0.5

SOURCE: UNIDO

has produced no strategy in the true sense for the Sahel. To devise a comprehensive strategy, the Team must take account both of the training objectives set by the other teams of the Working Group, as well as the extant education/training plans formulated by each of the eight CILSS member countries. To date, both sets of essential materials are wanting. Instead of pressing to help produce these materials, the Team has canvassed the Sahelian governments for a list of top priority human resource projects which bear on rural areas and which require donor assistance. However, the Team did produce, in late 1976, a long-term strategy for addressing the problems of health, water, and nutrition. A conceptual framework rather than a detailed planning document, the strategy is designed to link interventions in health with socioeconomic development throughout the region. A key goal is "to improve the health status of the population, particularly the health of mothers and children ... and the active and productive members of the population" by making basic health services available throughout rural areas of the region.[40]

Emphasis in the strategy is placed on the development of village-based health services involving the active participation of the communities themselves and the recognition and utilization of traditional insitutions and sociocultural patterns. The strategy calls for the use of village health workers who are trained to provide health promotive, disease preventive, and simple curative functions. These skills can go a long way in addressing a distinctive and tragic feature of the health situation in the Sahel and in most developing countries, namely the high proportion of the illness and death that occurs in infants and young children. Most of these deaths are preventable. The required technology is well known; its application is neither terribly complicated nor expensive. A careful and large-scale study carried out recently by the Pan American Health Organization showed that much of the excess childhood mortality in the Western Hemisphere is associated with or due directly to malnutrition.[41]

The case for nutritional surveillance, analysis, and intervention strategies cannot be overstated. Food is the single most important variable in the Sahel and probably the basic limiting factor for development of the region. A nutrition strategy focusing on nutrition policy and planning on a regional scale must be developed. Such a strategy would be an important step toward comprehensive nutritional planning and the ultimate relief of nutritional deficiency syndromes. There is a need for more site-specific intake data and dietary analysis to increase the understanding of caloric and protein requirements and food intake on age-and sex-specific bases-- data which would be valuable in planning and implementing nation and regionwide nutritional strategies. Lastly, little is known about the peoples of the Sahel. Demographic data are severely lacking, including the mortality and fertility rates and nutritional and health levels of both the sedentary and migrant populations. No accurate census has been taken of the region. The gathering of accurate demographic data is an essential prelude to economic and social planning under any development program.

5
The Structure of Social Change

Development as a paradigm cannot be made logically or even probabilistically compelling for a society which refuses to step inside the circle of change. Thomas S. Kuhn has said: "As in political revolutions, so in paradigm choice -- there is no standard higher than the assent of the relevant community."[1] The question before development architects is whether their preferred strategy should be pursued aggressively, by impressing a seamless orthodoxy, a development fundamentalism or, whether the approach should be quite the contrary: adaptive, absorbent, and gradualistic. In other words, should target groups in developing areas be shoved or otherwise forcefully implanted within our circle or should they be issued a polite invitation, allured, and patiently awaited until they decide to drop in?

A popular theoretical recourse in reaching a decision on the pace and manner to adopt in implementing development efforts has been to look for clues in the past. Historical processes have two aspects relevant to development: the specific path or sequence of transformations of a society and the way in which a new order is inaugerated. The central question as to whether the sequence in the movement toward what we vaguely and somewhat equivocally call modernism matters is admirably addressed by Barrington Moore, Jr.[2] History has traced out alternative sequences, some of which are more likely than others to lead to integrated development and, thus, to facilitate the transition toward a society that has registered not only physical but conceptual change. But even if the development architect was to limit his imagination by history and common sense, he would surely discover and invent more paths than anyone could deal with. It is, indeed, a long way from precolonial Sudanian empires to balkanized francophone and anglophone nation-states. The most obdurate traditionalist sees that. The problem is to understand how, given such endings, we can catalyze new beginnings.

For accomplishing this task, so that we may approach the future with more understanding, our intellectual resources, the scientific explanation of cultural change, are rather meager. Systematic discussions of the transformation of societies from what we gather they used to be like to what they seem now to be like generally follow one or another of a small number of strategies, which have been categorized by Clifford Geertz under the rubrics indexical, typological, world-acculturative, and evolutionary.[3] These various strategies for studying change may, of course, be combined, and some of them, for example the evolutionary and the typological, commonly are. However, taken either together or separately, they offer little guidance for policy makers concerned with the structure of social change.

Neither indices, stages, traits, nor trends are conclusive indicators of the extraordinary transformational phenomenon loosely labeled as modernization. To estimate the approximation toward and the obstacles in the path of the formation of a society and polity that are accommodative to modernization requires a macrodevelopmental perspective that is process-oriented. When we turn, for instance, to the Sahelian countries, we find it difficult to distinguish enduring social and political features from transitory ones. As old orders disintegrate and new ones emerge, we are made conscious by surface symptoms of a great ferment about which we know very little. While the literature on development is replete with cause and effect propositions that purport to explain stages of transition from "underdevelopment" to development, they rarely interlock to give us the train of events that can carry developing countries to their increasingly remote destination.

It has become "de rigueur" for social scientists contributing their services to development efforts, after outlining what they believe to be rational and feasible development strategies, to insert an escape clause stressing that without a demonstration of "political will" by the targeted society, any course of action would meet with failure.[4] At first glance, this seems to be a fair exoneration in case of failure. But when we stop to define "political will," and ask why individuals would be unwilling to actively embrace a program from which they might benefit enormously, we find ourselves confronted by a nexus of cultural currents and cross-currents. This failure to comprehend transcultural equivalents of "political will" and to catalyse them, has been the dangerous undertow of developing areas, overwhelming even the most well-executed and pragmatic-appearing development strategies.

Although it is true that economic growth cannot take place without capital accumulation, to what extent is this factor indicative of association rather than causation? Better health is associated with development, but who is to say whether better health produced economic growth or "vice versa?" The socioeconomic factors fundamental to integrated development can be enumerated at length and include population pressure, balanced growth, investment criteria, urbanization, natural resources, terms of trade, monetary and fiscal policies, and so on each with staunch supporters. The difficulty with these factors arises when inferences are drawn from them as to the dynamics of development. In a subsequent process that may be called social defibrillation, shock tactics of sorts are used to shed the apathy that impedes progress. This approach is grounded in hard theoretical firmament. Social psychologists have shown through the theory of cognitive dissonance that changes in beliefs, attitudes, and eventually in personality can be entrained by certain actions instead of being a prerequisite to them.[5] And even prior to the findings of Festinger, et al., Hirschman argued that the Protestant ethic is not the cause of entrepreneurial behavior, but arises as its consequence.[6] Somewhat earlier, Pascal had pointed out that religious feelings can be the consequence, rather than the cause,of devotional acts, such as kneeling.

A recurrent theme in general theories of cultural growth holds that adversity breeds strength and innovation. It is most eloquently put forth by Arnold Toynbee in his theory of the "challenges of the environment." As he employs the term, "environment" refers not only to geography, but also to social conditions. What is important is the "appropriate stimulus" which may arise from environmental harshness, from living in a frontier position, from being penalized as a minority group, and so on. The problems with this very plausible theory stems from its vagueness, since gearing an appropriate stimulus is no mean task. Such a theory has little explanatory power and certainly no predictive power. That is, if a Sahelian country were to ask what should be done to promote integrated development, one would have to answer in Toynbee's terms that the society should be provided with just the right amount of stimulus. Can this theory not be fleshed out to make it somewhat more robust?

While necessity is the mother of invention, exposure is its father. Harsh circumstances alone could spell annihilation. A dash of native intelligence would be valuable but not invaluable. Civilized man did not attain his present status without the sacrifice of many who could not benefit from the experience of others, from the savage groping in the dark of life-or-death experiments, and from the ensuing exposure to witnessing and subsequent generations. While experimentation and experience are integral to this overarching process, in time, exposure is its keystone.

The effects of exposure on mental processes remain fairly abstract to the social scientist. However, we can identify three distinctly disparate polarities of exposure. In the polarity of "over exposure," a society, when confronted by exposure, will reject the phenomenally new in its entirety. This may result as a consequence of a bombardment of alien phenomena of such intensity that the society in question cannot distinguish between what is germane and beneficial to its needs from that which may be detrimental. Literally turned off, the society rejects as a package the array of exotic wares thrust upon it. Subsequently, the society erects a conceptual wall and continues to function strictly within the parameters of the residual paradigm. More commonly over exposure is a defense mechanism triggered by subjection. Thus, we have witnessed in most African countries the assertion of the dignity of things generically African against the backdrop of European colonialism. The sentiments underpinning this reaction are profound and widespread for colonialism has, in Africa even more than elsewhere, often taken forms that were particularly damaging to the sense of integrity and self-esteem of indigenous cultures. Geertz illustrates this polarity in the colonial context:

> Beyond the economic and political, the colonial confrontation was spiritual: a clash of selves. And in this part of the struggle, the colonized, not without cost and not without exception, triumphed: they remained, somewhat made over, themselves.[7]

Some social scientists are wont to speak of a state of incoherence during the interim between the modern and residual paradigms. This is not necessarily the case because man is equipped, even in the midst of the most harrowing upheaval, with the capacity to internalize contradictory notions.[8] This is the thrust of the polarity of "double exposure." Michael Polyani has commented on the presence of this paradoxical condition in the West:

> A new destructive scepticism is linked here to a passionate social conscience; an utter disbelief in the spirit of man is coupled with extravagant moral demands. We see at work here the form of action which has already dealt so many shattering blows to the modern world: the chisel of skepticism driven by the hammer of social passion.[9]

Polyani refers to the crux of a modern dilemma: two essential but conflicting world views; one science-centered and the other faith-centered. Internalizing the two concurrently has been the attractive option for many. Members of any society can learn to use the language of science and to master technology without surrendering established beliefs in superstition and the supernatural. Amulets that once protected camels in the Sahel from malicious spirits have not been discarded by urban cab drivers, who now adorn their vehicles with phylacteries for the same reasons.

Lastly, there is the polarity of "cognitive exposure." This polarity is critical to laying the foundation for integrated development and is characterized by such prerequisites for progress as the transcending of negativism and the definition of hope in programmatic terms. In this polarity, a society enters into exposure on its own volition, discriminately selecting those wares that it can utilize. Japan offers an example of this stance of neither complete insulation nor wide-open integration that differs greatly from the process of subduction that the phenomenally new often undergoes in societies that have not entered into cognitive exposure despite claims to the contrary. Japan is the "model country" for developing countries attempting to adjust to the modern paradigm. Japan effectively and dramatically exploited technology and consciously reshaped the matrix of its society to accommodate it, demonstrating the value of cognitive exposure to genuine and integrated development.

David E. Apter states: "Once the social scientist discovered that there is a discrepancy between behavior observed and behavior felt, between the act and the rationalization, between the conscious and the subconscious, and between virtue and conduct, he fashioned a new role for himself -- the theoretically omniscient observer."[10] To be content with being a collector of empirical materials as an end in itself is to sell short the role of the social scientist in modernization. The social scientist is a natural mediator in the perennial conflict between the "expositor" and the "perpetuator," a conflict that I have referred to elsewhere as the Expositor-Perpetuator Reaction Series. According to this construct, exposure to the phenomenally new destroys the conceptual containers that encase individuals caught in the residual paradigm, i.e., perpetuators, and transforms them into expositors who, as the etymology of the word in Latin ("exponere") suggests, put forth, expose, and expound the ideas of a new paradigm. Unfortunately, the strategy of conflict between expositor and perpetuator, i.e., the Expositor-Perpetuator Reaction Series, is imperfectly understood. There is a present need for expositor and perpetuator in developing areas to pull out their bargaining chips and to enter negotiations more comprehensive and constructive than those few that have been held hitherto.

Part of the problem rests with identification of representatives from both sides of the cleavage. Where perpetuator input is solicited, development efforts often exhibit a "take me to your leader" optic, which posits that once traditional chiefs have given their blessings for any proposed changes, the rest of the community will fall in line. In point of fact, few Sahelian societies are so hierarchically organized. For instance, among the pastoralists the more likely situation is that there is no authority figure who can dictate his will over his fellows. Many pastoral societies have no centralization of managerial decisions relating to access to grazing lands and water and, therefore, to herd size, composition, and movements. Such a people are the widely dispersed Bororo or Wodaabe in Niger, who demonstrate a remarkable egalitarianism that goes a long way in exploding the myth of "oriental despotism" pervading views of societies "sans" Western imprint.

Throughout the Sahel, religious perpetuators are key agents of socialization, the process by which a community preserves and transmits its social traits. Religion can secrete attitudes and actions that corrode and undermine progress. There remains throughout the Sahel, the vigorous remnants of an ancient theocracy, and at times, it would appear that "leadership and authority are part of the seamless web of both politics and religion."[11] In Senegal, a handful of maraboutic leaders command the allegiance of powerful religious brotherhoods as well as much of the country's population and expect commensurate power in government. Indeed, President Senghor has granted more audiences to marabouts than any other group outside of his administration. On the other hand, donors to the Sahel, expositors "par excellence", have made few if any contacts with religious perpetuators. Yet, as I have argued in "The Protean Marabout" (<u>Psychopathologie Africaine</u> No. 1, 1973), the marabout's involvement in practically every aspect of the lives of his congregation makes him a central participant in development efforts.

Social scientists can help identify key perpetuators and the best forms of encounter in which to engage them in the development process. As we mentioned earlier, the major problem relating to health has been designing systems which are effective in the delivery of health services to the bush at a low cost. Various proposals for the training of paramedical or medical auxiliary personnel have been put forth; many of them have shortcomings or are too costly to make a real improvement in access to health services on the part of the remote villager or pastoralist. Yet, there exists a traditional health delivery system with representatives in the smallest villages and camps: these persons including barbers, herbalists, and marabouts, paralleling surgical, medical, and psychiatric specializations, have a vested interest in success, and provide a ready-made resource which enjoys some confidence on the part of the people. Unlike many paraprofessionals, they are willing to live in the hinterland.

Similarly, there exist well-established traditional educational systems, ways of passing on the knowledge and skills crucial for survival in harsh, marginal environments. We know very little either about the content or the methods of instruction of these systems, yet it would seem clear that we have much to learn from them, especially about the design of effective informal educational programs aimed at improving the quality of life of the rural poor.

Given the delicate balances in life styles of Sahelians, much finesse and appropriate forms of encounter are required for exposure to take. Otherwise, there is risk of halation or double exposure. What donors and other expositors need is a kind of exposure meter for measuring the intensity of whatever is being put forth to the target group. Of course, there are other ways, in the absence of such an unlikely instrument, to determine the correct exposure. They include any number of democratic processes that increase general participation in decision making, such as poll-taking and thorough research studies. To offset the impression given by the light-meter metaphor that what the expositor gives off is light, i.e., good, the evident should be stressed: exposure can be harmful. As Sahelians are all too aware, not everything in the Western scheme of things is benign, and many Western concepts, techniques, and products must be modified to suit Sahelian realities. Moreover, exposure is a two-way street. Indeed, for Senghor the global bargain of our times involves bartering the spiritual for the technological. His view is that the Third World is economically underdeveloped but the West suffers from a spiritual underdevelopment no less debilitating. "The civilization of the twenty-first century . . . will surely be superindustrial, that is, technological. It will be humanism or barbarism, depending on whether or not the peoples of the Third World, and among them the black peoples, will have brought to it their contributions."[12]

SOCIAL ORGANIZATION AND DEVELOPMENT

Social organization and values of rural Sahelians offer security and mutual support in times of crisis. Traditional forms of land distribution and usufruct can provide for an equitable distribution of either pasture or crop land, grazing or cultivation rights, and equitable distribution of output. Traditional organization and values can inhibit change as well. Small farmers experienced in dealing with government services and regional development organizations responsible for export crop production and marketing are receptive to changing traditional practices when economic incentives are present. Herders dependent primarily on their livestock for subsistence milk production are less open to using their herd for meat production. In general, traditional social organization and values in the Sahelian countries serve to mitigate the worst effects of the poverty that is pervasive in the region, but they are undergoing change in response to development interventions.

Greater governmental intervention in Sahelian life derives in part from the view that there has been inadequate regulation of the commons; that a kind of inherent logic remorselessly leads to tragedy "à la" great drought. Garret Hardin sums up the argument:

> Adding together the component partial utilities, the rational herdsman concludes that the only sensible course for him to pursue is to add another animal to his herd. And another; and another..... But this is the conclusion reached by each and every rational herdsman sharing a commons. Therein is the tragedy. Each man is locked into a system that compels him to increase his herd without limit -- in a world that is limited. Ruin is the destination toward which all men rush, each pursuing his own best interest in a society that believes in the freedom of the commons. Freedom in a commons brings ruin to all.[13]

On the other hand, Michael M. Horowitz has riposted in a vigorously dissenting opinion on the "tragedy of the commons" interpretation of Sahelian woes that Sahelian pastoralists are dynamic and opportunistic, making the only possible use of marginal lands.[14] He alleges that the idea of the tragedy of the commons is a myth colored by an anti-nomadism that views pastoralists as rigid, conservative, destructive of the environment, and caring more about social value and prestige than about economics. With such diametrically opposed approaches to pastoralists, is it no wonder that there have been so many ill-fated attempts at compulsory sedentarization and range management? Plainly, we need to delve further into the socioeconomic ambience of an important segment of the Sahelian population.

A much better understanding of the complex interrelationships between herding and farming populations is needed, especially the ways in which multiple use of the same terrain is regulated. One needs to know a good deal more about political, economic, and social exchanges among these peoples. This kind of repository can alert us to proposals that might disrupt the system and cause a reduction in the amount of useful energy which may be generated by it. One needs to understand the ways in which conflicts between groups are resolved -- for example, when herdsmen and farmers compete for the same land, or when two groups of herders compete for water rights. What use is made of traditional authorities? Of customary law courts? Of the modern government's mechanisms for dispute resolution?

Horowitz has shown that herdsmen and farmers have developed elaborate codes to regulate their relationships. These relationships derive from the fact that nowhere in the Sahel do pastoralists exist exclusively on the produce of their herds. Herdsmen and farmers spend a good part of the year in close proximity. Although occasionally antagonistic, the relationships between them may be termed complementary, even symbiotic. One study has concluded: "While on the whole cattle are a profitable enterprise in the research area of Tenkodogo, Upper Volta, farmers do better to continue the traditional practice of entrusting their animals to specialized Fulani herdsmen, rather than to attempt to care for them themselves. This is principally the result of a labor conflict between crops and livestock during November which is aggravated by a widespread desire on the part of farmers to be self-sufficient in food grain production. Not surprisingly, sedentary agriculturists in the research area are reluctant to adopt mixed farming practices that are often recommended by expatriate advisors as desirable new farm activities."[15] The principal exchange between herders and farmers is the post-harvest conversion of cultivated fields into pasteur, where animals graze the cropped farms, and provide manure, much valued by the cultivators since they lack chemical fertilizers. Significantly, herdsmen are also extremely receptive to foreign assistance when new practices are introduced which can improve the quality of the breed and prevent disease in the animal.

There are many obstacles precluding pastoralists from entering the polarity of cognitive exposure, including "untimely measures decreed by a government in which the ruling mentality is usually that of an agricultural peasant."[16] Sahelian administrations often echo the sentiments of donor agencies that the herdsmen, harmful to the environment, must be settled for their own good. These efforts usually fail, mainly because they lead to over exposure. Few attempts have been made to bridge the lacuna in life styles by putting the pastoralists veterinary expertise to account on dairy farms. Instead, the pastoralist's world view, his knowledge, and most critically his bioethic are ignored. A critique of the Hardin thesis argues as follows: "When I first read Hardin's article, I wondered if the users of the early English commons weren't prevented from committing the fatal error of overgrazing by a kind of 'bioethics' enforced by the moral pressure of their neighbors. Indeed, the commons system operated successfully in England for several hundred years. Now we read that, before the colonial era in the Sahel, 'over-pasturage was avoided' by rules worked out by tribal chiefs. When deep wells were drilled to obtain water 'the boreholes threw into chaos the traditional system of pasture use based on agreements among tribal chieftains.' Thus we see the tragedy of the commons not as a defect in the concept of a 'commons' but as a result of the disastrous transition period between the loss of an effective bioethic and its replacement by a new bioethic that could once again bring biological realities and human values into a viable balance."[17]

The problem, then, is to assist Sahelian pastoralists with adaptive strategies to preserve environmental capacity to sustain them by drawing on their ethic of resource conservation and the apparent strength of their culture. Indeed, we need to know more about the hardiness of traditional Sahelian herdsmen and farmers, identifying this strength (knowledge, skill, willingness to invest labor) as the basic resource for equity-based rural development. Also, these strengths are not randomly distributed across the region, but vary within groups and from group to group. Two general kinds of study are implied by these variations:

a. to identify the characteristics of exceptionally successful herders and farmers within groups (what are the factors which lead certain individuals consistently to outproduce others: i.e., better land, better use of tools, better capacity to mobilize labor in production, increased ability to moderate consumption, better entrepreneurial grasp of the characteristics of the market, etc.); similarly, one could identify the characteristics of those individuals who regularly appear unsuccessful. Once the analysis has been done, a number of actions relating to the possibility of raising the overall capacity of the group to produce or to invest more effectively may be recommended.

b. to identify populations which seem to make more effective or productive use of resources than others, or whose use of the environment appears to be less degrading. For example, across the region, certain ethnic groups are reported to have weathered the drought with less loss than others. The Dogon, for instance, claim to have had surplus harvests even during the most rainfall-deficit years. Why are the Dogon so markedly more productive than their neighbors? What can be learned from a study of Dogon productive sociology and productive economy that might be diffused to other people?

Among the sedentary ethnic groups a number of deep-rooted social and cultural variables represent impediments to agricultural development. One of the most important limiting factors is land tenure. The prevailing land tenure system and traditional method of inheritance, without titles to the land, give little incentive to long-term investments. Although there are some variations in the Sahel, communal tenure is the most widespread. It exists in a variety of forms, with certain fundamental features in common. Land is held on a tribal, village kindred or family basis, and individuals have rights in this land by virtue of their membership in the relevant social unit. Thus, title to land is usufructuary, rather than absolute. A chief or patirarch may be the custodian of the land but he is not its owner. The normal unit of land ownership is generally the extended family and, once the land has been granted to this group, it remains its property. In theory, land may be pledged and redeemed, but only in such manner that it shall not be permanently lost.

The prevailing land tenure system has adverse effects also on the distribution of population, which indirectly affects mobility of labor and, hence, agricultural development. H.A. Oluwasanmi, the perspicacious Nigerian social scientist, has opined that the scale of operation is a combination of the tenure system and the social organization, which render it virtually impossible for farmers to move freely from regions of high population density to areas where land is in excess supply. Oluwasanmi does not see how the impecunious peasant farmer with his three-acre holding and deeply ingrained habit of shifting cultivation can be a likely vehicle for accomplishing the urgent changes desired in agricultural productivity. As a result, he has recommended the adoption of farm settlements or plantations as more suitable units of production.[18]

In the Sahel's patriarchal and matriarchal cultures, the dominance of elders leads not only to a well-entrenched gerontocracy but also gives authoritarianism an authentic ring -- without exposure, it is a logical political system to the individual who continues to be ordered around in his middle age by family members. In general, the extended family impedes not only mobility but cognitive exposure. David C. McClelland demonstrates that the separation from the father is associated with higher achievement motivation in the son.[19] In a part of the world where polygamy flourishes, exposure is further limited by lengthy dependency relationships in mother-son households.

The ideal family organization in the Sahel is the "joint family." This term refers to a family which functions as a corporation and survives generation after generation without division of the family property. Members of such a family who do not live in the family compound are expected to contribute part of their income to the family funds. In return, all members of the family are entitled to support in old age or in case of disability. Economic improvements present specific problems to this kind of family organization, while changes in the residual economic system are unusually disruptive socially since opportunities for individual economic profit are usually accompanied by weaker ties of extended kinship. The village, which is composed of a nucleus of families descended from a common ancestor, is yet another determinant of social cohesion, which fairly rigid marriage rules are calculated to strengthen.

Similarly, obligations to one's kinfolk to share in agricultural work is a potent means of preserving group solidarity. However, the system of sanction may actually be counterproductive to agricultural productivity. Among Zarma perpetuators, the system of reward for efforts in production is generally based on ascriptive criteria like age, sex, position within the kinship unit, rather than on achievement criteria. In other words, within the production unit, members of the social system continue to be rewarded in their capacities as boys, girls, men, women, husbands, and wives, rather than on the basis of their respective contribution to the total output.[20] This type of structural incentive can act as a barrier to entrepreneurship.

Perhaps the most significant force in the reformation of

this antiquated system of sanction is the sexual revolution just beginning to make itself felt in the developing areas. Increasingly, "liberated" women are spearheading the development effort of the Third World, and for good reason. W. Arthur Lewis states: "It is open to men to debate whether economic progress is good for men or not, but for women to debate the desirability of economic growth is to debate whether women should have the chance to cease to be beasts of burden and to join the human race."[21]

The sequestration of women has been, for a long time, the ultimate precaution taken by perpetuators to eschew exposure--effectively precluding the possibility of new attitudes being taken back to the home and passed on to the next generation. Women have little or no access to even primary education in the Sahel. As mothers, they are forced to remain sterile insiders inside as opposed to more noetic outsiders inside. This has important ramifications for the education of a society, particularly at those critical early years. McClelland has found that early "training" in group interaction contributes immensely to making people more other-directed and willing to go along with new procedures introduced by strangers from outside their immediate experience.[22] The extent to which socialization instills an early respect for the perpetuator is illustrated in a study of New Haven school children conducted by Fred I. Greenstein. Greenstein found that children as young as seven years old, who had very little or no factual knowledge about what political leaders do, nevertheless evaluated fairly accurately the relative importance of various political positions and socially prestigeful occupational roles. Already affective-evaluative images of model perpetuators had been inculcated by parents and familial relations.[23] This obtains "a fortiori" to reinforcing a position of female inferiority in the minds of young Sahelians.

Many studies are now available which document the importance of women as decision makers, as well as a labor source in Sahelian agriculture. Several studies document how commercialization of agriculture has reduced the role of women, and further impoverished and made them more dependent on males. Other studies demonstrate the key role of women in any attempt to improve nutrition, and identify women and children as having the poorest health status.[24] Consequently, it is vital that new development programs avoid previous pitfalls, when it was tacitly assumed that a woman's place is in the home. An AID memorandum states:

> CILSS development plans and AID country strategy statements give little or no attention to what women do to provide basic needs to rural people, or to the kinds of training and supplies Sahelian women require to perform their tasks more effectively. Nevertheless,

> AID Sahel posts are giving increased support to projects which prepare women for work on the farm and in the community, as is evident in a recent AFR/SFWA report summarizing examples of projects involving/benefitting women.[25]

SDP installments should build upon this experience by outlining approaches that would ensure that the role of women in multilateral and bilateral development projects is adequately addressed.

The problems attendant to social change in the Sahel often require development architects to go beyond the utilitarian model. For instance, when a modern mill was built in Maradi, Niger, to save women the backbreaking task of grinding millet by hand, the women chose to boycott the mill since it deprived them of the social hour they enjoyed after finishing the job together. Much of the literature of economic development rests upon the assumption that all societies and most individuals would like to improve their economic condition. But what is sloughed over is the fact that most people welcome improvements in well-being as long as such improvements are economical, i.e., do not entail more trouble than they are worth and do not controvert too many values. W. Arthur Lewis has lucidly pointed up the influence of distinctly nonrational factors on development. He has effectively demonstrated that the "desire for goods" is an obvious psychological factor determining how hard people strive to increase their material welfare, and that the desire for goods may be decreased by limited knowledge of what is available for purchase to the consumer.[26] Farmers don't demand improved technology if they prefer the rigorous exercise they get out of their hand implements, or if there is no advertising to make them aware that improved technology exists.

Sahelian leaders, most notably Senghor, have consciously shaped the development environment to include noneconomic variables. Senegal's "socialist stand" or "African Road" asserts the primacy of culture and spiritualism. The works of the French Catholic philosopher, Pierre Teilhard de Chardin, accenting man's subliminal desire for wholeness, has greatly influenced Senghor. In his philosophy, Teilhard advocates material progress only so that materialism may be ultimately transcended by spiritual unity. Teilhard wrote, in 1939, that the "foyers of human development" always seemed to coincide with the points of meeting and synthesis of several races.[27] This observation underscored the importance of synthesis for Senghor, a product of cultural synthesis himself, and has been a guiding principle for all of Senghor's theoretical constructs from the "African Road" to the "Civilization of the Universal." Teilhard's philosophy enabled Senghor to bridge an impasse by elaborating a theory of socialism without renouncing any of the spiritual values of African civilization. According to Senghor, Teilhard carried the theories of Marx to their logical conclusion, achieving the "neo-humanism" sought by Marx. Teilhard, albeit a scientist, was also a devout Jesuit who refused to "mutilate" man by ignoring his spiritual nature.[28] Senghor is able to reject Marxism because he has found what he feels is higher philosophy as well as more knowledgeable science. Senghor has long argued that we must draw a distinction between immediate objectives and final ends. Marx only concerned himself with the former refusing to deal with the problem of ultimate purposes. Yet, Senghor demands: " ... on what is founded the obligation of duty? Progress of science and technology places between our hands the instruments of an incalculable power. For what should we use them?"[29]

The "African Road" is a harvest of the principal sources of inspiration discussed above and many more. It has been described as "a doctrine which is still confusedly seeking for itself, an amalgam of very diverse elements" both foreign and indigenous.[30] Because of its emphasis on a syncretic approach, it is non-dogmatic. Echoing the bastardization of Islam in the Sahel as it was blended with animism, Senghor has attempted to adapt a much watered-down, academic Marxism to African realities. While Senghor is a vocal critic of capitalism, he accepts it in practice, at least insofar as crucial sectors of the economy are concerned. The "African Road" permits the economic coexistence of both private and public sectors. Never, claims Senghor, has he opposed "capital investment" -- only the capitalist system.[31] As a realist, Senghor saw that his country could not industrialize without the help of French private capital. He has stressed the need to concentrate on the collectivization of agriculture rather than on the nationalization of industry. Senghor believes that the worker in Senegal is privileged and not a true proletarian. Because of his income he represents an affluent social group when compared with the peasants who make up the bulk of Senegal's population. It is natural therefore, that the "African Road" attempts to improve the lot of this important segment of society. Senghor wishes to transform "traditional village organization without having to pass through the capitalist stages."[32]

Senghor's first step towards implementing the "African Road" was to invite the development group Economie et Humanisme and its leader Father Lebret to undertake a study of the Senegalese economy. In 1960 Lebret's Twenty-five Year Plan, which attempted to put into practice Senghor's ideas on reviving the traditional cooperative, was accepted by the Senegalese government. To bolster the "weak dynamism of the traditional economy of Senegal," the Plan advocated the establishment of a "Service of Animation" (Animation Rurale) to expedite decentralization in an attempt to stimulate widespread participation in the effort for self-development. Animation had the function of putting into effect techniques adapted to Senegalese realities. Above all, however, its task was to form "animators" -- people selected from among the most dynamic and enterprising volunteers from each village. The volunteers were to receive training in technical and managerial skills useful for development, as well as relevant political ideals and skills of communal progress. Then they would return to their villages as "pioneers of renewal" to spread their knowledge, helping the peasant to discover himself as the essential meter of the nation's economy, and hence create a "revolution from the base."[33] Animation was conceived as the vehicle for realizing socialist development as the cooperatives were intended to provide the institutional framework.

Plainly, the first goal of the "African Road" is psychological. A "prise de conscience" that self-progress is possible had to be sparked prior to technical "encadrement." This disarmingly simple approach cannot be fully appreciated without taking into account one of the major obstacles to social change and economic development in Senegal: the pervasive worldview of fatalism in the face of the harsh conditions of life, strengthened by Islam with its submission to the will of Allah. With a strong appreciation for the social sciences, Senghor wishes to sensitize all Africans to the pivotal role of culture. He states: "Contrary to the notion of numerous African politicians, culture is not an appendage that can be lopped off without damage. It is not even a simple political means. Culture is the precondition and the goal of any policy worthy of the name."[34] From the beginning, Senghor made it known that he felt this facet of development to be more important than economic growth. On the eve of independence, he reported with delight to his people that the Russians were reading a novel entitled Not By Bread Alone. Senghor believes that he is proceeding in a manner compatible with current economic premises. "As for the cultural means, contemporary economists have given these an importance they did not enjoy in Marxian economics, though Marx stressed the role of consciousness and will in the transformation of the world."[35] He quotes the French economist Francois Perroux as saying, "Development is the combination of a people's mental and social changes, which makes it apt to increase its real global output cumulatively and durably."[36] The problem, therefore, is to awaken "dormant energies," to combat prejudices, routine, inferiority complexes, and the fatalistic spirit. Hirschman too emphasizes that the obstacles to the perception of change can turn into an important obstacle to change itself:

> The matter can also be put in the form of a vicious circle: to the extent that a country is underdeveloped, it will experience special difficulties in perceiving changes within its own society; hence, it will not

> notice resulting opportunities for even larger and more decisive changes. A country that fails to perceive these opportunities is likely to remain underdeveloped.[37]

One of the principal fallacies of integrated development arises from comparative socio-politics. A kind of factoring out process is used to determine which characteristics are shared by the developing country and the developed country. Subsequently, an attempt is made to introduce the missing characteristics in an aid program. While Western donors are necessarily bound by the limits of their own development experience, this does not preclude acknowledgement of the fact that to achieve comparable levels of capital formation, productivity, and consumption, there is no injunction to duplicate Western institutions. Non-Western societies are quite capable, "a la" Japan, of finding ways to accommodate economic growth and of entering into their own versions of integrated development.

Brought into connection with a dynamic conception of social systems such as it has lacked earlier, the comparative standpoint can "serve both the broadened human sympathies of this age and the requirements of the more coherent social theory appropriate to this extension of the imagination."[38] Perhaps the most encouraging aspect of the Sahel Development Program is its avoidance of an ethnocentric tint to development by respecting the development goals of Sahelian governments. Consequently, there is greater recognition of the legitimacy of many forms of human organization, and the particular kinds of cohesion, consensus, and stability that they invoke. In other words, the traditional background music can still be heard through the blaring polyphony of Western music. The question is whether they can be harmonized in the polarity of cognitive exposure.

CONCEPTUAL TECTONICS

Integrated development must be concerned with "conceptual tectonics," that is to say, the organization of mental motion as it flows from one conceptual system to another. A conceptual system or worldview is defined as a pattern of beliefs and values that permit man to relate to the universe, to the world around him in which he must act, judge, decide, and solve problems. Conceptual systems encompass ideology, and are composed of symbols that enable the individual to formulate an image of the world's construction and a program for his conduct that are at once reflexive. David E. Apter offers an appropriately generous definition for ideology: "It links particular actions and mundane practices with a wider set of meanings and, by doing so, lends a more honorable and dignified complexion to social conduct."[39] Men must form ideas about the material universe and embrace definite convictions that satisfy the metaphysical need for cosmic orientation. For example, traditional Zarma retain a conception of the earth ("labou") as a plane suspended in space with seven planes at equal distances above it called "baynay iyay" (highs) and seven planes, "ganda iyay" (lows), suspended beneath it. Each of these fifteen planes is infinite in area, dwarfing the inhabitants of a depopulated land.[40]

Varied and vibrant, Sahelian conceptual systems are indistinguishably meshed with the vitality of the region's spirituality. There is always the danger that foreigners interacting with Sahelians will exhibit a certain callousness in this respect. An unfortunate example of this failure to acknowledge non-Western conceptual systems is provided by one writer when he states: "Japan, unlike some parts of the non-Western world, did not come into the modern world 'tabula rasa,' and therefore the legacies of the past were certain to color the new order." No society enters "the modern world 'tabula rasa.'" Mutual awareness of the disparity in intellectual content and climate could facilitate wider acceptance of the persistent sway of ideologies, their not so infrequent originality, the fact that they are usually less rigid than they first appear, and are themselves in a continuing process of adaptation, susceptible to cognitive exposure and other influences. It has been pointed out that the Ghana of twenty years ago possessed an amount of capital equivalent to Japan's.[41] Thus, an ascendant school of economists, African-based or partial to Africa, have concluded that Japan was able to develop from a capital base not greatly superior to that of some of the better-endowed African countries since it was able to exercise a far-reaching sovereignty over its economy. Neocolonialism has been pegged as the evil culprit victimizing the African continent. While neocolonialism is an evident and detracting economic feature on the African scene, equally striking is the difference between the conceptual underpinnings of Japanese and African development.

At all stages, ideology has played a dynamic and creative role in Japanese modernization. While much has been made of the Japanese ability to develop rapidly within the shell of traditional culture, we tend to forget that existing beliefs allowed a bending and shaping of well-understood institutions which, despite their alteration, provided a sense of continuity. Some of these beliefs are represented in an emphasis on education for instrumental ends. Robert N. Bellah notes that in Japan learning for its own sake "tends to be despised. The merely erudite man is not worthy of respect. Rather, learning should eventuate in practice."[42] Furthermore, as Apter has shown, the primacy of political values and the emphasis on the polity allowed modification of economic organization without dramatically rupturing the accommodating values and social beliefs of the Japanese.[43] Thus, a state of conceptual tectonics, reminiscent of the one underpinning Europe as it anticipated the industrial revolution, enabled Japan to enter the polarity of cognitive exposure and, subsequently, to flourish in the modern paradigm.

The time element between paradigmatic shifts in the Expositor-Perpetuator Reaction Series has been a source of much confusion and frustration to integrated development. The interval between entering the polarity of cognitive exposure and consolidating a new paradigm can be a lengthy one. Although, the transition can be accelerated, it is evolutionary. Needless to say, the industrial revolution was not a spontaneous event. It came about only after much aggregative change, which extended from the end of the fifteenth century to the second half of the eighteenth century, covering well over two and a half centuries, characterized by as phenomenally new a discovery as the New World. This breakthrough, leading to a significant increase in knowledge development and production, was itself a consequence of improvements in science and technology, bearing upon navigation, ships, and weapons, and perhaps more significantly, of advances in social philosophy, reflected in the political organization and domestic production of Western Europe.

Simon Kuznets' concept of "economic epochs" is instructive with respect to time periodicity:

> An economic epoch implies an interplay of technological and economic changes not only with institutional modifications but also with shifts in beliefs entertained by the societies that participate in it; and the time and effort required to overcome the resistance of old beliefs and to evolve the new and more appropriate spiritual framework may partially account for the length of epochs. [44]

In his sixth characteristic of epochal economic growth, Kuznets elaborates that an epoch is marked by a substantial addition to the stock of knowledge, and those societies that take advantage of it necessarily undergo "a prolonged process of learning"; that "changes must ensue in the system of views that dominate and govern the behavior of men."[45] Views on the relation of man to man, on social organizations, on natural conditions, on established religion, in fact, on the validity of many long-held beliefs are violently rocked by cognitive exposure.

New attitudes must be fostered to permit the exploitation of science-based technology. The nature of the nexus of views, a veritable "Weltanschaung," essential to the application of technology to economic well-being is unclear. Vague as this proposition is, and difficult as a precise formulation of the requisite outlook might be, it is an area that merits greater attention: "the dominant views of an economic epoch are as distinctive and as important as the technological and social epochal innovation that characterizes it."[46] John Dewey has insisted that a genuine acquisition of knowledge can take place only by "acting upon the world"; it cannot be passively absorbed. "Men have to do something; they have to alter considerations."[47] Yet, there are powerful factors favoring a passive epistomology.

In a thoughtful piece that appeared in The New Yorker, William Pfaff observed: "For individuals as for nations, our (Western) sense of values has been based on a belief in consequence and development, in causes having effects. And Industrialism and technology are phenomena of cause and effect par excellence."[48] In contrast, deprived majorities in many developing areas view their condition as an intrinsic part of the order of things, legitimized by religion, subject to change only through some ultimate and perhaps apocalyptic redemption. India's Hinduism is perhaps the archetypal religion of natural order, inculcating a belief in the **transmigration** of souls in union with the Absolute Spirit, which is the ultimate reality. "It is hardly an accident that so many of India's great modern enterpreneurs and industrialists have come from the Parsi community -- Zoroastrians from Persia, believers in the resur- of the dead."[49] And yet, it is true that among the disadvantaged segments of society, a self-denying outlook may help to make a haggard, at times, humiliating existence more bearable.

After centuries of poverty and both natural and human oppression, apathy and hopelessness tend to become a way of life. Recurrent failures to obtain small material improvements, together with the broken promises of politicians, support a strong propensity toward fatalism. In the face of seemingly ineradicable inequalities, gratification is delayed indefinitely and wants are kept to a minimum, bringing them into line with the harsh limits of the possible. "In a situation of limited and static aspirations, if a man should feel that his requirements are just two bags of paddy rice per year, he works for two bags, but not for more. If he looks to the stars, it is only to worship them, not to pluck them."[50] In the Sahel, the widespread phenomenon of "limited aspirations" is at the crux of the development quandary, and highlights the need to introduce and/or emphasize mechanisms through which a conceptual system more amenable to integrated development can be fashioned. The internalization of conceptual variables necessary to integrated development is a delicate business, especially where symbol systems which construe experience are internalized to such a degree as to be axes of human existence.

One of the most intriguing facets of African religious history is the study of transition, wherein a more dominant system of belief becomes superimposed, often after a period of coexistence. This theme has been widely treated in the history of the Nilotic Sudan and may be fruitfully investigated in the Sahel. The adaptations of cults in pre-colonial history is a more neglected theory, but equally important and suggestive. The dissemination of development ideology could benefit from the precedent set by the penetration of Islam in the Sahel.

It is important to bear in mind that the principal impulse for evolution of a highly structured culture -- true state organization, long-distance trade, sophisticated art, and universalistic religion -- grew out of a centrally located peasant society upon which less developed outlying regions pivoted, and that Islam penetrated this axial social structure well after the latter was securely established. Religions rarely sell themselves diffidently. Islam benefitted from proselytism of a hard-core, quasi-fanatical lot of Fulani pastoralists who became forceful (literally) missionaries. However, it is necessary in the Sahel to refraim from teleological and deterministic suppositions. Animism and Islam are genuinely plural in the Sahel, not merely because different communities retain separate rituals and beliefs, but because there are layers of belief coexisting in many individuals who may physically participate in several ritual spheres, i.e. religious double exposure.

The role of religion accents the protean and embrangled nature of the cultural kaleidescope in our area of inquiry. Sahelian Islam is remarkably maleable, syncretistic, and most significantly of all, multivoiced. What for so many parts of the world has been a powerful, if not always triumphant, force for cultural homogenization, for the social standardization of fundamental beliefs and values, is for the Sahelian countries a no less powerful force for cultural diversification, for the crystalization of sharply variant notions of what the world is really like and how one should therefore go about living in it. Such a milieu offers endless possibilities for a cross-fertilization of ideas and experiences in the polarity of cognitive exposure. Perhaps the greatest obstacle to the meeting of minds is foreign perceptions of the immutability of indigenous ideological constraints. Unfortunately, the development implications of religious activity have been neglected, and many facile formulations have yet to be discarded.

A legal or fundamentalist interpretation of religion is of course possible, and the pervasiveness of such an ideal in Islam accounts for the general lack of attention by Moslems to their own religious history, but it should not dissuade those in the business of development assistance from entering into a dialogue and feeling out areas where there is a capacity for ambiguity. Greater understanding of "syncretism" would flow inevitably from such a dialogue and, perhaps, the term will lose its currency, not because the mixture of different religions is to be denied, but because syncretism's implications that there is a pure form which is devalued by accommodation to other values, will be viewed in a more sympathetic light. Moreover, there are heartening instances of religious reform for development. The Pakistani reform group that grew around that country's poet, philosopher, and religious leader certainly sets an example that parallels Turkey's. The aim of the movement was to purify Islam of folk-religious encrustations, which in Iqbal's view made it a conservative force working against social and economic progress.

Part of the conceptual hindrance to effective intercourse between outsiders and Sahelians has academic origins. The influence of assimilation is anathematic to many theorists in the social sciences. According to Talcott Parsons, an actor must commit himself wholly to one side of the basic Parsonian dichotomies of pattern variables (universalism-particularism, ascription-achievement, etc.) before he can even act.[51] Whether or not this postulate is accepted, it is evident that traits are acquired in any number of exposure polarities. However one succumbs to exposure, gradually or by one-time choice, commitment, and turnaround, synthesis is inevitable . Ali A. Mazrui remarks: "The idea of a thesis colliding with an antithesis and resulting in the improvement of a synthesis is sometimes taken for granted in current theories of modernization."[52] In assisting to bring about integrated development, donors must pierce the integumentary beliefs of target groups, remembering the while that even the strongest held convictions are rarely mutually exclusive, not always externalized, or clearly articulable. With characteristic good sense, W. Arthur Lewis concludes: "... truth is not to be found by identifying virtue with one only of two opposites. For just as materialism and spirituality are both desirable, so also society needs to have both reason and authority. The good life is founded in weaving a pattern of opposite principles, not in rejecting some and using only the others."[53]

Alterations in the machinery of conceptualization, in the character of cosmological sensibility, are more than just intellectual reorientations or shifts in emotional climate, bodiless changes of the mind. They are also, and as fundamentally, social processes, transformations in the quality of collective life. In the Sahel, motivations essential to integrated development are being laboriously acquired "ex post" and "en route." Consequently, the development process is more halting and circuitous. Caught in the polarity of double exposure, Sahelians are experiencing strong tensions between residual and modern values. Likewise, there is the omnipresent danger that should contradictions grow, with a much smaller pie, elites will be less generous in prorating the national wealth, and the chances of a "revolution from above" will diminish proportionately to shrinking resources.

CONCLUSION

Institution bashing in the residual paradigm by no means guarantees integrated development. A sort of artificial insemination can result in the creation of iconoclastic entities juxtaposed to traditional institutions which preserve themselves with a veneer of reform in the polarities of double exposure and over exposure. Transformation must be process-derived if it is to be meaningful. In the context of modernization, change is not something which comes in small doses. Many Third Worlders have discovered that it is not possible to pick up a few words from the language of the modern paradigm and get by. Languages must be mastered if they are to be used coherently. Indeed, the few words one learns casually are frequently of a scatalogical nature. The disastrous effects of modernization to the fragile eco-system of the Sahel is a dramatic example of what happens when improved health and technology packages are introduced to regions that cannot sustain them -- at least not without more holistic support systems.

Progress in many traditional societies is construed as a function of greater physical exertion, a notion reinforced by the idea that suffering must somehow be recompensed. This is a stubborn mind-set to alter. Even the most intimate exposure to innovation often does not justify alterations in conceptual tectonics, much less tinkering with the traditional order. Ideological obstacles to integrated development, like the propensity to view achievement in physical terms and the delicate nature of social change, have contributed to some of the thrumming in international development efforts. In many cases, these efforts are in need of reorientation, with more conscious focus on the conceptual systems which dictate people's actions and which can facilitate genuine integrated development. One of David C. McClelland's most significant findings in The Achieving Society has particular relevance to those who would pull integrated development off:

> The achievement sequence more often dwells on obstacles to success and specific means of overcoming them, rather than on the goal itself, the desire for it, and the emotions surrounding attaining or failing to attain it. The adaptive quality of such a concern with means is obvious: a people who think in terms of ways of overcoming obstacles would seem more likely to find ways of overcoming them in fact.[54]

This fairly clean-cut observation has been patently ignored. Too frequently both recipient and donor governments are anxious to realize a development objective without being wholly pervious to the possibilities that inhere at the implementation stage. Hirschman observes, "the term 'implementation' understates the complexity of the task of carrying out projects that are affected by a high degree of initial ignorance and uncertainty. Here 'project implementation' may often mean in fact a long voyage of discovery in the most varied domains, from technology to politics."[55] In short, the process of development can often have more impact on conceptual systems than the mere physical presence of a "fait accompli."

One of the major stumbling blocks to integrated development in the Third World is the restriction imposed by traditional values that circumscribe interaction between particular groups of "others" (relatives, strangers, friends, superiors, inferiors, etc.). In the most generic terms, these restrictions create imperfections in the market, the very center of the modern economic society, since individuals are committed to trade certain goods or offer their labor only under certain conditions to certain people at certain times. The most generalized solution, then, to the problem of particularistic commitments is to transfer the individual's loyalties to the "generalized other." One way to do this is through development projects, especially those contributing to the creation of public centers and public enterprises that bring diverse groups together. Unfortunately, this is rarely a principal criterion for project identification or design. The social interactive value, similar to that derived from U.S. domestic racial integration efforts, should be central to the ethos of a project. The degree to which a project imparts critical themes to those who participate in its implementation stage and, subsequently, to the target group, is a benchmark that should be incorporated in project evaluation.

Implanting a project in a developing country implies (1) a decision to accept some "status quo" traits as temporarily unchangeable characteristics of the environment that will mold the project, and (2) a decision to consider others as subject and ready for the kind of changes that are required for making a success of the project. With the help of some apt terminology from price theory, Hirschman has coined the terms "trait-taking" and "trait-making": the decision which traits to "take" that is, to accept (because they are considered unchangeable) and which ones to make (by changing existing or creating new traits). Hirschman queries:

> Would it perhaps be useful for the project planners to ask themselves whether changes in project design might not make it possible for them to act a bit more as trait-makers and a bit less as trait-takers or vice versa? Could not an implicit analysis of this unusually implicit decision reveal to them on one occasion that they would be rash in assuming the role of traitmakers while on another they would be throwing away a precious opportunity by not doing so?[56]

At present, the most common kind of trait-taking ignores indigenous cultural assets and, with few exceptions, imports traits from abroad or from the more advanced parts of the same country, which seems to be more feasible than generating needed skills and inputs locally. Consequently, an exclusionary policy evolves and immigrants or "expatriates" become the "indispensable" occupants of elite positions. However, if we could find out how to utilize local values properly and set them to work for integrated development, they would put more power behind a momentum for self-improvement than all the imported capital and institutions. This is a particularly awesome challenge to development architects, who may otherwise lazily follow the line of least resistance and go on importing machines and organizations conceived and designed for Western cultural settings.

To return to the question we posed earlier: "How does one transcend paradigmatic thinking and enter into the circle of change?" An attempt has been made to show that there are three critical polarities of exposure that have much sway in determining whether or not an invitation to enter the circle will be accepted. The actual invitation and the manner in which it is tendered is almost as important as the occasion for the invitation. In the past, good-doers have not been sufficiently aware of this seemingly trivial aspect of development. Delivering the goods and not how they are delivered has been everyone's preoccupation, at times, to the utter neglect of what we have called cognitive exposure.

If transitions in conceptual tectonics accompany the transfer out of the residual paradigm, we must not expect the target group to attest to these changes immediately. That is not to say that this is always a long-term transformation. The Senegalese training program for animators has been an amazingly successful experiment in social engineering. By forcing animiators to have complete trust in one another via a number of exercises, a sense of comraderie develops over a short time between strangers with diverse backgrounds. On a larger scope, the social value potentialities of strengthening secondary towns in the Sahel cannot be overstated.[57] As centers of culture, education, science, and technology, as well as finance, business,and government,urban centers should be dynamos for socioeconomic progress in all parts of a modernizing country. Towns offer fertile ground for cognitive exposure. This does not mean that policy makers must elide rural community development. On the contrary, without a stable, internal balance of power, there is little hope of developing either industry or agriculture, the city or the country.

The open-ended, "in search of truth" type of education, because it ideally instigates cognitive exposure, is one of the chief mechanisms for achieving socioeconomic development. Yet, such bold components of knowledge and its application as science and technology can unleash an unexpected set of ramifying issues counterproductive to integrated development, indeed, reinforcing the very attitudes and static assumptions that have subverted progress in the past. Many fuzzy concerns can suddenly come sharply into focus, and hope, prayer, and superstition become egregiously outmoded methods for confronting stark and complex realities. This gloomy scenario hardly suggests the emergence of an activist epistemology. By the same token, it does not seem that the individual who has received much exposure in the polarity of cognitive exposure can retreat into the cocoon of tradition for his wings have now spread. He must fly.

To fly can be a dangerous proposition and a frustrating one if your wings are clipped shortly thereafter. One African observer has stressed the perils of importing advanced technology and Western education from the standpoint of unemployment. He offers a countervailing argument to some of the points espoused by the author in the present work:

> It is I think slightly utopian to suggest that one can pick and choose which elements in a culture you should retain and which you should give up. The evolving of a culture is largely a sub-conscious process, most of it beyond control. The greatest danger to any culture is mass unemployment, as it was to German culture when Hitler rose to power on the backs of seven million unemployed. ... If you really want to ruin a culture, take a lot of people and educate them for jobs which when they leave the schools and universities and technical institutes, do not exist. This is an excellent recipe for turning everything upside down and creating unemployment. This is the road to bloody revolution, and produces disinherited people with disinherited minds who have lost all sense of identity and sense of purpose. If we can adapt education and technology to the African cultural and economic environment, so as not to create mass misery and mass unemployment -- if we can find the intermediate and middle way -- we shall solve these problems. If we go on importing Western technology and institutions, then everything will go to pieces.[58]

When ideologies enter, as they must, into a debate about choice of ideology, their role is necessarily circular. Each party uses its own ideology to argue in that ideology's defense. Given the diverse but concrete manifestations of solidarity in ideological form, conceptual systems offer important clues that could help vitalize the pursuit of integrated development. This task is not without a sense of urgency. At a time when so many countries want to develop rapidly, but have failed to move from condition A (a low level of integrated development) to condition D (a high level of integrated development) despite political and socioeconomic reforms, it is essential to have a better handle on indigenous conceptual systems if processes inculcating over time optics like interest as opposed to passion motivation, achievement motivation, other-directedness, self-confidence, and optimism are to be effective.

In the realm of social attitudes, the lesson to be drawn and emphasized is this: **material development is not the** only thing which developing countries are seeking. Bread is desirable, but their concept of the good life includes more than bread, and agricultural development should be seen as part of the quest for a greater whole, the quest for the "good life." This is differently conceived in different cultures, and aspects of it are assigned different weights. It goes without saying that there are values for which people are ready to sacrifice material efficiency as calculated from rationalized economic considerations. The best and most potent incentives to improvement are those that people accept as leading towards the good life as they conceive it; and the best social attitudes to inculcate for agriculture, as for development generally, are those that lead to the realization of individual and community aspirations towards their conception of the good life. To ascertain this conception is a duty that lies primarily with effective national leadership. Social scientists can be of assistance in this task by illuminating large-scale social change. Social scientists have much to contribute in the business of offering the experimental results and experiences in general that donor countries already possess to target groups via the most effective and accepted channels of exposure. What this should represent is not a "take it or leave it" transfer of resources or casual cultural diffusion but a sincere effort to exchange development recipes.

6
Agriculture on a Pedestal or as Development Keystone?

The Sahel's struggle to achieve a radical economic transformation is apt to be won or lost in the countryside -- not because rural problems have some sort of intrinsic priority in a development program over such other issues as industrialization and urbanization but because of the rural problems' combined quotient of importance and difficulty.[1] Not only does the agriculture sector perform a dual role of supplier of labor to industry and of food for the industrial labor force, but for the majority of Sahelian countries, agriculture is the primary source of capital formation and employment. Three-fourths of the population is engaged in dryland farming on the arable land covering 29 percent of the region, in most years yielding only enough food for subsistence. Only 10 percent of the population lives on that 3 percent of the area which can obtain river flow water either by flood recession or by irrigation methods.

For the Sahelian countries poor economic performance is directly related to lack of progress in the agriculture sector. Food grain production, which accounts for well over half of the value added in that sector, has not kept pace with population growth. The regional index of per capita food production declined 10 percent during 1970-77. Regional food self-sufficiency declined in some countries substantially over the same period through-out the region. The development prescription which calls upon agriculture to finance industrial development, provide cheap labor, and eventually be pulled into modernization by a dynamic manufacturing sector, continues to have its strong adherents.[2] The policies commonly used to implement such a strategy -- cheap urban food prices, heavy export taxes on agricultural products, protective tariffs against foreign manufacturers, import substitution, overvalued exchange rates, emphasis on heavy industry, concentration of government investment in urban centers, subsidization of credit to large industries and for agricultural mechanization -- frequently have led to intolerable social, political, and economic situations in terms of employment, income distribution, rural-to-urban migration, and the provision of basic services to the population. Thus, an ascendant school has evolved which holds that while it is true that the ratio of non-agricultural to total population tends to be highly correlated positively with "per capita" income, the degree of industrialization may be and often is a consequence rather than a cause of the level of prosperity, and that where agriculture is prosperous tertiary or service industries tend to grow spontaneously.[3] William Letwin enumerates as his first fallacy (defined as a truism that has been misunderstood) of economic development the widespread notion that manufacturing is more productive than agriculture. This fallacy underlies the argument for industrialization as a panacea for underdevelopment. Letwin observes: "...the truth is that agriculture and industry have always co-existed; extraction and fabrication both have gone on together ever since the beginning."[4] The theoretical complementarity between the two sectors rests on any number of mutually reinforcing objectives. Yet, this symbiotic relationship is frequently sloughed over by impatient development architects, who forget that agriculture is perhaps the most fundamental industry. W.W.Rostow would note at the beginning of the first Development Decade:

> The processes at work during the preconditions generally yielded both a general rise in population and a disproportionate rise in urban populations. Increased productivity in agriculture has been generally a necessary condition for preventing the process of modernization from being throttled.[5]

Taking note of the need and the potential, the Sahelian countries have consistently listed increased agricultural production as one of the major goals in their national plans. Technical assistance in agriculture has ranged from 4 to 40 percent of total assistance to the Sahelian countries during recent years. Yet, Sahelian estimates of food produced per capita in 1975 were less than in 1955. In particular, yields of staple food crops (cereals and rice) in the Sahelian countries are low. Millet yields for 1977/78 were approximately 44 percent of those in the developed countries, 72 percent of yields in Asia, and 78 percent of African yields. Similarly rice yields in the Sahel were 24, 55, and 78 percent of those in developed, Asian, and African countries respectively. Between 1965 and 1978, food crop yields declined by 2.7 percent per year.

The major factors responsible for this poor productivity performance in Sahelian agriculture are low and/or declining soil fertility, vulnerability to pests, and weather variability. Population pressure has either caused marginal lands to be brought into cultivation or caused over-farming and reduction of the fallow time required to restore natural fertility.

Pests and diseases perennially attack crops and reduce yields. After the recent drought, predators caused unusually severe grain crop losses. Grain yields vary also by ecological zone, the lower the expected annual rainfall the higher the yield variability. One study estimates that in the Sahelian countries only four kilos of sorghum are produced per day of labor, and only 10 percent of the cereals are marketed.[6] Frequently, the labor requirement for this subsistence crop is concentrated into a critically short period; therefore, production cannot readily be increased. In many areas ecological degradation is reducing the resource base per family and the number on the very edge of survival in increasing.

The performance of export crop production was better than for food grains and provides the basis for whatever economic improvements have occurred among rural people in the region. The major export crops, groundnuts and cotton, account for most of the Sahelian farmer's income. Progress, however, has not been dramatic and has been limited mainly to higher rainfall areas (above 800 mm) of the Sahelian countries. Improvements have come from introducing animal traction, chemical fertilizers, and modified cultural practices. Export crop production has been successfully introduced and diffused in The Gambia and the central part of Senegal for groundnuts, southeast Mali for cotton and groundnuts, and in the southwestern parts of Upper Volta, Chad, and Niger for cotton. In these areas, a relatively high percentage of farmers use animal traction (almost 50 percent in The Gambia) and most use some fertilizers and other inputs produced off the farms. It should be emphasized, however, that farmers benefitting from these programs receive only modest gains in productivity and income.

The levels of technology in export crop production is higher than for food crop production but is still not far advanced. The rate of application of fertilizer (Table 21) is indicative of the level of technology that exists for export crop production. The rates for The Gambia and Senegal are illustrative of fertilizer consumption levels in areas where export crop production efforts have been concentrated. Although these levels are many times higher than a decade ago, they are low by world standards. Consequently, export crop yields remain low (940 kg/ha. for groundnuts in The Gambia and Senegal and 200 kg./ha. for cotton in Chad) as do money incomes. Despite several intense outreach efforts, the majority of Sahelian farmers are not served by export crop production and marketing agencies because of relative inaccessibility and poor natural conditions.

While this introduction is believed to be a fair and reasonable assessment of the situation, there are differences among countries, areas, and crops. Illustrations of high productivity do exist. First, dualistic agricultural economies have emerged in many countries -- a commercial sub-sector and a subsistence sub-sector. Yields per hectare, production per man

TABLE 21: Fertilizer Application Rates in Sahelian Countries - 1976 (kg/ha cropland)

Cape Verde	4.0	Mauritania	0.5
Chad	1.0	Niger	0.1
The Gambia	10.0	Senegal	16.0
Mali	1.0	Upper Volta	1.0
Regional Average	3.8		

Source: Annual Fertilizer Review (FAO; Rome), 1977.

year of labor, and return to investment in the export-based commercial sector are occasionally satisfactory. Second, numerous successful projects can be cited where productivity has been increased and small farmer/herder incomes raised. Finally, areas close to urban markets have fared reasonably well and productivity is above outlying areas.

FARM PRICES AND FARM INCOME

In the 1960's, the Sahelian countries, with the exception of Chad, showed a general decline in the real level of per capita income in the farm sector and a real increase in per capita income in the non-farm sector. The indices of farm prices, corrected for the rise in the cost of living, showed stagnation or decline. The disparity between per capita farm and non-farm income grew considerably. Increases in the world prices of export crops were, in general, not passed on to the farmers largely because Sahelian governments increased export taxes as a source of public revenue. The declining rate of return to farm labor has a number of important consequences: (a) farm incomes are kept low; (b) employment of non-family labor to meet peak seasonal labor demands has been discouraged resulting in the maintenance of large families and underemployment of family labor for the rest of the year; (c) there has been a premature exodus of labor from the rural areas to the urban; and (d) agriculture remains a low-status "way of life."

It is generally accepted that food crop production is and must be limited by the price formed in the market place. If more food production is desired, it can best be accomplished by improving the marketing and pricing systems. However, regulation of cash crop prices for export is a function of government policy and cannot be altered without the substantial institutional changes which would be needed in order to alter prices of locally produced grains through their import policies of grains such as rice and wheat and to varying degrees, through price stabilization programs.

In the past, inadequate attention has been given to pricing policies of food and cash crops and their interrelationship since the majority of Sahelian farmers engage in both types of crop production. Low export prices tend to cause farmers to shift their resources to food crop production, thus increasing the general food supply and lowering food proces. These actions weaken the ability of agriculture to produce a surplus for investment in its own development and to pay for modern inputs without subsidization. During the 1968-1974 drought, the high prices of cereal crops, due to market forces, drew extra resources into food crop production. With good weather conditions some places, e.g., western Upper Volta, recognized that the return per man day, was greater in sorghum production than in cotton, and farmers reacted accordingly, producing a surplus sorghum crop in 1975-1976.

Sahelian governments have attempted to influence the price of food grains in at least two major ways: (1) by subsidizing imported cereals such as rice and wheat and (2) by government price stabilization programs:

Cereal Imports. There are two striking features in the cereals imports picture of the region. First, only Mauritania and Senegal import a substantial part of their total cereal supply. Second, in every Sahelian country as bread consumption (a recent addition to the standard fare of porridge) grows, wheat imports are increasing at an alarming rate. In the interim between 1961-1965 and 1966-1970 periods, Mauritania increased wheat imports by 7 percent and Senegal by 5 percent, while the rest of the region increased cereals imports an average of 13.5 percent. The total supply of domestically produced grains of the four interior countries declined slightly in the decade of the 1960s, but still amounted to 96-99 percent of the supply in 1969-1971. At the peak of the great drought, this figure declined measurably.

Grain Price Stabilization. The objective of seasonal grain price stabilization programs is to provide sufficient price incentive to producers. In general, price stabilizing programs are not designed to replace the grain dealers because the government does not have the means or structure to do so. In practice, price stabilization programs have been expensive to maintain unless accompanied by some form of production control, and then only for a crop the major part of which is marketed. This way the year to year differences in the quantity marketed are diminished by controlling the area of crop produced (the model). A country or trading area with a cereal deficit can also stabilize the price as long as it stays above the world price by applying a levy to the imports, which can be used to subsidize whatever occasional surplus cereals need to be exported (the EEC model).

When a government grain board sets cereal prices too high, it runs the risk of accumulating stocks in excess of what it can store and it will also draw surplus stocks into the market that would otherwise have been stored on farms. If prices are set too low, the supply will be insufficient. Where only 10-20 percent of production is marketed, a small percentage increase in production can double the quantity available to be marketed. Curves of probable production indicate a 50 percent probability of getting a yield 80 percent of the average in the Sahel and 86.5 percent of the average in the Sudano-Sahelian zone. So the fluctuations in a country like Niger (about one million tons a year supply) may be on the order of 150,000 tons in 50 percent of the years. In order to avoid destroying commerical trade and producing chaos in the marketplace, the government would have to set up a price network in relation to the transfer cost, taking into account the cost of transporting grain to market and the cost of its storage. Otherwise, the producers would all expect the government to buy their whole market surplus at harvest time, thus permitting them to avoid the costs of storage and tying up their money in stocks.

It is doubtful that Sahelian governments can stabilize the price of grain via a buy/sell operation, considering the size of the countries, the transportation problems, and the limited financial and technical means at their disposal. Given the substantial problems involved in the pricing system, there is a need to study the interrelationship between the price of food and cash crops and the production decision of the farmer. Studies of costs of production of different crops produced in different ways and in different regions are basic. There is also a need to study the effect of government pricing policy of imported and concessionary foods on the price of domestically produced grain.

OTHER CONSTRAINTS

To increase food production and generate employment and income in rural areas, a number of difficult but tractable sectoral problems must be overcome. These include low and declining crop and labor productivity, inadequate incentives, inappropriate marketing and storage policies, and weak institutions serving agricultural and rural development. It has been observed that improved, irrigated rice production increases the productivity of land area per season by a factor of 3-4. "If the productivity of the scarce factor, labor, is to be increased by a similar magnitude, major changes in production systems will be required ... Despite the relatively high cost of African farm labor, the cost of new techniques, other than perhaps animal traction, remains sufficiently high to preclude their extensive use as a means of raising the productivity of labor in rice. If they are to be made attractive to farmers, policies must in most cases be tailored to offset their high costs." 7 Incentives to purchase the fertilizers, improved seeds, and other modern inputs needed to increase food production are weak. Official producer prices, established by governments for major cereals, cannot be supported effectively at the farm level because of inadequate storage facilities, transportation networks, communications, and management capability. Related to this is the inadequacy of input delivery systems, except for export crops, to provide farmers with modern production requisites. Those Sahelian countries that have established marketing boards to regulate grain prices and trade must reverse tendencies to discriminate against producers in favor of urban consumers. Insufficient data on basic factors which influence farmer's production decisions and attitudes toward risk, coupled with the lack of capacity by Ministries of Planning or Rural Development in the Sahelian countries to assess the costs and benefits of alternative agricultural development policies, render it difficult to establish appropriate price or input subsidy policies at the present time.

Extension services are ill-prepared to tackle farm-level problems. The common view in the Sahel,with the exception of Senegal, is that the rural population is unable to participate in decision-making. This perception is deeply entrenched at all levels of national ministries and results in highly centralized, authoritarian extension services. Such a structure provides inputs for farmers and support to extension agents, but it also discourages independent, innovative efforts to adapt to local requirements and demands. While extension agents are in direct contact with farmers, the rigid organizational hierarchy obliges the agents to be more responsive to administrative requirements than to farmers' problems. This approach has been successful in increasing the production of export crops, but it has failed to result in self-generating growth through farmer initiative. For example, after some 40 years of activity, the CFDT (a major French agribusiness) still depends upon a high ratio of extension personnel to farmers. In contrast, the degree of local initiative in vegetable production and other areas, generally neglected by the Sahelian governments, is impressive.

Agricultural education and training are largely theoretical. Agricultural education and training parallel and reinforce the paternalistic and nonadaptive approach of the extension services. Observers have noted that while professional agricultural training courses at the various training schools in the Sahel are comprehensive and well-organized, they rely on educational materials in use in francophone West Africa for the last 15 years. These courses are insufficiently oriented toward the application of agricultural principles farmers are already applying. Adequate staff and instructional materials for some agricultural courses is lacking; other courses, such as economics and management are often neglected; staff/student ratios are unrealistically high; practical fieldwork is either limited or improperly integrated with classroom studies. In sum, professional agricultural training is too bookish and does not sufficiently prepare extension personnel for what they are going to find in farmers' fields.

The capacity to carry out research on complex technical, biological, economic, and social problems in Sahelian agriculture is weak or absent. For the most part, agricultural research has been oriented to export rather than to food crop production. Few resources have been allocated to agriculture research. In 1972, only 187 scientists years (SYs) "in toto" were devoted to agriculture research in all the Sahelian countries, with a low of 4 SYs in Mauritania and The Gambia and a high of 90 SYs in Senegal. Moreover, most of these SYs were devoted to research on export rather than on food crop production. However, there is reason for optimism. Applied agriculture research is beginning to demonstrate the potential to increase yields. Millet yields obtained on farms in Senegal, where improved varieties have been introduced, indicate yields double traditional averages. Estimates of the effect of crop protection measures on millet and sorghum yields in Chad and Senegal hover around increases of 25 percent over traditional yields.

Recognition of the need to build national capacity in agricultural research is growing in all Sahelian countries. The number of activities destined to strengthen national research organizations in the first generation program for agriculture adopted by the Club du Sahel at Ottawa reflects this recognition of the potential contribution of research. That international research centers such as ICRISAT, IITA, ILCA, and ILRAD have recently turned their attention to food (and livestock) production problems in the Sahel is encouraging. Recognition of the need to strengthen extension services and training institutions is growing. Efforts to make the programs of training institutions more practical and to prepare extension agents to deal with farmers' problems are underway or proposed.

There is considerable potential for increasing food and agricultural production by bringing underexploited areas with high rainfall into cultivation. As problems of endemic diseases, land use planning, and resettlement are overcome, exploitation of new lands could relieve population pressure on overfarmed areas and provide employment for the growing rural population. Sensitive food policy issues are beginning to be addressed. Since the drought, official prices for major food grains have been increased by about 60 percent. A dialogue has begun within the framework of the Club du Sahel on price and marketing policy issues. The Sahelian countries and donors participating in this dialogue are building the foundation for more equitable agricultural development policies.

THE CLUB DU SAHEL AND AGRICULTURE

Agricultural development is central to achieving Club du Sahel goals for food self-sufficiency and self-sustaining economic development in the Sahelian countries. The Club strategy for agriculture emphasizes three main themes:

- Raising productivity of land already under cultivation, both rainfed and irrigated.
- Development of the underexploited potential of sparsely populated "new lands," including vast areas of underutilized lands laying within the watersheds of the three major and two minor river basins of the Sahel.
- Developing the capability of Sahelian institutions at the regional and national levels to effectively plan, manage, and evaluate their development programs.

Raising productivity through intensification of production of land presently under cultivation is a key theme of the Club strategy for agricultural development. This strategy involves intensification of production under two quite different farming systems -- rainfed and irrigated agriculture. For the near or medium term and probably through the year 2,000, attaining self-sufficiency in basic foods will depend on expanding production of traditional rainfed crops, despite their vulnerability to climatic hazards. Intensification will vary by climatic and ecological zones. In areas of low rainfall, programs will focus on improvements within traditional farming systems. Where rainfall is higher and soils better, intensification is to be achieved through production technologies based on fertilizers, draft animals, pest management, better varieties, and improved cultural practices.

The Club's crop intensification strategy also devotes attention to the possibilities for increasing production under existing, irrigated agriculture systems in the Sahel. Of the 165,000 hectares of irrigated agriculture in the Sahel, over 60,000 hectares are producing well below worldwide averages. Many of these irrigation systems have been abandoned or have deteriorated to the point where they can hardly be classified as functioning irrigation systems. CILSS has advanced a five-year program of irrigation system rehabilitation coupled with creation of farmer controlled irrigator associations to operate and maintain the rehabilitated systems. This program, which would consider rehabilitation of up to 60,000 hectares at an estimated cost of $57 million, offers the greatest potential in the short and medium term for increasing production of basic food cereals produced under irrigation. AID declared its intent to finance up to 25 percent of the cost of this program and Holland and France along with the World Bank have expressed their interest in financing the rehabilitation of existing irrigation systems of importance.

The Club agriculture strategy recognizes that the greatest gains in production in the short term can be achieved from intensification of production, both dryland and irrigated, on presently cultivated lands and that, over the long term, there remains two million hectares of "new lands" which could be settled and developed. At a Club seminar held in Ougadougou with the topic of "La Mise en Valeur des 'Terres Neuves'", the notion of new lands was put this way: "Within the "new lands" idea what is new is not the land, but the desire to develop with the available human potential the underdeveloped or untapped natural resources of some regions."[8] Settlement of new land would serve to relieve pressure in some of the more densely populated areas, e.g., the Mosai Plateau in Upper Volta and the Groundnut Basin in Senegal, and would expand the agricultural production base of the Sahelian countries. However, new lands development, while offering considerable potential, involves major capital investment in infrastructure and resettlement of populations. This potential can only be tapped over the long term and after careful study. New lands do not exist as purely random phenomena. These lands have not been previously settled and exploited because of (a) severe environmental problems, such as poor soil or low water tables, and (b) the existence of disabling disease problems such as bovine trypanosomiasis or onchocerciasis. Therefore, before land can be settled, careful planning must be completed to identify and overcome previously prevented settlement. The work of the Club's Dryland Group in this area has resulted in an analysis and comparison of the needs and potential for new land development in each country. The Group has not proposed new projects. Instead, it has limited itself to recommendations for further actions by the countries. The recommendations for the countries are separated into two categories:

Countries with New Land Development Plans. Senegal and Upper Volta have new lands projects that preceded Club activity. Their focus is on several large and densely populated areas and the presence of considerable new land areas. In Senegal, the Societé des Terres Neuves (STN) had developed around 3,000 hectares with 300 families by 1976. By 1978, there were 13,000 hactares with 900 families. In Upper Volta, L'Autorité des Amenagements des Vallées des Volta (AVV) developed around 1,200 hectares with 648 families by 1976. By 1978, 1,095 additional families were resettled. The STN and AVV offer a wide contrast in management styles. The STN style reflects an emphasis on light capital technology, with low investment in infrastructure and low administrative personnel to settler ratio. The AVV is antipodal, with high infrastructure investment and high administrative ratios.

Niger is developing the Say Region. Compared to Senegal and Upper Volta, both the new lands area and the population pressures in Niger are less. In all these countries, the Dryland Group has determined the primary problem to be one of management. Both "light" and "heavy" management structures have good and bad features. For example, the organizational frictions arising between the AVV and the Offices of Regional Development (ORD) in Upper Volta might benefit from more awareness of the STN approach. A further complicating factor is that spontaneous settlement is proceeding along with organized settlement.

Countries with No New Land Development Plans. Chad, Mali, and Mauritania have considerable potential for new lands. However, their lack of areas with high population density gives them more time for analysis of available options. The Club has recommended that these countries generate and organize their new lands data base in anticipation of future development of these untapped lands.

River basins constitute a special category of new lands. The three major and two minor international river basins hold the key to development of irrigated agriculture in the Sahel. These basins account for close to two million hectares of potentially irrigable and untapped agricultural soils in the Sahel. Recognizing this potential, Sahelian governments have organized regional river basin planning commissions for most of the river and lake basins. Organization of these planning and regulatory bodies by the various riparian states has sprung not only from an awareness of the agriculture, power, and transport development potential of the basins but also from the recognition that mismanagement of these great hydrological resources could destroy this one great natural resource of the Sahel. Although Sahelians have attached great importance to the development of the river basins, donor interest has been restrained. The Club du Sahel has attempted to awaken donor interest in the rational exploitation of Sahelian river and lake basin potential. Since the formation of the Club, several multi-donor assistance programs have been organized under the general direction of the United Nations Development Program (UNDP). Recognizing the limited ability of donors acting independently, the UNDP, acting on behalf of the Club du Sahel, is organizing donors in a common technical assistance effort in support of the Niger, Lake Chad, and Gambia river basin commissions. Studies financed under this technical assistance will provide Sahelian and donor policy makers the data base and empirical framework for selecting the most rational and efficient planning strategy for development of the region's river basin potential.

It will take several years for the results of the planning underway to result in tangible, on-the-ground results. This is unavoidable when tackling problems as complex and large as those involved in development of the Sahelian water resources potential. Suffice it to note that in the years since formation of the Club du Sahel, a planning process has been set in motion which increases the prospect for frequent interstate collaboration among riparian countries and enables multilateral and bilateral donors to collaborate in support of these river basin commissions.

Several components of the Club's strategy can be considered together as strategy support programs. These components include price policy, marketing and storage, agricultural research and extension, training, and transport. The Working Group on Agriculture established a special team to work on price policy, marketing, and storage problems. The discussions in this group and the consultants' report highlighted the sensitive nature of price and marketing policy issues. No definitive strategy has as yet emerged on price policy. The team did recommend, however, that before deciding on a systematic policy to increase producer returns to production efforts, intensive studies were required on alternative means to raise producers incomes. More exhaustive research on the effects of price, input subsidy, and other food policies on the level and distribution of rural and urban incomes was recommended. Unfortunately, a definitive marketing policy did not emerge from the deliberations of the special team. The Sahelian representatives on the team felt that increased human, financial, and material support for official grain marketing boards over the long run was the best way to protect producer interests despite the hindrances they have often posed for expanding grain production. The consultants' report suggested regulation of the private trade and formation of producer cooperatives as the most efficient way to guarantee adequate returns to farmers. The Sahelians on the team favored regulating private trade in the short term. Although a plan of action did not materialize, the debate surrounding the Club's report sensitized the Sahelians to alternative approaches to marketing policy.

A major strength of the Club's strategy for agriculture is its emphasis on programs to strengthen institutions and organizations serving agriculture, i.e., national research organizations, technical agricultural services, extension services, and input delivery systems. The Club Working Group on Agriculture treated these programs as integral to the various components of the strategy, not as separate items. The first generation list of projects reflects this concern with building institutions and organizational capacity to deal with major sectoral problems. The recognition of the need for training of personnel at all levels is also a strength of Club strategy. The dearth of qualified agriculturalists was identified as a major constraint to development of Sahelian agriculture and training is being accorded the highest priority.

One major shortcoming, however, of the Club's work has been that planners in the Sahel have tended to be preoccupied with production of food staples "per se" rather than with stimulating growth of the rural economy and farm income. With the memory of the drought still fresh, it is easy to understand this concern for food self-sufficiency, but more attention should be directed to programs which open the possibility for expanding food production while at the same time stimulating increased producer income and rural economic activity in general. A further weakness of the work of the Club du Sahel, which again reflects the strong preoccupation with production of traditional food staples, is that it ignores the fact that there is almost no research underway in the Sahel which is directed toward developing new crops and cropping systems.

LIVESTOCK

The performance of the livestock production sector is somewhat analogous to that of staple foods. During the 1960s and early 1970s, there was a relatively rapid growth in livestock production in the Sahel, largely due to favorable weather, improved animal health services, and programs to increase water supply. Since the great drought, priority attention has been focused on ways of increasing livestock production while at the same time reversing the deteriorating condition of the rangeland. Within bounds and with supportive measures, pastoralism may be the most appropriate life style in parts of the Sahel. W. David Hopper remarks:

> Large areas of Africa are and will continue to be mainly devoted to the raising of cattle. The development of watering places, improved ranges, disease-control centers, meat-packing establishments and other facilities could dramatically enlarge Africa's ability to add to world food supplies, particularly to the supply of protein.[9]

In a bid to keep the nomads from being squeezed into the desert, the government of Niger in 1961 set a northern boundary of legal cultivation. But the northward advance of farming, set back only temporarily by the years of severe drought, has continued all the same. Today, farming takes place on sites at least 100 kilometers past the legal limit and is practiced illegally in the protected zone by both nomadic groups and others moving up from the South.

Pastoralists, especially in the North, depend almost entirely upon natural forage for their animals. Rangeland animals are of two types: the grazers that feed primarily upon low grasses and herbs, and the browsers that feed primarily on leaves and stems of more woody, often perennial vegetation. The differences between the two result in markedly different impacts on rangelands. An area overgrazed by cattle can still be utilized by sheep. Goats can thrive on areas overgrazed by sheep, and camels can survive on areas overgrazed by goats because they can utilize even woodier or more spiny browse. A comparable scale exists for endurance without water. Albeit they are in a privileged place on this scale, the cattle in the North, generally Zebus, may, on occasion, go two or three days without water on the long drives.[10] Reports of camels being driven, without water, for up to nine days across barren deserts are not at all uncommon. One study reaches the conclusion that the endurance of livestock aside, diversification of herds in the Sahel should be encouraged:

> Livestock development programs for the pastoral zone should take into account the important role that goats play for the zone's least wealthy residents. Such programs should not unilaterally promote the development of one animal type in the pastoral zone at the expense of others. An equilibrium among the different types of animals raised is required for efficient exploitation of forage resources, risk avoidance through diversification of herds, and provision of a steady supply of milk to livestock producing households."[11]

Nomads subsist largely on dairy products. In one study, off-take from the herd is reported, as a yearly average, to be three-fourths milk and one-quarter meat.[12] Such offtake has many deleterious effects on productivity. Cows, as a result of their poor lactation characteristics and the low availability of feed, generally produce barely enough milk to support their calves. Hence, taking milk for human consumption results in malnourished, slow growing calves. During the dry season, because forage is scarce and often at great distances from watering points, animals undergo a period of no growth, and, often, of actual weight loss. Consequently, much of the weight gain is lost each year in sustaining the animal until the next wet season. The combination of genetic traits and poor environmental conditions results in slow maturation, requiring four or more years to reach adult size and sexual maturity; extended nursing time for calves often lasting eighteen months to two years; low fecundity with mature cows generally having a calf only every other year; and high mortality rates because of decreased resistance to diseases and parasites, especially during the first year.[13] A significantly less efficient system of converting ecosystem productivity into meat is the outcome. Modern cattle raising systems require only about 8 kg of feed to produce 1 kg of meat. The ratio in the Sahel may run 20 to 1 or higher.[14]

In response to the Club's mandate to develop a unified development strategy for the livestock sector, teams of livestock production and marketing specialists comprised of consultants, donor agency and host country professionals were formed. Several "key elements" emerged as a strategy to guide the development of the sector:

Integrated Natural Resource Management. Except in the arid zone and in some specialized grazing zones, grazing does not occur in isolation but as part of a complex socioeconomic system involving livestock and crop dependent families. Therefore, the accent is on the reversal of negative environmental trends by setting aside selected land units for limited use such as forestry, natural conservation grazing, or a combination of these. Development assistance programs are expected to foster integrated resource management among decisionmakers, farmers, and herdsmen. The adoption of alternative forms of land tenure, water use rights, and vegetative use rights is viewed as essential if further natural resource degradation is to be prevented. The Club recognizes that regulation of pastoralists is the most difficult area in which to bring about needed improvements. However, it has concluded that substantial improvement in feed availabilities per animal can be made via improved range and grassland management.

Integration of Agriculture and Livestock Production -- Mixed Farming. Because natural range and grasslands are overexploited, improvements in output per animal -- meat, milk, and tractive power -- will require the use of harvested feeds. Some additional "stratification" of meat production is envisaged with grazing areas providing immature stock for growing out and fattening on small farms and on specialized feeding and fattening units generally in higher rainfall zones. Farm units in "new lands" areas would be assisted in becoming "mixed farms" where feasible. In areas where integration between crop farming and feeding are feasible, farmers need to be encouraged to conserve fodder, crop residues, and to add fodder crops to crop rotations. Bovine traction and small unit feeding of cattle and sheep are important enterprises on some Sahelian farms. Farming systems and basic applied agricultural research are required to support and expand these activities.

Livestock Marketing. Livestock in the Sahel is usually marketed by small and medium-size private traders. Because of growing shortages, prices of cattle and meat have increased rapidly since 1973. As a result, coastal countries, notably the Ivory Coast and Nigeria, are turning to extra-regional (mainly Argentinian) sources for meat. Activities which reduce losses and shrinkage in marketing, particularly between Sahelian (inland) areas and coastal markets are required if Sahelian countries are to retain their most profitable export markets.

The Club has adopted a posture of entrepreneurial advocacy for improved marketing services and access to markets, with emphasis on activities which improve the efficiency of the livestock trade, lower the cost of marketing, reduce the environmental damage caused in some instances by cattle concentrations near transshipment points, and improve the availability of animals for use in traction and animal feeding programs.

FISHERIES

The growth potential of marine and fresh water fisheries in the Sahel is good. Fish is at present an important source of protein in the Sahelian diet; more importantly, fish and fishery products have the potential for supplying a greatly expanded percentage of the protein requirement of the Sahelian population. However, a number of constraints inhibit growth in the fishery sector. Chief among these constraints is the preservation of the catch. Approximately 30 percent of the present freshwater fish catch is lost due to improper handling and spoilage.[15] Rapid growth in the sector will also require concerted efforts to upgrade fishery support services, improve research on fisheries biology and expand the available fishing craft and equipment. Attention will have to be directed to the implications of river basin development for aquaculture both in terms of integrating fisheries into basin development programs as well as to minimize the disruption to fisheries for construction of dams and irrigation infrastructure.

The goal of the Club's fisheries sector strategy is to ensure the development of fishing in both the coastal and inland areas during the next 10 to 20 years. Analysis of available fish stocks indicates that considerable expansion can be accomplished within this time frame without overfishing existing stocks. On the basis of anticipated population trends, protein needs, and increases in individual incomes, demand for fish within the region is expected to increase from the present 370,000 tons to 700,000 tons by the year 2,000. Exports of fish from the region are also expected to increase to at least 1,000,000 tons by the year 2,000. Total catches must be increased from 620,000 tons per year to 1,700,000 tons representing an annual increase of 7 percent in landings. It is expected that 25 percent of these catches will come from inland waters, 40 percent from large industrial seagoing vessels and 35 percent from small-scale coastal fishery.[16]

Development on this scale will be possible only if substantial assistance is provided in the way of fishing techniques, fish processing techniques, marketing techniques, strengthening fishery directorates and services, improving research, and training fishery officers and staff. The program outlined by the Club would cost $700 million during the period 1977-2000. The elements of the initial 3-5 year phase of this program (cost $65 million) have been worked out on a country by country basis. The strategy adopted by the Club is to strengthen all aspects of the fishing industry since this represents the best opportunity for short-term increases in fish production. The development of skills necessary to manage and operate the fishing industry will require a substantial educational element. Aquaculture is viewed as having some potential in certain areas. Training, research, and large-scale fish farming activities will be initiated as a second portion of the program with long-term payoffs.

CONCLUSION

Given the world food situation and, specifically, scarcity of food in the Sahel, development of agriculture is a priority objective. Increased productivity (hence income generation) in agriculture will not only lessen the risk of famine and improve diets, but create a demand for urban-produced industrial goods and services. Increased productivity will stimulate and accelerate the rate of overall economic growth and development. Unfortunately, in few Sahelian countries is agriculture receiving as much as 30 percent of the total new investment for development.

The low farm population incomes relative to urban incomes in the Sahel are due not only to low productivity, but also to unfavorable terms of trade. More favorable terms of trade for the agriculture sector would encourage investment in the rural areas -- reducing the tendency for capital to gravitate towards non- or low productive ventures such as rental houses for high-income groups in the urban areas. It follows that food and rural poverty are primarily, but not entirely, problems the individual countries must face. National self-sufficiency in food production is not necessarily sound policy. Resources vary greatly, and comparative advantage indicates some countries should be major exporters of food products (Niger, for example), while others should probably continue to import (Mauritania, for example). The problem must be approached regionally as well as nationally, and the logical point of entry is through the planning process. Sound planning will determine where and how the various products should be produced, and who should export and import. Sound national plans will recognize the regional implications and include linkages among the Sahelian countries as well as to countries outside the region. The Sahelians must, in the last analysis, front and thrash out for themselves many of the compelling issues of their rural sector. But this does not mean that the array of constraints to development in this sector lie beyond the appropriate range of international concern. Roger Revelle observes:

> A large capital investment will be necessary to realize the potential for irrigation and high-yielding agriculture in the developing countries. ... Because of the shortages of capital in the developing countries, a large part of this investment would need to come from the developed countries. It would seem to be a small price for the transformation in the lives of the world's poor (probably one of the necessary conditions for reducing birthrates) that

> could be brought about by the modernization of agriculture.[17]

The agricultural conundrum is complex, and there are many constraints not localized to the region, which are beyond the capability of most Sahelian countries to remove quickly without external assistance.

Rainfed agriculture is the principal source of the world's food. Careful management of cultivated land to control water and wind is essential to avoid excessive soil erosion, reduce downstream flooding, and sediment damages. Practices like contour planting, terracing, strip cropping, and appropriate cropping patterns make up the conservation management system for humid regions. The erosion control thus provided assumes major significance in maintaining sustained crop production. Similarly, in semi-arid regions of the world capturing and holding water on the land is essential for obtaining acceptable crop yields. Vegetative barriers, pitting, crop selection, and fallowing are some of the practices currently used in the Sahel. New techniques to aid water conservation by storing water in the soil until a successful crop can be assured merit further research. Throughout the arid and semi-arid regions, water conservation is essential, particularly in marginal areas bordering on deserts. While the Sahel is a well known high-risk farming area, similar problems exist in such Latin American countries as Chile, Mexico, Argentina, and nearly every other country where dryland farming is practiced.

Combined with forest and range management techniques, hydrologic manipulations can provide for effective use of the environment. Careful, technically sound water management would aid greatly in providing agriculture with long-term, stable production. According to one report, there are 92 million hectares of irrigated land in the developing countries. While only about one-eighth of the cropped land in the world is irrigated, crops produced on these lands account for one-third to one-half of the value of agricultural products.[18] Production of rice seldom rises beyond 1.5 T/Ha, without water control on these fields. By utilizing water control alone this can usually be doubled. Moreover water control opens the potential for other inputs which might otherwise be of nominal value, such as fertilizer, pest management, etc. The combination of water control and these inputs can result in rice yields of 7 T/Ha and up.[19] The situation is similar for upland crops grown under irrigation. If irrigation is employed in wet-dry tropical, subtropical, and even temperate areas, two or three crops can be grown where only one would be possible.

Past programs in which development agencies were involved have sometimes transferred technology which was adapted to conditions in the United States or in other developed countries, i.e., labor -- scarce and expensive, capital -- plentiful and low-cost, energy -- cheap and plentiful, management -- capable of fine tuning operations, and infrastructure -- extensive, flexible, and responsive to new needs. These conditions do not exist in the Sahel, and research attuned to local conditions is required. A problem inherent in technology transfer to the Sahel is the tendency for new, efficiency-increasing technology to be adopted first by the farmer-stockman with an adequate acreage of land, access to capital and management skills; therefore, widening the rich-poor gap. An evaluation of two AID projects in Senegal, the Senegal Cereal Production Project (SCP), which is rainfed, and the Babel Small Irrigated Perimeters Project (BSIP) illustrates this skewed outcome:

> Preliminary investigations indicate that, in both projects, a disproportionate share of project benefits are earned by large, high-income farmers. In SCP, officials note that adoption of recommendations is much more common among large farmers than small farmers. Several factors inhibit intensification by small farmers: the surface cultivated is too small to supply feed for a pair of oxen, the amount of credit available to a farmer is tied to the quantity of groundnuts sold in the past, and credit is not available to cultivators other than the compound head. BSIP seems to offer greater possibilities to improve incomes of within-project poor farmers because of its greater accessibility to the group (liberal credit, low equipment costs, etc.). [20]

However, unlike parts of Latin America, the Sahel can attain the combined objectives of rural equity and output growth without deploying as puissant a policy instrument as land reform. The "latifundia-minifundia" landholding structure, which compresses excess labor into very small properties ("minifundia") and into an underemployed landless labor force, cannot assume the scapegoat's onus in the Sahel since there is a restrained sprinkling of "latifundia."[21] A more serious problem is the danger of certain technologies being misused with irreversible environmental impacts. Nevertheless, mechanization "per se" cannot be shunned. Selective mechanization may be appropriately utilized to break constraints caused by seasonal labor peaks, to eliminate sheer drudgery, or to increase production and, thus, yield benefits beyond labor and other power saved.

Needless to say, technological advance in agriculture is not solely a function of research in the natural sciences. At its simplest, each discipline group depends on the others. For example, the technical conditions for innovation must be met by breeding better varieties of crops or discovering new agronomic practices. Subsequently, the economic conditions of acceptance by farmers must be discovered through research on price analysis, credit conditions, and marketing conditions. Finally, the cultural conditions of rapid acceptance must be found through research in conceptual tectonics, leadership patterns, value structures, and so on. Among the concurrent changes in socioeconomic ambience needed for advances in agriculture, Rostow enumerates:

> ... a willingness of the agricultural community to accept new techniques and to respond to the possibilities of the widened commercial markets; the existence and freedom to operate of a new group of industrial entrepreneurs; and, above all, a national government capable not only of providing a setting of peaceful order which encouraged the new modernizing activities but also capable and willing to take a degree of direct responsibility for the build-up of social overhead capital(including its finance); for an appropriate trade policy; and often, as well, for the diffusion of new agricultural and industrial techniques.[22]

One does not have to accept a new high-yielding wheat variety with unfavorable characteristics of taste. On the other hand, one can discover human preferences and then breed a high-yielding wheat with the desired characteristics. Collaboration between social and natural scientists can ease the process of application by adapting technology to human conditions and wants. Likewise, when technical conditions are difficult to meet, social scientists can discover means of speeding the changes in human conditions and wants. Thus, a strong argument can be made in support of the proposition that the problems of rural development will not be solved until agriculture has achieved a more compatible marriage than now prevails with the social sciences.

The Sahelian hinterland is especially insusceptible to the importation of ready-made Western "solutions." Fortunately, the Sahelians have been wary of the extant molds provided by the international community to save its members the trouble of forming their own. In rejecting prefabricated models, Senghor has said:

> We have not allowed ourselves to be seduced by Russian, Chinese, or Scandinavian models, ... we have observed that formulas like "priority for heavy industry" or "agrarian reform" have no magic power within themselves; applied dogmatically, they have produced partial failures. That is why we established priorities as follows: infrastructure, rural

economy, processing industry, heavy industry, in line with reasonable requirements and our realities. To transform, one must first produce something to transform; before producing machine tools, we must produce living men -- that is to say, we must have consumer goods. The distribution of land to the peasants does not get them very far unless they have previously been given the means to make the land fertile: modern knowledge and modern instruments.[23]

7
Turning the Environment Around or Giving Ground?

The so-called interaction fallacy holds little water before the ecological principle that any change in one part of the environment ultimately affects other parts of the environment. At the outset of the 1968-1974 drought, cattle in the northern Sahel were dying of thirst. Engineers and ecologists decided to try to save some of the animals by delivering water to them, and numerous borehole wells were dug to tap subterranean water. The initial problem was solved: cattle could drink their fill. When word spread, however, herders from all over the region brought their animals to the wells. What followed was an ecological disaster. The hungry herds consumed the ground cover and then began to die of starvation. New borehole wells were dug approximately 30 kms from the first ones; herds migrated to the new water sources and the same thing happened again. This process was repeated over and over again, and when the drought finally ended huge portions of the northern Sahel had been left denuded and highly susceptible to wind and water erosion. Soil fertility was thus severely decreased, leading to desertification and permanent ecological damage. The water table had been lowered and land was lost to the desert, all to virtually no gain.

In its efforts to protect soil fertility, ecology/forestry overlaps with the agricultural sector. Ecologists have an interest in maintaining adequate fallow periods, rotating crops, and growing crops whose nutrient requirements put minimal pressure on the soil. Reforestation projects and the planting and maintaining of ground cover prevent erosion and increase the water-holding capacity of the soil. Because of the nature of the ecosystem itself and the interrelated goals of the ecology/forestry sector, it is ecologically counterproductive to concentrate, for example, on growing trees at the cost of exhausting the soil, or preserving ground cover at the expense of food production. Ecology projects thus tend in general to have multiple uses and multiple goals. Problems tend to arise less from inappropriate choices of method "per se," as in the case of village water supply, than from excessive single-mindedness, overmanipulation of the natural environment, and extreme changes in land use, which can cause severe and avoidable damage in pursuit of large-scale benefit.

Because they are especially well-equipped to foresee and interpret the effects of particular environmental changes, ecologists are uniquely qualified to serve as "watchdogs" over the environment, alerting others to potential dangers, preferably before they arise. In particular, ecologists can share information and insights with other sectors' planning officers during the predesign stage of their projects. Ecology's total-perspective approach equips the ecologist particularly well to promote intersectoral complementarity and cooperation in the interests of integrated development.

The means for avoidance of major negative impacts lie in sectors other than that of ecology. Ecologists cannot, for example, build sanitation systems or adequate housing, provide food, undertake health surveillance, or supply clinics. Nor are there any standard procedures for bringing about these kinds of efforts or avoiding negative outcomes. It is largely a matter of stressing to others that problems will inevitably arise and explaining how, where, and why they are likely to occur. In order to do this effectively, ecologists must be familiar with the other sectors of the economy and their activities. In particular, ecologists should be fully acquainted with the major diseases that occur in the Sahel. Since disease transmission is an ecological phenomenon, ecologists can play a valuable role in disease prevention and control. If it is convincingly presented, the ecological perspective can rally people from different development sectors to work together to formulate a coordinated long-term plan designed to prevent and/or combat threats to environmental and human health while promoting sustained economic growth. This perspective is central to the war that is being waged against desertification.

In a provocative article that appeared in The Economist, Barbara Ward minces no words in describing the level of urgency brought on by the impending crisis of desertification in the world's drylands:

> The risk of these regions literally 'giving ground' to their menacing desert neighbors could become a permanent disturbance in world food supplies. Above all, there are 600 million people living on the desert fringes, on the most vulnerable of all the planet's lands. The advance of the deserts -- desertification -- can mean higher costs and lower food standards for everyone. But for a seventh of the human race, it means quite simply famine and death.[1]

The real deserts are, of course, the result of variation in

the world's climate. The distribution of heat, wind, and water freezes the extreme north and south and creates a vast waterless belt across the eastern hemisphere, with few intermissions, from the Sahara to the Gobi. However, the issue that needs to be addressed is not whether these areas will spread because of changes in world climate; weather modification is not yet a viable response. The issue is whether man is exacerbating matters, in which case his bahavior must be modified.

Several interdisciplinary seminars have been conducted in recent years concerning various aspects of mankind's effect on the environment. One was "Inadvertent climatic modifications-report of the study of man's impact on climate," sponsored by the Massachusetts Institute of Technology in 1970. The following statement was included in their conclusions.

> In relation to the earth's history our recent climatic fluctuations, covering less than 300 years, are only small-scale noise, are seemingly random, and are certainly not well understood . . . In fact, as has been frequently pointed out, it will be difficult to identify any man-made effect because, first, with our present state of knowledge, we do not know how to relate cause and effect in such a complex system, and, second, man-made effects will be obscured by the natural changes that we know must be occurring.[2]

A significant natural change precipitated the recent Sahelian crisis. Favonian weather conditions beginning in 1966 resulted in increased productivity in the region in both the natural vegetation and in the field crops. This caused several marked changes, as far as human activities and expectations were concerned. The areas being cultivated increased during the wet period and sedentary farming activities expanded to the north. Export cash crops became an important percentage of the agricultural output, replacing part of traditional cereal production. The result of pressure for increased production was a decrease in average fallow time (to five or even one year) and consequently a lowered fertility, poorer soil structure, and less erosion resistance. However, the increased rainfall masked at least part of the effects of the decreased fertility as enough marginal land was brought under cultivation so that the total production of cereals actually increased. The growth in cultivated lands could only decrease that available for the nomads and their livestock.

By the end of this benign period known as the "little pluvial," the expectations of Sahelians had risen tremendously only to be dashed by just less than average rainfall conditions in 1968-1969. Widespread reductions in forage production (especially the ephemeral herbs) coupled with the all-time high animal population resulted in extensive overgrazing and even further reduction of the perennial grasses and shrubs. Desertification of rangelands began and northern grain fields were abandoned. Soil erosion and gully formation became more common in central and southern zones. The stage was set for a major crisis. Even though the 1968-1974 drought was no worse than many that have occurred in the Sahel's history, its effect was a human and livestock catastrophe far exceeding any recorded previously.

Little is known concerning the history of the degradation of the West African sub-Saharan region. More is known about the pre-Saharan and coastal regions of North Africa. At the time of Herodotus (484-424 B.C.), North Africa still had large populations of elephants along the coast and in the forest-covered Atlas Mountains. Hartebeest, wild donkeys, addax, antelope, ostrich and other such animals were widespread. The Sahara was a desert at the time but it appears to have been smaller and the oases were surrounded by large areas of thornbush and coarse grass. In the subdesert, streams ran longer in the dry season and provided some grazing in their beds, even when they dried up. Under Greek and Roman exploitation, the coastal and desert edge regions were cultivated, with dams, cisterns, and aqueducts to increase the production from the limited rainfall. Goats were introduced into North Africa about 194 B.C. At about the time of the birth of Christ, Polybius, reported that "the number of horses, sheep, and goats in the country (North Africa) is so large that I doubt if so many could be found in the rest of the world." Camels were introduced into the region from Syria between 193 and 211 A.D. In 429 A.D., the Vandals invaded and Roman control of the region was lost. Most of the intensive water control devices of the Romans were allowed to fall into disrepair. The continued exploitation of available vegetation by grazing and browsing animals resulted in extensive desertification. As a result, many of the old Roman farms are now bare rock and moving sand dunes.

With appropriate measures, a similar history of long-term overgrazing and resulting desertification will not someday be documented for sub-Saharan West Africa. However, that continued overgrazing, especially by goats and camels, is a major factor in vegetation destruction and resulting desertification has been demonstrated many times in recent decades by exclosure studies. Basically, such studies involve putting fences around sites, thus protecting them from grazing. Most have been in the sub-desert and savanna zones where significant changes have been observed in periods of five to twelve years. A fenced ranch in Niger that was so visible in ERTS satellite photographs is but another example as to how limited grazing permits the restoration of native vegetation and, if properly managed, can

TABLE 22 : The Ecological Balance in the Sahel

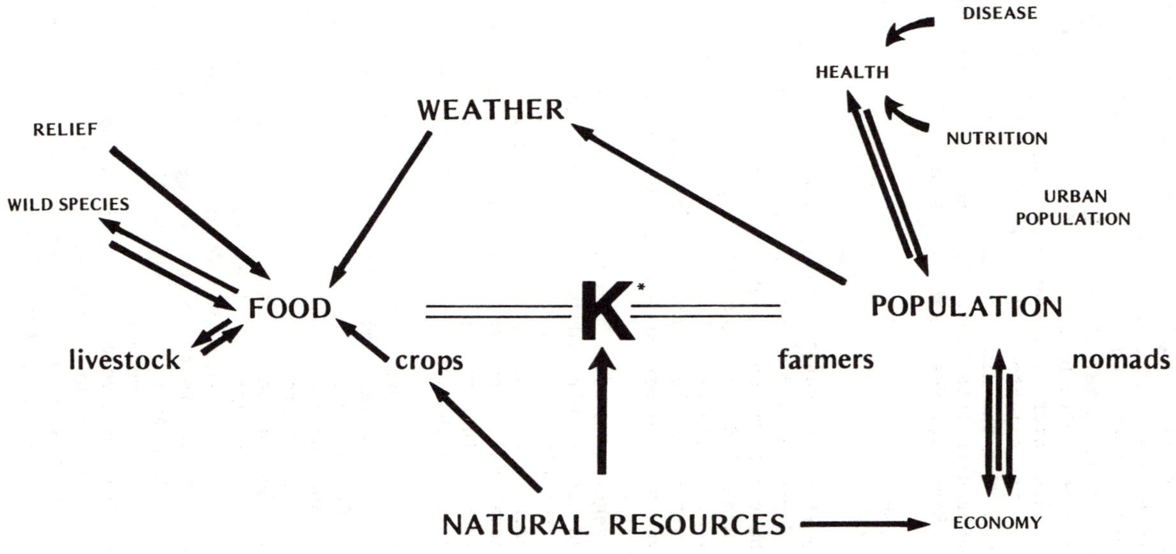

*K = carrying capacity

result in long-term, sustained yield of forage.

In a report prepared for the President of The Gambia, a novel benchmark is used to illustrate the deterioration of the Sahelian environment.[3] Dust fallout data was analysed revealing that increasing quantities of African topsoil are being recorded over a greatly enlarged distribution zone in the southern Atlantic. A map of dust recorded by ships at sea based on data collected before 1942 indicates that a two hundred square mile patch of the Atlantic juxtaposing the West African bulge was affected. More recent dust fallout data has been obtained from the Nimbus weather satellite and from the geosynchronous satellite SMSI. African topsoil fallout density recorded in Barbados, West Indies, was as follows:

	1968	1972	1974
micrograms per cubic meter	8	15	24

Increased dust in the Sahel reduces rainfall by suppressing rain-cloud formation and retarding the normal northward progress of the summer monsoon systems. During the 1978 dry season, dust-laden winds continued blowing across Senegal and The Gambia long after the usual February to April period. Ground-level dust was particularly heavy in mid-June, and high-altitude dust was still observed pouring out across the Atlantic as late as mid-July.

Where vegetation cover is continually reduced, resulting in increased dust levels and lower rainfall, streams dry up and the water-table is lowered beyond the tree-root zone. In northern Senegal, for instance, the loss of gum tree forests (Acacia Senegal verek) has ranged from 20 percent to 80 percent in recent years. This has had a telling affect on the Sahel, where trees and vegetation play an important role:

- Fruits, nuts, leaves, sprouts and roots are a valuable source of food. These by-products are available during the dry months and therefore are an important reserve in time of drought;
- Leaves, bark, and fruit of some trees provide forage for livestock and are available precisely when fodder is scarce;
- Firewood is the major source of energy, providing over 90 percent of the region's energy requirements;
- Trees and vegetation protect the soil from wind and water erosion. And in some instances, as with the acacia albida, trees increase soil fertility.

This valuable resource is being systematically destroyed. Wooded areas are being cleared for cultivation to meet the increasing demand for food. Trees are also being cut at a tremendous rate to satisfy local requirements for firewood and timber. Wooded areas around large population centers have almost completely disappeared. Virtually all trees within 70 kms of Ouagadougou have been consumed as fuel by the city's inhabitants, and the circle of land "strip-mined" for firewood--without reclamation--is continually expanding. Consequently, firewood prices have risen even faster than kerosene prices.

Firewood and charcoal prices are climbing throughout most of Asia and Latin America as well. Those who can, pay the price, and, thus, must forego consumption of other essential goods. Wood is simply accepted as one of the major expenses of living. In Niamey the average manual laborer's family is now spending nearly one-fourth of its income on firewood, according to foresters in the region. In Ouagadougou, the portion approaches 30 percent.[4] Even though fuel costs in Chad are about twice as high as in the United States the cost per unit quantity of water pumped by human labor is thirteen times the cost of mechanical pumping with a low-speed diesel engine and the cost of pumping using animal power is nearly three times as high.[5]

The indiscriminate, unplanned cutting of trees has depleted the cheapest energy source and destroyed the protective tree cover. The national forestry services of the CILSS countries have identified 170,000 hectares (225,000 acres) urgently in need of erosion control and restorative measures. However, lack of data precludes a detailed assessment of the full nature and extent of natural resource deterioration in the Sahel. An encouraging reforrestation prototype is The Gambia's National Tree Planting Program, which has brought bush-fire control legislation into effect; identified the types of trees most suited to each part of the country; established central tree-nursery facilities in each Division of the country; and established simple tree-raising nurseries at the village level to provide planting stock for compounds, roadsides, shelter belts, and field boundaries. The development of tree plantations throughout the Sahel is one of the most sound investments that can be made in the ecological future of the Sahel.

Tree plantations can serve the crucial function of increasing the Sahel's reserves of renewable fuel, which in turn means that less damage will be done to natural vegetation during an urgent search for fuel. When firewood becomes scarce, for example, people cut down darite trees, which yield nutritious fruits during the rainy season and nuts that are processed for oil. Also vulnerable to use as emergency firewood is the Acacia albida, a valuable farm tree which contributes nitrogen-rich organic matter to the soil, improving yields of millet. It also drops a seedpod that is eaten by livestock. Plantation adjoining farmland can also have a beneficial effect on the soil by acting as windbreaks. All these processes can indirectly but decisively affect nutrition by contributing to higher agriculture yields. Fast growing tree varieties that can be culled for firewood inside of a decade are available. The concept is simple, but its implementation is not. One of the major conceptual stumbling blocks is the sheer magnitude of the need for wood, and the scale of the growth in demand.

Population growth, which surprised many with its acceleration in the 1950s and 1960s, has swallowed the moderate tree planting efforts of several countries and whatever noticeable impact. The problem of scale is closely linked to a second major problem: the perennial question of political priorities and decision-making time frames. Even when the political will is there and the funds are allocated, implementing a large-scale reforestation campaign is a surprisingly complex and difficult process. Planting millions of trees and successfully nurturing them to maturity is not a technical, clearly boundaried task like building a dam or a nuclear power plant. Most of the areas with too few trees have too much cattle. The leaves of a young sapling present an appetizing temptation to a foraging animal, and a herdsman, even if he keeps careful control of his own animals, may reason that if he doesn't let his eat, someone else will let theirs. Marauding livestock are prime destroyers of tree-planting projects in the Sahel.

Indeed, it is clear that the most severe problems facing the Sahel today are ecological: poor soil, erratic and inadequate rainfall, a serious imbalance between people and resources, growing human and animal populations, and uneven population distribution. Overuse of the land resulting from the rapid population growth over the last fifty years, coupled with a fluctuating climate, have rendered the Sahelian ecosystem extremely fragile. Under such circumstances a relatively mild environmental assault could have extreme consequences. In response to these pressing problems, ecologists and foresters are pursuing three interrelated goals: preventing further deterioration of the ecosystem, maintaining the quality and increasing the quantity of renewable resources (forests and water), and enhancing the region's carrying capacity -- the number of people and animals it can support without incurring damage. Successful efforts to protect the environment in turn have pervasively beneficial effects on human health, life expectancy, and general well-being.

Sahelian institutional capabilities to arrest and reverse the process of desertification are generally underdeveloped. The forestry services are, in most cases, badly organized and are understaffed. There is a general lack of adequately trained personnel. Expertise in forest, range, and agricultural land management is limited at all government levels. Material and financial support required to undertake important activities is often nonexistent. Many Sahelian countries have no schools to train low and mid-level personnel. Individuals seeking higher levels of training have no option but to leave the Sahel to attend universities in France, the United States, or another foreign country.

The ecological problems stated above have direct implications for the Club du Sahel goal to achieve food self-sufficiency. If environmental deterioration is to be reversed, the CILSS countries must begin to develop and strengthen their institutional capabilities: to plan and manage their natural resources; to monitor the changing condition of the natural domain; to forecast crop yields; to detect erosion of land and pollution of water; recognize alternatives in land use; give early warning and assess damage of drought; and observe other relevant aspects of environmental change. This is an embryonic state for most of the Sahel.

In 1976, the Club du Sahel established the Ecology and Environmental Working Team to formulate a long-term development program for addressing the reforestation/antidesertification problems in the Sahel, as well as to ensure that the whole of the Sahel Development Program is environmentally and ecologically sound. During the initial planning phase, the Ecology and Environment Working Team focused its efforts on formulating a regional program to satisfy needs for forestry products and to combat desertification in the Sahel. The long-term goal of this program is to achieve food self-sufficiency through the sustained and balanced management of the Sahel's natural resources. More specifically, the program is designed to: (1) satisfy needs for cooking fuel, posts and poles; (2) stabilize pasture output; (3) arrest soil deterioration; and (4) conserve the region's flora and fauna. In order to achieve these goals, the program includes 83 projects submitted by the various CILSS governments. These projects represent a wide range of interventions which have been grouped into four general sub-programs: wood production, integrated agro-sylvo-pastoral activities, wildlife conservation and utilization, and training research. The total cost of the first generation program is estimated to be $173 million; of this, donors have been requested to provide $146 million, with national governments contributing the remaining $30 million. The total cost of the long-term program (20 years) is estimated to be $450 million.

ENERGY

There is grim but apt meaning in applying the term "dark continent" to Africa today: per capita commerical energy consumption for much of rural Africa is less than one-sixtieth of the global average, less than one three-hundredth that of North America, and barely one-sixth that of India. Without the ability to harness increased amounts of non-human energy to useful purposes, rural parts of the Sahel will not be able to develop. More available energy could permit increases in the cultivation, irrigation, harvest, storage, and transportation to market of food and cash crops, as well as in the productivity of non-agricultural activities such as cottage crafts or small industries. Currently, villagers spend a large fraction of their days gathering firewood, carrying water, and pounding grain. Since these activities must go on even during periods of the crop cycle when the demand for labor is greatest, they interfere with production.

Farm output as a function of energy input shows the familiar S-shaped curve. Additional energy input in the lower ranges increases output markedly but yields little or no increase at higher levels. If development plans fail to consider the availability of energy both present and future, their success will be limited. To be sure, Sahelian energy demand shows no sign of abating in the near future, magnifying the difficulties attendant to the reproduction of renewable energy resources and threatening the feasibility of the entire Sahel Development Program.

Increased availability of energy would improve the quality of village and rural life by supplying clean water for drinking, hot water for sanitation, lights, radio and television for communication and education, and release from onerous physical tasks. The upshot of this point is that energy can be the engine for increased rural productivity and improved quality of life, helping to reverse the growing trend toward emigration by rural Sahelians to already crowded urban areas and encouraging the new generation of educated Sahelians to work toward developing the economic and cultural strengths of their countries' interiors.

The present reliance on fuelwood and charcoal for most rural energy needs is leading toward an agricultural and environmental disaster. Women and children in many rural areas are finding it necessary to devote one or more days a week simply to seeking and gathering wood to cook with. These rural uses combined with urban consumption of firewood and charcoal and the need for lumber in construction are rapidly outstripping natural growth and replanting programs. At present rates of deforestation in Niger, for example, the last trees will be consumed within the lifetime of the present generation's great-grandchildren. The need for considerably increased energy availability in the Sahel is therefore compelling. But extension to rural areas of the electrical grids and other modern energy forms remains agonizingly slow. Recent studies of energy use in rural areas of developing countries in Asia, Africa, and Latin America have shown that non-commercial energy sources -- fuel wood, crop residues, dung -- supply between 61 and 96 percent of the total energy used. Between 69 and 97 percent of this energy is used for domestic purposes the major part of which, by far, is food preparation.[6] Wood has become "the poor man's oil." At present, the need for firewood in the Sahel is estimated at 26 million cubic meters per year. In 1990, it will reach at least 35 million cubic meters even if other energy sources or more efficient use of wood is taken into account.[7]

Like most developing countries the Sahelian countries have two distinct energy-technology needs. On the one hand, economic growth is dependent on conventional urban energy systems that utilize commercial energy sources and technologies already in use, or being developed, in the industrialized countries. Agricultural development schemes pegged to irrigation, mechanization, and manufactured nitrogen fertilizers also depend on these energy sources and technologies. On the other hand, the majority of the population lives in rural areas, isolated from central power distribution. They continue to rely on firewood or dried dung, and would particularly benefit from development of technologies to exploit renewable energy resources based on solar energy used directly (e.g., heating and distillation) or indirectly (wind and hydropower).

Work is currently underway in several Senegalese organizations to develop and perfect technologies which use renewable sources of energy. The Institut de Physique Météorologique (IPM), the Institut Universitaire de Technologie (IUT), and the Ecole Polytechnique de Thiès are experimenting with ways to pump water using energy from the sun and wind. This work is heavily supported by the French. Experimental solar collectors, photovoltaic systems, and windmills have been installed and are in operation in a number of sites in Senegal. Caritas, a private voluntary organization, has developed a hand pump which has been successfully installed in several villages. In the area of food preservation, IPM is working closely with the Institut de Technologie Alimentaire (ITA) to perfect a prototype of a solar dryer. And IUT is experimenting with cooling systems (refrigeration) using solar cells.

The rapid rate of deforestation in recent years has caused the Senegalese government to encourage the use of butane for cooking through subsidizing the importation of butane and butane burners. In addition, it has placed strong limitations on the production of charcoal. It is too early to assess the impact of these policies on the consumption of firewood and charcoal as opposed to butane. Some experimental work is being done by Caritas to produce methane for cooking and lighting. IPM is constructing a prototype for a solar cooker.

The development of indigenous energy resources is a matter of indisputable significance to the Sahel. The choice of energy technology and energy resource -- renewable or non-renewable, indigenous or imported -- made by Sahelian countries will have a long-term impact on their development. This impact is perhaps more widespread and significant than that of any other technological choice currently facing them. Choosing the path of large-scale, capital-intensive, centralstation technologies will have important short and long-term repercussions in every sector, and on urban development, industrial expansion, and environmental impact. It will also mean increased dependence on non-renewable fossil fuels.

On the other hand, the choice of small-scale decentralized energy systems (e.g., solar heating and generation of steam and electricity; windmills, small-scale hydroelectric plants) will have a different set of short- and long-term effects. Such systems are conducive to, for example: de-emphasis of Western-style industrialization, dispersal of industry and perhaps encouragement of cottage industry with attendant changes in financing approaches. All of these factors could contribute significantly, in the long run, to a self-sufficient and resilient but distributed population instead of concentrated urban growth.

It seems clear from past experience that elimination of the worst aspects of poverty in rural areas will necessitate much higher per capita consumption of energy. In those developing countries where substantial progress toward this goal has been made, it has been accompanied by increased use of petroleum fuels in all sectors. Thus, increased per capita energy consumption coupled with expected population growth means that achievement of this goal by the turn of the century with conventional commercial fuels alone would require more petroleum than known world resources can possibly provide.[8] If the Sahel sustains a moderate population rate, by the end of the century it is likely that energy consumption of non-wood sources will become seven to to ten times the 1970 level. The Sahelian countries are almost all in the United Nations category of "most severely affected" by the 1973-1974 world oil price increases, which have made energy a major drain on foreign currency. This trend is likely to worsen, since the foreign currencies needed for energy production and distribution will increase at rates between 9 and 11 percent, while exports are projected to grow at a rate of less than 6 percent, unless very major mineral finds are exploited.[9] The resultant conclusions point to a serious dilemma for the Sahelian countries.

Local resources can be developed to reduce these balance of trade problems. Prospecting rights are being exploited in Chad by Conoco, DIREP, and Shell (Conoco and Shell have found some gas and oil in the Doba basin and north of Lake Chad, but commercial possibilities are not known); in Mali by Texaco, Sonarem and Mobil (with no results, so far); in Mauritania by ESSO and AMOCO offshore and Tennesco, Shell, Planet, and Agip on land (no reported finds, to date); in Niger by Texaco, Continental, Bishop, and Global (with uneconomic small finds, so far); in Senegal by ESSO, Copetao and Shell in the South and offshore (finds, but not exploitable as yet); and in Upper Volta no interest has developed because of poor prospects. On the basis of available information there is little hope of early large exploitation of oil, although some gas might eventually be produced. One possibility for a low-cost solution revolves on whether Algeria would either bottle or pipe, trans-Sahara,

TABLE 23

ANNUAL CONSUMPTION OF PETROLEUM PRODUCTS (1970)

Country	Quality (MT)	Thousands of Tons of Coal Equiv.	Value ($000)	Unit Cost ($US/T)
Chad	69,345	87	8,581	124
Mali	71,300	99	3,975	56
Mauritania	116,551	156	3,782	32
Niger	51,623	75	2,239	43
Senegal	416,870	523	9,549	23
Upper Volta	50,843	69	3,774	74
Totals	776,532	1.009	31,900	41

SOURCE: UNSSO, 1974.

TABLE 24

ENERGY CONSUMPTION PER CAPITA

Country	Fossil & Hydro (million BTU)	Wood (million BTU)	Wood as & of Total
Chad	0.44	6.44	93
Mali	0.55	4.30	89
Mauritania	1.56	4.30	73
Niger	0.36	4.60	93
Senegal	3.80	4.40	54
Upper Volta	0.26	5.50	95

SOURCE: MIT, Energy & Minerals Resources, Annex 9, 31 Dec. 1974.

gas for liquification in the Sahel.

Some of the balance of trade problems could be alleviated if the Sahelian countries could obtain special oil-pricing agreements (as Senegal has succeeded in doing with Iran) or could arrange to buy hydroelectric power from excess capacity available in the coastal area at long-term stable prices. This latter possibility is good, given the growth of regional cooperation, because Ghana and Guinea are developing projects for 768 MW and 625 MW respectively, which can produce electric power greatly in excess of domestic needs for a number of years. High cost of transmission could be substantially reduced by using high voltage DC lines, similar to the Pacific NW-California tie line. A transmission line from Kainji in Nigeria to Niamey has recently been constructed.

While more than half of Niger's exports are now from uranium, and there are important known uranium reserves in Chad and, to a lesser degree Mali, it is unlikely that area demand will be sufficient for many years to justify an economically sized nuclear power plant. Export income to offset fuel imports and development costs are a more appropriate use of this resource. The hydroelectric potential of the Senegal and Niger Rivers is substantial, but not impressive when compared to other major rivers. Although annual flow is of considerable volume, the total fall through the Sahelian countries is small and economic dam sites are very few and far between. For example, the Kandadji dam site in Niger could produce up to 200 MW of firm power, but since to do so, the dam must be 30 m high and 12 km long, the power production cost would be as high as that of current oil-fired generation unless a very large percent of the dam cost could be charged to irrigation, navigation, and flood control.

Development of increased capacity to formulate and implement energy policies is critical for long-term planning in the region. National energy policies should consider the long recovery times occasioned by different forms of land over-exploitation. Balance of trade problems could hamper development and, in the last analysis, must affect the choice of energy policy. Clearly, regional cooperation and coordination of energy policy is desirable. Coordination of urban growth and energy policy is needed to optimize utilization of local resources. A primary tool to assist Sahelian governments and regional institutions in acquiring a handle on the techniques of making and implementing energy policy is the power and energy surveys proposed to be implemented through each of the major river basin development commissions in the region.

WATER RESOURCES

Based on the World Bank, FAO, AID, and UNDP studies to date, it is clear that, although the extent of irrigable land in the Sahelian river basins is not yet known with absolute certainty, considerable advanced planning has been undertaken in the three principal basins -- Senegal, Niger, and Lake Chad. In the absence of definitive land capacity and irrigability studies, most of the planning is based on estimates of 430,000 hectares in the Senegal basin (OMVS program) with IBRD current costs for development running at an average of over $5000/ha; 2,700,000ha. in the Niger basin (IBRD rough preliminary estimate); and 680,000 ha. in the Lake Chad basin (FAO 1974 survey of prospects).[10]

The World Bank, FAO, and most other donor evaluations for a development strategy in the agriculture sector recognize that in the higher rainfall areas of the Sahelian countries, rainfed agricultural production must be expanded to assist in meeting the food requirements of growing populations. There are, though, large areas where rainfall even in normal years is insufficient to grow food crops without irrigation. It is estimated that 600,000 ha. are currently being used for irrigation including traditional flood recession cultivation. The potentially irrigable area by the year 3000, assuming the construction of regulatory dams, totals 1,830,000 ha. Modern irrigation technologies exist that could probably be adapted for use in the development of Sahelian river and lake basins. However, making use of these technologies will require substantial investment in physical and social overhead capital, in the form of dams, irrigation systems, roads, social services facilities, adaptive research, and training of managers and farmers. Because of the relative ease of transferring capital intensive technologies, there may be a neglect of the more difficult job of developing technologies that employ small farmers as large-scale infrastructure is built.

Average annual rainfall throughout the lower Senegal basin in Senegal and Mauritania, the Niger inland delta in Mali, the Niger course in eastern Mali and part of Niger, and the Lake Chad basin north of N'Djamena in Niger, Nigeria, Cameroon, and Chad is below 500 mm, and in a major percentage of these areas there is quasi-desert. With high evapotranspiration rates and severe variability of rainfall, very low yields of under 400 kg/ha. of drought-resistant cereals such as millet are obtained now. While some improvement of these yields is feasible through better practices and the use of modern inputs the ultimate potential remains very low, estimated at less than the 1000 kg/ha. now realized from rainfed production in the higher rainfall areas of the region.[11] This is the reason that wherever in these parts of the Sahel there is no irrigation, rainfed farming is restricted to very low-level subsistence type operations or flood recession cropping that is very high risk and limited in time and growing season. If the Sahelian governments, assisted by donors, pursue the rainfed alternative in the Savannah or Sudanian portions of the region, irrigation development will not detract from worthwhile investment in rainfed production.

Although there are apparently huge underground resources of fresh water, much of this is geologic in origin and is not recharged from the surface. It has been estimated that some 3.6 trillion cubic meters are exploitable, but in order to maintain the equilibrium of the water tables, annual use must be restricted to no more than 12-15 billion cubic meters.[12] However, considering exploitation costs and the requirements for both community water supplies and livestock, the annual usage of groundwater for irrigation could not prudently exceed 2 billion cubic meters, or enough to irrigate only 20,000 hectares in the course of the next few decades.[13] Thus, the primary sources of irrigation water will have to be from efficient management of rainfall and from rivers and lakes. In the Senegal, Niger, Lake Chad, Gambia, and Volta basins, international basin authorities have been established with membership by all or most countries riparian to the surface water system. This regional synergy will become increasingly important once the potential of the basins is realized and irrigation projects become operational. The exchange of information and cross-fertilization of ideas in the early, experimental years will be invaluable to governments and farmers, who both stand to gain necessary experience in adapting to irrigated farming techniques.

The people of the Sahel have always lived with the fact that their crops often fail because of lack of water. Therefore, there is always some interest in a technology such as irrigation, which promises to insure sufficient water supplies for their crops. However, this interest is tempered by the harsh realities of life in the Sahel. The people of the Sahel, above all else, are proficient in the art of basic survival. Generations of experience in the difficult climatic conditions of the Sahel have conditioned the farmers to avoid risk as much as possible. Therefore, even though irrigation is perceived in a favorable light as "water availability insurance," it is a new and in many cases unknown quantity. Thus, the farmer views irrigation as a mixed bag at best and its suitability probably depends on how well it can be integrated with his other survival activities. Irrigation presents somewhat of a paradox as well to the governments of the Sahelian countries and to aid donors. It is viewed as the salvation of the Sahelian countries because it lessens reliance on the capricious rainfall for production of basic food crops. It also offers the potential for greatly increased yields through intensive management and lends itself to increased mechanization and subsequently to increased labor productivity. On the other hand, irrigation schemes are very expensive to construct and operate, and require rather sophisticated management expertise if they are to operate at a reasonable profit.

Technical aspects of an irrigation proposal can usually be resolved with little difficulty by competent irrigation specialists and engineers. Of course, even though irrigation schemes may be technically feasible, they may be so costly as to be economically unfeasible. With irrigation costs per hectare ranging from $2,000 to $5,000, and in some cases up to $10,000, the returns from each hectare must be very high in order to amortize the investment costs. Additionally, annual operating costs of the irrigation system and recurrent costs for the government services can range from $100 to $400 per hectare. All of these costs must be covered by revenues from the crops grown and leave a large enough profit for the farmers so that they have an adequate incentive to participate.[14]

To a far greater extent than any of the above, it is the social considerations which most often prove fatal to a project. The records of AID, IBRD, and the Asian Development Bank (ADB) are replete with instances of irrigation systems which were well planned, designed, and implemented which, within a few years, were floundering at best. In most instances agencies have attempted to overlay a traditional culture with an extremely complex system or systems that are little understood by the traditional cultivators. The result is that the cultivator has little vested interest in running the system beyond his own headgate and it is somebody else's fault when water does not arrive in proper amounts and in a timely fashion at his headgate. Also, since he is not directly helping to manage and run the system beyond his headgate, the government or agency concerned must supply all the management staff and facilities necessary to operate and manage the system. This results in excessively high overhead costs that are one of the principal factors contributing to producing a non-viable activity.

A fee may or may not be levied to cover the overhead costs to run the system and this leads to other difficult aspects. The cultivator, who is usually not operating in monied economy has no cash to pay the management costs. Consequently further government organization is needed to handle the collection of fees in kind. These activities only further increase the overhead costs of the activity. For instance, in the Haute Valee project in Mali and in various perimeters in the Senegal River Basin the cultivators observe that their government is usually notoriously inefficient and they wonder if the taxes or levies they pay yield commensurate economic results. Thus they place full blame for any problems on the government. If the activity is to be successful, the cultivators must be involved more intimately in all management and operational aspects, particularly in those elements of the system that directly impinge or affect their holdings.

The lessons learned from AID experience over the years indicate that if irrigation projects are to become viable, only about 20 to 30 water users should be included in the farmer groups involved in managing a water delivery system. Projects involving more farm families will require a more sophisticated layered management structure including representatives from each farmer group. The management capability to run the system will have to be provided by the sponsor until the farm water users become capable of managing and running their systems.[15]

THE TECHNOLOGY SALIENT

Achieving environmental equilibrium rests in large measure on striking a technological balance. In precolonial times, the Sahel saw little application of machinery to cultivation, to water control, or to transport. Practically the only machine was the loom. In agriculture, animal power was not used for any form of traction. This was partly due to the absence of a fundamental invention that spread throughout Eurasia but never reached Africa south of the Sahara, with the exception of Ethiopia: the plow.

What is the significance of the plow? In the first place, it increases the area of land that can be cultivated and, hence, makes possible a substantial rise in productivity, at least in open country. This in turn means a greater surplus for the maintenance of specialist crafts, for the growth of differences in wealth and in styles of life, for developments in urban, that is, non-agricultural, life. Secondly, it stimulates the move to fixed holdings and away from shifting agriculture. Thirdly and, not independently, it increases the value of arable land despite the fact that farm land remains in many parts of the Sahel "extra commercium."

The absence of even elementary mechanization has important implications for the economic development of the Sahel. In planning the rate and progress of development, we have to take into account the base line from which we start. In the Sahel, the small-scale technology of Eurasia is lacking; at the village level there are wood-carvers but few carpenters, ironworkers but no mechanics, potters but no wheels or kilns. The basic craftsmen have still to be trained in many not so remote parts of the region.

The traditional methods of crop production are strongly indicative of the symbiotic relationship between man and nature in the Sahel. An unwritten pact stipulates a harsh tradeoff: human sweat for nature's rain. While nature has at times been deceitful, notably during times of drought, the Sahelian farmer, entrenched in his ways, has been presented heretofore with few opportunities for change. The conceptual system which dictates his actions, continues to assign the highest priority to dependence on both nature and self. From the rains that nourish the seeds to the winds that winnow the ripened grain, nature is an omnipresent participant in traditional agriculture. The farmer and his family for their part, spend countless laborious hours on the land. It has been observed that even when a farmer possesses a draft animal, he relies on himself as a load carrier. This stems from a world view that regards survival and improvement as a function of greater effort and increased skill in using old tools rather than the development of new ones. Needless to say, progress is more likely to come about from the introduction of better tools and power systems than from greater dexterity in the use of old ones.

Potentially one of the most important jobs for animals, but one that has not been successfully promoted in most of sub-Saharan Africa, is hauling by carts and wagons. "The addition of a cart to the farmer's tools can be a very important stimulus in helping him to adopt other new practices. With load-carrying mobility, he has incentive to raise more crops and to seek out new and more distant markets. He can do custom hauling for neighbors to enhance his potential cash return and acquire additional resources to purchase more of the proven production-increasing inputs. In other words, a simple cart can greatly broaden the farmer's horizons and increase his income."[16] Similarly, many improved implements can radically alter the small farmer's lot for the better.

The shortcomings of the traditional cultivation methods are highlighted by the travails of weeding. Irregularly-spaced and haphazardly-located, plants can be weeded only with a great deal of time and effort. In combatting weeds, the traditional farmer has few options once he has taken the preventive measure of soil burning to kill all grasses and their roots prior to preparing fallow sod land for cultivation. Mustering the largest number of people that can be had, the farmer takes to his field with hoe or bare hands to begin the painstaking job of eliminating weed competition. In an AID project paper for the Sahel Food Crop Protection Project, the project development team reported:

> In all countries (Cameroon, Chad, Mauritania, and Senegal), and for all crops surveyed except for rice, weed caused losses matched or exceeded losses caused by pests or diseases. Some 45 percent of total losses for all crops was directly attributed to weeds, with maize, millet, and sorghum most affected.[17]

The tendency at present is to let the weeds get too large before controlling them. However, this may well be an expression of the farmer's frustration with his ability to clamp down on what he has come to regard as a futile situation. Weeds are in fact one of the major deterrent factors in expanding agricultural production, and traditional attempts to control them and increase fertility levels are responsible for the ensuing crop management bottleneck. Traditional harvesting and processing tools and techniques are generally very functional and unrefined. The widely used machete is a heavy knife used for harvesting large, thick-stalked plants like maize and sorghum. Also used for general clearing and brush cutting, they appear in a wide variety of shapes and are affixed to a wooden handle. Before the grain can be consumed in various porridges, the mainstay of the Sahelian diet, it must be processed by the womenfolk who pound it into flour. Using a mortar hewn out of a section of tree trunk and pestles made from heavy slender poles, the women rhythmically pound in teams. This frequently seen community activity undeniably emits the heart beat of the African continent.

The low level of technological developemnt in food and agricultural production is a major constraint to increasing productivity, raising real incomes, and improving the welfare of small farmers and herders. Research and development of technologies for food crops has been generally neglected while development of technologies for export crop production has proceeded somewhat more rapidly. Despite limited investment in research on staple food crops, there are technologies involving integrated export and food crop production both for rainfed farming and small scale irrigation that can result in modest productivity and income gains for small producers. These existing crop technologies are more promising in areas of higher (800mm) and less variable rainfall. Much remains to be done, however, to develop substantially higher-yielding varieties of millet and sorghum, the principal sources of calories for the rural poor and to develop highly profitable farming systems for small farmers.

Similarly, research and development of technologies in livestock production have been neglected with the exception of research on animal diseases and on rangeland species. Closely associated with the neglect of research has been the slowness to develop institutions for delivery of information, services, and inputs to food and livestock producers. Regional development organizations established to provide technical support to export crop production and marketing have been slow to broaden their role to encompass food and livestock production. In an annual research report for AID, John W. Mellor states:

> The initial empirical research on this contract has confirmed the crucial importance of the relationship between technological change in agriculture on the one hand and the distribution of income on the other hand. The analysis has also shown that the relationship between these variables are extremely complex.[18]

The interdependence of numerous factors and the tremendous effort, organization, and resources required to increase participation of the small farmer in growth demand wholehearted government commitment. Such a commitment is found in Senegal's program to accelerate and intensify agricultural production by introducing a package of inputs, including improved animal power and implements.

APPROPRIATE TECHNOLOGY SENEGALESE STYLE

Intermediate technology -- a concept that has taken off on self-sustained growth in development circles -- has not passed unnoticed in the Sahel and, particularly, in Senegal. In fostering improved agricultural technology, the Senegalese authorities have given careful attention in the extant system to the level and scope for mechanization, innovation, entrepreneurial activities, and infrastructure. In short, Senegalese officials elected to aid the small farmer within the context of his environment. At the most recent meeting of the Association for the Advancement of Agricultural Sciences in Africa, the following characteristics, which largely define this environment for all Africa, were enumerated:

1. predominantly subsistence farming
2. small size of holdings (on the average between 3 and 4 acres)
3. use of predominantly human labor
4. limited cash resources
5. widespread use of natural fallow techniques
6. absence or limited use of costly inputs such as fertilizers
7. widespread use of intercropping to minimize risks
8. low productivity
9. principally rainfed cultivation
10. crop production improvement limited to cash and export crops rather than food crops[19]

Recognizing the great effort involved, the need for adaptive research, the importance of an able extension service, and the long-term nature of agricultural change, Senegal established a systematic, carefully integrated program of agricultural intensification. A scheme of progressive development was planned to gradually upgrade the traditional subsistence agriculture into a market-oriented system. Different levels of progress were defined which could be reached by most farmers without costly investments.

The Senegalese government originally planned the program in three stages. The first stage utilized oxen for traction and carts for transportation. It also introduced the use of oxen for plowing and harvesting and other animals for planting and weeding. Within its four year duration (1963-1967), it succeeded in "popularizing" these schemes systematically to the point where 70 percent of Senegal's farmers were applying them to their crop production. The second stage established a stationary agriculture by annually applying fertilizer deep into the soil of the preceding year's fallow land with the help of bovine traction. Improved animal care was also emphasized at this stage. The present and third stage is the complete integration of animals and crop production. Farmers are taught the rational use of crop rotations, improved fertilization, selection and care of high-yield varieties, production of temporary pasteur, and planting of annual field crops.

Senegal's intensification program has required the allocation of significant resources. The magnitude of Senegal's commitment to agricultural development is reflected in the number of specialized organizations it has established to provide the necessary infrastructure to launch and sustain this program:

SODEVA. An organization which specializes in promoting agricultural development was commissioned to work with research institutions and organize the "popularization" of the intensification program at its inception in 1963. This French firm, Societe d'Aide Technique et de Cooperation (SATEC), provided extension services until 1968 when it was succeeded by the Societe de Developpement et du Vulgarisation (SODEVA). By 1967, SATEC had met with considerable success in its campaign to introduce improved implements and practices for groundnut and millet production. In this peak year of its existence, its staff consisted of 770 persons including 695 Senegalese extension agents, 35 French technicians, 24 Senegalese technicians, and 16 engineers. The results they achieved were very encouraging as is indicated in Table 24.

TABLE 25 - RATE OF IMPLEMENT INTRODUCTION IN SENEGAL

Improved Inputs	Units	% Utilization by Farmers	Units	% Utilization by Farmers
Sowing Machines	65,000	50	124,000	95
Hoes	20,000	15	80,350	55
Plows	2,400	1.5	14,800	17
Fertilizer	kg		kg	
Groundnuts	18,700	16	44,250	37
Millet	2,300	2.5	11,116	10.4

SODEVA has its headquarters in Dakar, with three principal field operations offices in Kaolack, Thies, and Diourbel. The majority of SODEVA personnel are directly attached to the three field offices. SODEVA is the responsible development agency for preparing a regional outreach strategy to deliver new technology to the farmers of its designated servicing area. This is a function which must be sensitive and responsive to the particular needs and character of each region. The groundnut basin, which has three disparate soil and moisture zones, requires a specific approach suited to each zone. Operational programs in each region vary, but they generally promote one or both of two types of emphasis: diversification when appropriate, and intensification. Diversification of agriculture is promoted by introducing or expanding the production of such crops as maize, millet, sorghum, tobacco, and rice in conjunction with the traditional peanut crop. Intensification is promoted by initiating applicable cultivation techniques which have been proven by research to have significant socioeconomic value. The overall orientation of SODEVA is geared to the following procedure:

> Individual farmers are brought into the program at various levels of intensification, and are led through progressive stages of application, and assisted to advance from one level to the next over a period of years, toward full adoption and application of all the techniques. For example, the three principal stages planned for this project are termed (1) Exploitation Theme Leger (semi-intensive), (2) Exploitation Traction Bovine (oxen traction) and (3) Exploitation Intensif (Intensive Exploitation). This type of program offers a level of participation for nearly any farmer regardless of his means, and at the same time presents a challenge to each farmer to progress from one level of achievement to the next higher level.[20]

The farmer does not, however, actually receive a supply of inputs from SODEVA. These must come from his local cooperative. The elaborate network of local cooperatives imposed on the rural sector by law creates a marketing network, which has not existed, at a stroke. There is at present, approximately one cooperative for every five villages in Senegal. A staff of civil servents works at each outlet. A local elected body manages the cooperative but, given the lack of local skills, the public employees bear most of the burden. In point of fact, cooperatives operate as an arm of the government and often have little local autonomy. SODEVA plays an important supportive and advisory role to the cooperatives and is represented on the local board of each cooperative.

ONCAD. Agricultural credit and the subsequent delivery of animal-drawn equipment, seeds, and fertilizers to farmers is the responsibility of the National Office for Coopertives and Development Assistance (ONCAD), which is also the national marketing agency for groundnut and cereal staple crops. The Government of Senegal created ONCAD in 1966 to assure a commercial outlet for the increase in crop production. ONCAD purchases any amount of cash and staple food crops offered for sale by the farmer. ONCAD is also responsible for importing and distributing staple foods when there are national shortages.

Cooperating extensively with regional development organizations, ONCAD assists in the formation of farmer cooperatives. The cooperatives do not function as producers or marketing cooperatives. They are, however, the only way individual farmers can secure government credit. Certain indebtedness limitations are fixed by ONCAD for each cooperative, and this is based on a percentage of the value of the cereals and cash crops marketed by the cooperative in the previous three years. Orders for material are grouped and given to ONCAD, which is responsible for placing the orders with suppliers and in seeing that deliveries are made. ONCAD is also responsible for the purchase and distribution of seed, and regional units known as "seccos" have been constructed to store the seed.

ISRA. The Senegalese farmer is the object not only of input supply and marketing organizations, but equally important, he benefits from an effective research and technical support base. Behind the development structures in the country stands the Senegalese Institute for Agricultural Research (ISRA), which is responsible for fundamental and applied research for the whole of the country. Better known as IRAT (Institut de Recherches Agronomiques Tropicales et des Culture Vivrieres) until the recent change in name in 1975, this research organization has been in operation since the turn of the century. ISRA currently integrates the findings of ten research stations spread throughout the country where researchers pursue endeavors in fields ranging from agronomy to oceanography.

One of the oldest and most established experiment stations is the Bambey Center for Agronomic Research, which was founded in 1921. This research center's budget for 1978 was 900 million CFA, of which 650 million CFA was financed by the French government in accordance with the Franco-Senegalese General Agreement. Bambey employs approximately thirty French scientists who collaborate with the Senegalese counterparts and assistants. Extensive work is being conducted there on animal-powered techniques and equipment. A series of agronomic research projects in the early 1950s on cultivation techniques, fertilization, and implements found that bovine traction was necessary for getting the fertilizer deep into the soil. ISRA scientists have devised new equipment including Jean Nolle's "polyculteur" (a tool bar adapted to bovine traction).

For the hand farmer, primary tillage and timely land preparation is a critical task. Animal power with its ability to break, turn, or ridge larger areas more rapidly enables the farmer to overcome this bottleneck. However, if the plow is his only tool, he is immediately confronted with another serious problem: he cannot look after and weed by hand all the land he can till and plant with animal power. Weeding becomes the limiting factor in intensified and expanded animal-powered production, when all operations subsequent to tillage must be done by hand. The need for an animal-drawn implement specifically designed for this purpose becomes evident. To meet this and other requirements, the progressive Senegalese farmer is advised to choose the multiple-purpose toolframe or toolbar. With a basic toolbar, the farmer can add other attachments at very reasonable cost as he gradually enlarges his operations and begins to use other inputs to improve his farming system. Currently available are attachments for tillage, weeding, seeding, cultivating, and carting plus several harvesting tools for lifting groundnuts.

Perhaps the most important factor contributing to the success of the research component has been its orientation, with a marked emphasis on adaptability. Each new practice is thoroughly tested on farms and in pilot projects before being promoted on a large scale. Innovation packages are initially distributed among ISRA's 100 test farmers in the vicinity of Bambey. The farmers make use of these packages on the whole or part of their farms and through a feedback process enable the ISRA scientists to observe any difficulties which arise. In 1968, two experimental units were established which consisted of 150 to 200 farms each. Robert Toute observes:

> After five years of operation, many useful lessons could be drawn from this experience in research-extension relations. The introduction of ox-drawn plows; the adoption of cropping systems with rotation of cereals, peanuts, and cotton; basal dressing (phosphate) and fertilizer applications; the introduction of mechanical post-harvest operations; reforestation (windbreaks and borders); all contributed to vastly improved economic conditions on the farms concerned. Thus, from hand cultivation to semi-intensive ox-drawn cultivation, the data per farm is as follows:
>
> - total production value rose from 20,000 CFA to 65,000 CFA
>
> - agricultural income increased from 18,000 CFA to 49,000 CFA
>
> - the net monetary margin rose from 8,750 CFA to 37,000 CFA.[21]

The ISRA people can ill-afford to seclude themselves in an ivory tower. To be sure, they have had to cultivate the businessman's shrewdness and acquire the capability to gauge adeptly the consumer's psychology. Since 1961, the Bambey Center for Agronomic Research has been a partner in a venture to develop agricultural equipment commercially.

SISCOMA. The Société Industrielle Senegalaise de Constructions

Mécaniques et de Matériels Agricoles (SISCOMA) traces its origin to the first field day held at Bambey in 1958 to display agricultural implements and their usage. This fair brought together researchers, manufacturers, and extension agents and led to the establishment of a domestic agricultural equipment industry. In 1961, with financing from the Senegalese government and a number of French agricultural equipment firms, a factory was constructed in Kaolack. This factory proved to be incapable of meeting the demand for agricultural equipment. In 1963, a new factory was built at Pout at a cost of 270 million CFA. The Pout factory employs 200 full-time employees, who turn out annually over 100,000 items geared for animal power and thousands of diverse materiel used in the agricultural sector. However, the Pout factory is operating at only 65 percent of its capacity. To expand production, SISCOMA has actively sought new markets throughout West Africa. In 1973, exports surpassed 45 percent of the turn over. They have since increased considerably:

TABLE 26

SISCOMA EXPORTS (IN CFA)

	1973	1976
Cameroun		583,292
Dahomey	4,329,685	3,822,270
Gambia	13,058,318	74,462,502
Guinea Bissau		621,950
Ivory Coast	72,516,125	245,492,750
Mali	68,575,550	17,324,402
Mauritania	9,720,000	16,393,184
Niger	39,618	34,315,745
Upper Volta	23,235,288	51,380,745

Sales within Senegal have almost quadrupled since 1973, the 3 billion CFA mark having been attained in 1976. However, SISCOMA has been hurt by the establishment of a rival firm in the Ivory Coast, which is making inroads into the Sahelian market. In addition, it faces competition from French firms, particularly the Mouzon Frères Sociéte of Paris, which have pioneered work on animal-drawn toolbars. In general, the approach has been to meet the farmers' needs at the lowest cost with a skid-mounted tool which can be used for all basic field work. A more versatile and sophisticated toolbar is mounted on rubber tires which makes it usable for transport and cart work on any surface. The basic toolbar consists of a main frame on either skids or wheels, four tool clamps, two cart brackets, and a combined box spanner and tommy bar. To this basal structure, the following attachments can be fitted: a steerable toolbar, a moldboard plow, a ridger, four 13 and 25 cm center shares, a seeder, a groundnut lifter, and four sping tines for weeding. By putting the toolbar in the in-work position, a locally made cart platform can be mounted on the cart brackets and tongue. Five toolbar systems manufactured or assembled by SISCOMA dominate the Senegalese market. SISCOMA also successfully markets seed planters, cultivating and weeding implements, threshing and harvesting equipment, winnowing, cleaning, grinding, and other processing machines, farm carts, and wagons.

As with other catchalls, intermediate technology should not arouse unrealistic expectations. However, it may well be the long overlooked link between the residual agricultural techniques and implements in developing countries and the modern, often inapplicable agricultural innovations of the developed countries. Victor Lateef states:

> There is a significant missing link in the agricultural developmental levels of many West African states. Such a link would consist of simply and inexpensively designed implements which could increase output, speed, convenience, efficiency in time, cost and effort, and offer the progressive farmer a more satisfactory option.[22]

In Senegal, considerable effort has been channeled into the harnessment of intermediate technology to intensify agricultural production. The results, albeit marred by the Sahelian drought, are encouraging.

Millet and sorghum production in Senegal have been increasing again in recent years with the subsiding of the Sahelian drought, surpassing peak pre-drought production figures. In 1972-73, millet and sorghum production reached a nadir of 322,000 metric tons. Crop production data for 1974-75 was only recently confirmed by the Ministry of Rural Development and Hydrology at an unprecedented 795,045 metric tons. The national average yield per hectare rose to 689 kg. compared to 460 kg. in 1963. Groundnut production increased from 674,878 metric tons in 1973-74 to 994,222 metric tons in 1974-75. Rice production almost doubled from 64,340 metric tons in 1973-74 to 116,975 metric tons in 1974-75.

Even with the climatic vagaries taken into account, much of these increases in crop production levels can be attributed to the introduction of improved technological inputs in the country's agricultural sector. Agricultural implements in

1974-75 were estimated by the Ministry of Rural Development and Hydrology to total up to 67,271 items including 16,478 seeders, 26,140 hoes, and 12,178 plows. The 1975-75 inventory represents a 16.5 percent increase in volume over the 1973-74 inventory of 57,774 items. In 1974-75, there was a spectacular increase in the number of cattle being used for animal traction. Compared to the 3796 pairs of oxen being deployed in 1973-74, the number of pairs jumped to 12,936.

In 1963, before the intensification program got underway, fertilizer consumption was very meager for groundnuts and non-existant for millet. In 1974-75, distribution of fertilizers for both peanut and millet was fairly widespread, and registered substantial increases over the previous growing season. Fertilizers for peanuts rose from 19,930 metric tons in 1973-74 to 28,639 metric tons in 1974-75. Fertilizers for millet rose from 13,143 metric tons in 1973-74 to 24,908 tons in 1974-75. Total fertilizer consumption for all crops rose from 49,096 metric tons in 1973-74 to 62,845 metric tons in 1974-75, or a 28 percent increase. Pesticides also rose in consumption from 68 metric tons in 1973-74 to 108 metric tons in 1974-75.

The limits of appropriate technology are detailed by Harvey Brooks.[23] Unfortunately, many proponents of labor-intensive technology in the developing countries overlook a very important dimension of the labor situation in rural areas -- namely the sociology of the division of labor. The brunt of labor requirements in Sahelian food production systems falls on the members of the extended family. In grain production, the planting cycle affects family members as follows: _clearing the land_ is done by boys and young men; _in planting_, men make holes, women plant seed -- often women are responsible for selection of seed; _weeding_, which is the most labor-demanding part of grain farming, calls for mobilizing the whole family; _harvesting_ too means that every available person must lend a helping hand; and, finally, _threshing_ -- a woman's job, followed on a daily basis with pounding into flour, a gruelling process consuming two to three hours.

Of course children should be freed for school, wives should not be driven so hard, and even the poorest unemployed usually have their own small parcels of land to cultivate. In technology assessment, greater care must be taken in investigating the specific family and sex role responsibilities of target groups. Mellor encapsulates the problem well:

> The small farmer earns his income more from the labor of his family than from his small piece of land -- he is thus a cross between a landless laborer and a landlord, but weighted towards the laborer. It is for this reason that the labor intensity of farming is so important to the small farmer, and it is here that important interactions occur

with other elements of development strategy.[24]

New advanced technologies that appear out of place in the traditional settings of Third World villages can contribute to a "prise de conscience" that progress is possible by breaking out of the vicious circle of "nothing ever changes here." Progress means not just changing, but changing for the better. Thus, while "imbalance" in economic development, "lack of integration" in research and development, and "fragmentation" in policy making have distinguished proponents including Hirschman, Burton Klein and William Meckling, and Charles E. Lindblom respectively, the value of spontaneity in the face of new, often unique circumstances does not alter the very real limits of informal, unstructured approaches to development. Moreover, these limits are directly related to the level of development and, in the Sahel, which I have argued is undeveloped, the snags, tensions, and difficulties that hamper development require patient, concerted effort, in addition to occasional spurts and jolts.

TOWARD A SAHELIAN SCIENCE POLICY

A "science" policy (which really means a technology policy) is important to the Sahel for several reasons. A sound science policy with regional observance could contribute to environmental equilibrium. Such a policy and the bureaucratic apparatus required for its implementation could increase the diffusion of science and technology in the region. It could also reverse the typical situation where attention is focused on the sophisticated technological needs of modern industry to the neglect of traditional technologies that are central to the welfare of the poor.

From the standpoint of those engaged in the advanced sector a progressive integrated development strategy involves a conversion of the capital flow into technologies with a lower capital to labor proportion, on the average, than their present level. However, from the perspective of the majority of the labor force, which is found in the residual sector, it implies a substantial improvement in the number and value of machines and tools available. It is high time that development architects looked at the problem of technological choice through the optic of the poor rather than through that of the well-off.

This trying shortcoming reflects an extension of a gap in national policies and priorities. Those developing countries which have devoted the greatest attention to their science policies have focused on the technological needs of modern industry. Brazil, Korea, India, and Algeria, for example, have developed integrated national policies designed to build local technological capability in industrial sub-sectors considered critical to their economic development, e.g., steel, aircraft, petrochemicals, electronics, and nuclear power. These policies define sub-sectoral goals and derivative strategies for the mobilization and mastery of technology, as well as for scientific and technological research needed to keep that technology up-to-date. In contrast to these examples of science policies for modern industry, the integration of policy and technology at the national level in the pursuit of meeting the basic needs of the poor is unfortunately rare. Few developing countries have a development strategy which both calls for a direct attack on poverty and acknowledges the requirement for technology capable of providing for the needs of the poor within available budgetary resources and in a manner suitable to local conditions. The subject is correspondingly neglected in international discussions such as the North-South dialogue on technology. A stirring appeal to share technology with the poor is made by Chandra H. Soysa:

> Today it is a fact that technological responses to national and even global resources are in the hands of small groups who, both at the national and international level, control these resources to satisfy a demand pattern created in their own interests and who thereby prevent the technological participation of the masses in the exploitation of these resources. Since the nature and extent of a country's technological response to resources, and especially the quality and quantum of the participation within it, are central to self-reliant social and economic progress, it is essential to improve the technological capability of these masses, so that they may achieve, by an integrated and dynamic response to their resources, technological participation in achieving the human and social development which they seek.[25]

In the early 1970s, leaders of developing countries began to emphasize the key role played by technology in industrial development and in related programs for generating employment and expanding trade. Their stated goal, as expressed in the Declaration of Lima, was to increase their share of the world's output of manufactured goods to at least 25 percent by the year 2000. Growing interest in technology for industrialization coincides with the firmly held belief among many policy makers in developing countries that industrialization is a precondition of national economic well-being, adequate employment, and national autonomy. While it is possible to question the validity of such a generalization on analytical grounds (for example, in a developing country with strong comparative advantage in world markets for mineral or agricultural products), the belief itself is sufficiently rooted in the economic history of the presently industrialized countries as to stand beyond challenge. Hence, the logic that technology will foster industrialization, increase employment, and stimulate trade, leading to improved economic well-being has become a dominant intellectual theme in Third World public policy circles. Indeed, the critical interface between technology and development has snowballed into a key issue in the North-South Dialogue. Orville Freeman goes further: "Technology in the broadest sense -- including material, managerial, marketing, organizational and other skills, as well as advanced technical information such as secret know-how -- is at the heart of the difference between developed and developing countries."[26]

Economic growth through import substitution -- the thrust of which is to make domestic manufacturing profitable -- is a policy that must be embarked upon cautiously in the Sahel. The region's economy would have to absorb tremendous transactions costs if this policy was pursued zealously, as well as a significant opportunity cost: the danger that such a thrust will cripple on-going agricultural development. Moreover, the scarcity of skilled management and labor contributes to the inefficiency of industrialization. Expatriate managers and technicians who benefit from a high salary and wage structure, a holdover from colonialism, increase the cost of industrial production.

Science policy for the mobilization of technology to social objectives calls for a difficult meshing of measures designed to stimulate and diffuse technological change, with policies which direct these changes toward desirable social goals. This process is not simply a matter of technology transfer, on the one hand, and the development of indigenous capacity, on the other. Rather, it is a complex process involving technology suppliers, technology users, and a variety of intermediary institutions, all acting in response to inventions and within constraints set by a wide range of government policies, many of which were adopted for reasons having little to do with technology. In the Sahel, as with most developing countries, communication is lacking among relevant participants: enterprise managers and engineers in the productive sector (publicly or privately owned), officials of operating government agencies, planners, makers of economic policy, banks, makers of technology policy, managers of scientific and technological institutions and of engineering firms. The application of science and technology to social goals has ramifications far beyond science policy and involves issues not usually considered in discussions of the subject at the national, let alone the international level. For example, it often requires substantial reforms in the policies of financial institutions and those rendering essential services such as water, education, health, and extension, as well as attention to needs of the so-called "informal sector," with which formal technological institutions generally have little contact.

Kuznets stresses the need for structural shifts to result from the interplay of technological and social change: "Even if the impulse to growth is provided by a major technological innovation, the societies that adopt it must modify their preexisting structure."[27] In other words, the mere possession of N automobiles per capita or electrification of the hinterland has no inherent significance as an indicator of genuine development. Indeed, there is something cosmetic about Third World showplace communities boasting all the modern amenities; conceptual and social change often exhibits profundity comparable to the new corrugated tin roofs. The dismantlement of the residual paradigm cannot, even with the most vigorous exposure, hope to be total. While this is normatively a dubious objective since there is usually much in the residual paradigm that is culturally valuable, as we have argued earlier, ambitious attempts to bring about change can lead to the dominance of the polarity of over exposure.

Appropriate technology, on any scale, is technology that can be understood, implemented, used and maintained by local people using locally available supplies. It may involve a sophisticated idea, thoughtfully developed and applied by means of simple procedures and readily available materials. Though perhaps technical in the sense that it has been designed by skilled specialists, it is appropriate in that it used local materials and is readily understood and maintained by its users. This is not to suggest that "grass-roots technology " is the only type of technology appropriate for developing countries. Appropriateness is determined by taking into account a mix of factors, including needs, projected energy expenditures, social and political constraints, available resources of money and labor, possible benefits and drawbacks, unintended consequences, and often the unique circumstances of the particular situation.

Not all forms of Western technology should be adopted without modification to suit the needs of a particular developing country. Where adaptation is impossible or too costly, indigenous innovation would be encouraged. Many in the developing countries forget that, by and large, technological innovations in the industrialized countries were realized in what can be described as a "continuous flow consisting of a sequence of acts of insight which leads to a cumulative synthesis of individually small elements."[28]

A similar analysis has been made of technological change in Japan:

> If Japan's experience teaches any single lesson regarding the process of economic development in Asia, it is the cumulative importance of myriads of relatively simple improvements in technology which do not depart radically from tra-

dition or require large units of new investment.[29]

The Sahelian countries have the beginnings of a science and technology network. Most of these institutions have shown of late a strong interest in the area of appropriate goods and/or appropriate technologies rather than on frontier science-related activities. This redeployment of resources should be stimulated with outside funds to encourage a truly regional approach to the planning and setting of R & D objectives and decisions. To codify this necessary divorce from the statist model of R & D as a national enterprise, the Sahel requires a coherent regional science policy, that places emphasis on indigènous S & T capability and more vigorous R & D networking.

I have observed elsewhere that the extent and effectiveness of research and development to fit technologies to local circumstances is likely to be meager without extensive participation by local research and development institutions.[30] They are also essential to permit much use of outside scientific and technological talent, findings, and experience in finding solutions for local use. Local research and development institutions are among the most effective "gate-keepers" through which these external technological resources can flow to local users and through which local experience can flow out to other developing countries.

Experience has accumulated in recent years, primarily in agriculture but also in other fields, with systems for research and development collaboration among organizations that are doing research and related knowledge dissemination on a worldwide basis. These research and development networks concentrate on problem-solving in a discrete and widely pervasive problem area. They are characterized by voluntary, self-selecting participation, by organizations that are private or public, national or international (but not by governments as such), in whatever collaborative activities they find useful. They form a common pool of research and development results to which all participants contribute, based on the types of work that they want to do and are able to do for their own purposes, and from which all may draw for local adaptation, as needed to fit their own situations. The stimulus for the network's operations is provided by one or several of the more advanced participating organizations performing functions essential for this purpose, such as leadership in organizing collaborative programs or projects, logistical support, and information or materials management services. Although the research collaboration in such networks follows the traditional pattern of voluntary cooperation among scientists or organizations sharing common interests, the collaboration in the newly-emerging agricultural research network tends to be more extensive, systematic, and sustained than the casual and intermittent international research collaboration that has existed in the past.

Such networks foster increased research specialization and divisions of labor that could enhance the rate of progress of research and development on global problems. Appropriate divisions of labor permit economies of scale by concentrating much of the more expensive and difficult types of research at facilities that can serve international needs, particularly the needs of developing countries. The networks can provide both developed and developing worlds with access to worldwide scientific and technological capabilities far beyond anything that they could provide or organize for themselves on a country-by-country basis.

CONCLUSION

Mellor has remarked that agricultural production conditions in low-income countries are characterized by wide variation -- variation from conditions in high-income countries and great variation within their own agricultural programs. It happens, however, that most low-income countries are located in the tropics, whereas most high-income countries are situated in temperate latitudes. Differences in temperature, rainfall regime, length of day, and differences in soils contribute to low applicability of innovation developed for high-income temperate agricultures to those of the tropics. Further compounding the problem, economic differences in capital-labor cost ratios and capital-land cost ratios inhibit the transfer of agricultural technology from one set of conditions to another. And as if these formidable obstacles do not suffice, cultural differences in regard to work habits, attitudes, and consumption patterns, needless to say, also exert appreciable influence on the choice of the appropriate technology. Vernon W. Ruttan concludes:

> It might be argued, for example, that the dominance of the developed countries in science and technology raises the cost, or even precludes the possibility, of the invention of location-specific biological and mechanical technologies adapted to the resource endowments of a particular country or region. This argument has been made primarily with reference to the diffusion of mechanical technology from the developed to the developing countries. It is argued that the pattern of organization of agricultural production adopted by the more developed countries-dominated by the large scale mechanized systems of production employed in both the socialist and non-socialist economies-precludes an effective role for an agricultural system based on small scale commercial or semi-commercial farm production units.[31]

At the U.N. Desertification Conference held in Nairobi, the United States made an offer to consider requests for up to 1,000 Peace Corps volunteers to be placed at host country request in reforestation, arid land management, and local community education in anti-desertification efforts. This offer was repeated by Mary E.King, Deputy Director of Action (Peace Corps)before a Club du Sahel meeting in Paris on October 12, 1977. Subsequently, in Caracas, Venezuela, President Carter affirmed:

> To become more self-reliant developing nations need to strengthen their technological capabilities. To assist them, I am proposing a United States Foundation for Technological Collaboration. Through private and public foundations and through our increasing participation in the United Nations Conferences, we can make technical and scientific cooperation a key element in our relationship.

These overtures by the United States could address critical needs in the Sahel and might have maximum impact by consolidation into a technology corps. This would differ in focus from the suggestion for a technology corps for Latin America, where such a corps would function primarily to search and negotiate for foreign technology.[32] Instead, the more traditional Peace Corps orientation would be explicitly directed toward technology diffusion. The need for this kind of extension effort will grow as a corpus of appropriate technologies are developed and adapted to developing areas as a result of the attention this subject is now receiving. Formation of a technology corps should stem from a recognition that the impact of science and technology is not "ipso facto" a beneficial one and that much turns on the way new technologies are introduced to the target community. Foreign aid donors must demonstrate greater sensitivity to the linkage between technology transfer and income distribution. Technological choice can make an important contribution to narrowing internal income gaps.[33]

Failure to develop an integrated approach to this challenge probably represents one of the more striking examples of a mistaken impression concerning the extent to which foreign technology could be transferred to developing world conditions. We have now moved to the other extreme. All too often the existing culture and values are seen as absolute blocks to the diffusion and acceptance of innovation. This is a logical conclusion to draw if one assumes a large stock of unutilized innovation. However, a more careful look suggests that the study of culture and conceptual tectonics might better be directed at finding the features which lend themselves to innovation and diffusion of innovation. Many innovations have spread rapidly. Why? Little research has been directed at this question. Too often the question has been why did innovation not spread and the obvious answer that it was unprofitable was often overlooked. This is not to encourage an equally dangerous misapprehension -- that any profitable innovation will spread rapidly. The consequence may be neglect of the ways in which existing cultures and institutions may be used to facilitate the more rapid spread of innovation. Again, the influence of foreign aid donors, combined with inadequate information may lead to inappropriate advice and pressure.

Technology development that takes place through a series of "accidents" may result in successful diffusion if the innovation happens to coincide with an existing demand. But such results are rare and serendipitous. Other consequences are more frequent: (1) the new development is aborted early, or (2) the innovator has to engage in a marketing push to recover his investments, or, most seriously of all, (3) the users make inappropriate choices for want of known alternatives. These mishaps are commonplace in the commercial market, and their effects on both producers and consumers are often cited as flaws in the economic system. To the extent that competition eventually offers correctives to distorted demand-supply relationships, not much is lost by these innovative failures. But these correctives are usually not available for "public" goods like agricultural technology, health delivery systems, or educational services. In developing countries, especially in situations where government decisions replace market choices even regarding "private" goods, the luxury of "inappropriate" technology is a serious drain on available resources.

Current criticism of "inappropriate technologies" has supplied us with an inventory of these costs: unemployment; underemployment; people deprived of health care and schooling because the delivery systems are unable to serve them; irrigated farms producing one crop a year instead of two or three because water is distributed wastefully or inequitably; and enclave high-technology industries producing subsidized goods for export when the domestic market is undersupplied with essentials. With a considered science policy, government resources can adjust the decisions that lead to these distortions. The emergent science policies of both developed and developing countries should encourage collaborative ventures that meet a mutual benefits criterion, as when joint efforts reflect a special concern for the problems of the very poor.[34] By the same token, the demand for advanced technologies in many sectors of developing country life, e.g., population control and preventive health measures, is great and suggests the need for liberalizing the basic human needs strategy in foreign assistance and the desirability of allocating greater resources to front-end science and technology which, in many cases, may be deemed terribly appropriate. Moreover, where these technologies are "inappropriate," the opportunity costs that are typically cited may be exaggerated. To a surprising extent, it is the introduction of new, iconoclastic technologies which make the social change possible that permits, even necessitates, institution building. However, a relevant radicalism does not imply the need to resort to drastic solutions.

It does not appear that any of the conventional energy sources (with the possible exception of a vigorous and costly increase in hydroelectric development efforts) will have significant impact on the availability of energy and, therefore, on productivity, quality of life, or environmental deterioration in rural parts of the Sahel between now and the end of the century. If conventional sources are lacking is it possible to gain more useable energy from the wind, sunshine, flowing water, wood, and organic wastes that are available either within or near the villages themselves? Such a prospect is obviously appealing, particularly now that solar and other renewable energy forms are receiving considerable attention throughout the world. But is it realistic for the villages of the Sahel?

Small-scale technologies have been developed and used in the Sahel, with notable successes as well as some failures. Solar water pumps, which are successfully in use in a dozen locations in Africa (and in a number of other developing countries in Latin America and Asia), were first developed in Senegal with French cooperation. Recent applications of ancient Cretan windmill designs to local materials (with use of some modern parts) have allowed the introduction of irrigation in the Gambia. And in Niger, solar-charged batteries have been successfully powering school television sets in remote villages since 1968. In contrast, American-type fan windmills have been installed in some areas and then abandoned, sometimes because diesel pumps proved cheaper and more reliable, but more often because no one was trained to maintain them and no effort was made to make replacement parts available. Several attempts to introduce biogas digesters or solar cookers have also failed, again due to lack of sustained maintenance, and often because the technology or device simply did not "fit" into the local culture or economy. Generally, it seems that these unsuccessful attempts have been due more to inadequate or inappropriate transfer processes than to failures in the technologies themselves. Therefore, it is imperative that advances in the technical development of small-scale devices be matched by similar progress in the ability of governments or donor agencies to effectively introduce or transfer the technologies to particular communities.

If small-scale technologies prove suitable and adequate to meet a substantial portion of the Sahel's growing energy needs, it would be a development breakthrough on the scale of the Green Revolution. It would suggest that rural Africa and other developing areas could by-pass substantial investments in an obsolescing fossil-fuel economy, and thereby move into a world of twenty-first century energy sources ahead of the industrialized countries, which are largely entrapped by their existing conventional fossil-fuel investments and infrastructure.

Admittedly, this is today only optimistic speculation. Some devices, such as solar water pumps or wind generators are unlikely (at least within a strict financial analysis) to prove to be economical in the immediate future, although their prospects in the longer run seem promising. We can be almost certain however that some small-scale technologies, such as more efficient wood-burning stoves and charcoal kilns will prove to merit widespread dissemination now. Wind-powered water pumps, solar water distillers, and methane gas generators may already be economically viable in many situations. But the primary criterion in evaluating for small-scale (and conventional) technologies should be the extent to which each technology, or mix of technologies, can be incorporated into total rural development programs to improve quality of life, productivity, and environmental quality. With a concerted village test program, Sahelian governments -- and those of other developing countries -- might well find that they have available, within the next several years, a major boost in energy for their developement efforts.

8 The Administration of Development

Walt Rostow's Stages of Economic Growth epitomizes the "big push" theory. It is interesting to note that the metaphors of this school of thought are drawn from aeronautics and the space age. Once an aircraft has taken off into the air, it is much easier for it to continue in serene flight than it was to take off and gain altitude, as is the case with a rocket that has secured its orbit. What this school underestimates in its understandable impatience to get the show on the road, is the enormous and complex support system that thereafter monitors, regulates, and otherwise back-stops the pilot and his crew or the lone astronaut, who would be rendered helpless without the invisible umbilical cord which links him in the void of space to the earth.

The Sahelian governments have decided that it is their duty -- and one that cannot be shirked -- to initiate and foster that "growth perspective" which Hirschman has maintained is the one "sine qua non" for successful economic development. However, they are discovering that growth in itself is sterile and bears fruit only when assisted by a great number of changes -- structural, behavioral, technological, and organizational changes. They have learned that development cannot be reduced to a mere quantitative phenomenon, the scarcity of productive resources, any more than the growth of developed countries can be considered a simple question of capital accumulation. On the eve of the Third Development Decade, it is appropriate to examine the central qualitative factors that fall under the rubric of administration and that play an important part in the growth process of the Sahelian countries.

It is becoming increasingly evident that the effectiveness of foreign aid depends upon the efficiency of recipient governments. One of the essential features distinguishing the present-day context of development from that of pre-industrial Europe is the dominant influence which the state is capable of exerting on the evolution of the growth process with the result of economic inhibition or acceleration, according to the trends of development policy and the nature of government intervention. The state is now in the business of outlining comprehensive plans, often indicative and sometimes imperative. Thus, it defines the macro-economic and social aims, establishes priorities in sectors or regions, regulates imports and stimulates exports, selects investments, determines the setting up, the management and the objectives of various enterprises through its social, its tariff and taxation policies, etc. It acts more and more like an entrepreneur itself.

Political power and decision making in the Sahelian countries are highly centralized. The exercise of political power by government elites is constrained in some cases, e.g., in Mauritania, by influential traditional religious or ethnic leaders. Fiscal power is also highly centralized and local government units have little control over the use of revenues collected in their own jurisdictions. The net effect of the concentration of political and fiscal power is that the organizational and budgetary means for independent local action are extremely limited.

The failure to develop a system of farm credit is a special case in point of the weakness of monetary institutions. Institutional production credit, i.e., credit from sources other than family, friends, or merchants, is generally only available on a year to year basis from regional development organizations that deduct charges for operating capital from the price due the producer when he turns over his export crop to the official marketing agent. This system of seasonal farm production credit provides no opportunities for farmers to deposit savings in interest bearing accounts for subsequent investment in productive activities. Institutions such as official marketing boards which could serve farmers interests have become instruments for centralized crop collection and storage, debt collection for credit, and agricultural taxation. Marketing boards and government sponsored cooperatives serve mainly to extract a marketable surplus of export crops such as groundnuts and cotton from rural areas. Very little of the revenues or exchange earnings from the export of primary commodities has been reinvested in rural areas. Marketing boards and state cooperatives have been the prime movers behind the formation of cooperatives not farmers and herders organized at the grass-root levels.

The rampant military intrusiveness and take-overs of Sahelian governing processes derives in part from the organizational inadequacies of civilian regimes. Government problem-solving capacity is weak in the Sahel, seriously impairing socioeconomic development given the leadership role the state is striving to assume. This is a lacuna which, unlike the scarcity of foreign exchange or investment, cannot be overcome by foreign aid and to which aid donors cannot afford to be impervious.

The administrative machinery in the Sahelian countries is geared for limited public works functions. During the colonial period, most senior positions and key appointments were held by foreigners, many of whom have remained after independence. The extent of administrative evolution and the degree of development of indigenous educational and training institutions varied with different colonies, but in all cases it was inadequate for the responsibilities to come. A higher ratio of civil servants is found today in those countries that experienced outside domination longest. In 1978, Senegal had 100 civil servants per 10,000 inhabitants compared with 27 in Mali and 24 in Niger. Perhaps the greatest shortcoming of Sahelian bureacracies is their dearth of technical-oriented personnel. In an earlier epoch, the colonized were expected to go to the "metropole" for higher education and almost invariably pursued a liberal arts education. This trend continues into the present. The education imparted by the universities, especially in Western Europe, is still highly non-technical and prepares, to use an immediately relevant example, for economic analysis rather than for the methodical programming of actions in terms of decisions and long-range expenditures. This causes many inconsistencies between planning and implementation. When Sahelian governments saddle themselves with large-scale public sector development programs and extensive regulation of the private sector, inevitably delays and dislocations occur.

The operations of official marketing agencies, regional development organizations, and government sponsored cooperatives have discouraged the development of rural associations such as cooperatives that would give small farmers and herders a greater voice in the management of their own affairs. Aside from traditional social organizations, only a few local participatory institutions have emerged that would help ensure access by small farmers and herders to productive assets and promote a more equitable distribution of the benefits and costs of economic change. Local administrative and planning capabilities required to make producer associations effective are also weak.

Despite the seriousness of these political, administrative, and institutional constraints to accelerating growth and reducing poverty, some positive changes are in evidence. These include:

- the Senegalese Administrative Reform in which political and fiscal power and much of the responsibility for providing social services are being devolved to local government units;

- the establishment of rural communities also in Senegal that are intended to reach a larger target group in food and export crop production than the existing regional development organizations;

- the development of livestock producers associations in The Gambia and Niger for the management of herds and common grazing land;

- the rise of cooperative associations of women in The Gambia and elsewhere for the production and marketing of vegetable products; and

- broadened mandates of the regional development organizations to include providing inputs and information for food crop production in addition to export crop responsibilities.

The question of how development administration intersects with the Sahelian hinterland poses the follow-up question of what alternative management structures are available? Options are constrained by time limits. For while the long-term development program in the Sahel aims at the year 2000 as its horizon, some fundamental changes will be undertaken in the agricultural production systems of the area within the next decade. Plainly, a cadre of civil servants oriented toward rural areas must be turned out. Shear states:

> We must look at the village as the delivery vehicle in greater detail. Using the village as the principal channel for development programs will give us a safeguard against some of the dangers of the macro-planning which has taken place at the national level and sometimes even outside of the Sahel itself..... The proposed approach through the village has three primary advantages. First, it utilizes the existing, responsive, administrative structure at the local level. Secondly, it avoids the creation of large government bureaucracy with the resulting high continuing costs for its maintenance. Third, it assures sensitivity to local conditions which would be impossible if the program were primarily administered from the capital city. This is critical to the creation of an evaluation system so essential for the success of any long-term program which includes the need for relative ease of obtaining information feedback.[1]

It has been observed, paradoxical as it might sound, that many administrators in Third World countries, where poverty is all-pervasive, do not know enough about the poor.[2] Usually the administrators come from urban elites; the rural poor, who are ignorant of the ways of the city dwellers, generally hesitate to come forward to seek the assistance which administrators and their organizations are supposed to provide. This administrator-people gap partially explains why the package of welfare and development services meant for the poor is not always delivered to them and often ends up benefiting segments of society that are relatively well off.

The low priority assigned to rural development in the past has tended to produce both a scarcity of trained manpower for development jobs in the rural areas and attitudinal and behavioral patterns among the city-bred administrators which are wholly out of tune with the new directions in which these societies need to move. However, there is a growing awareness that all-round social and economic progress is to a large extent dependent on the efficient day-to-day management of development policies and programs, particularly at the grassroots level, and that administrative capability can be built up fairly quickly and at a modest cost by carefully planned training programs. Increasingly, appraisal reports on rural development projects prepared by international aid agencies and other funding insitutions now clearly specify, usually in a separate appendix at the end of the document, the training needs of the staff to be engaged on various assignments and the ways in which these must be met.

It is necessary to prepare qualified managers and administrators to serve at all levels throughout the government structures of the Sahelian countries. Unless this basic manpower requirement is addressed at the provincial and local government levels, as well as in the capital cities, it will be difficult to improve substantially the existing development efforts and it will be impossible to carry out with any degree of effectiveness expanded development programs.

Sahelian students overseas are one obvious source of potential recruitment for qualified managers and administrators -- students presently enrolled as well as students who have failed to return following the completion of their programs. While undoubtedly a substantial number of these students and former students are and have completed liberal arts and law programs, it is also true that world-wide a large percentage of graduates in these areas form a substantial core of the administrative cadre. In the Sahel, their utilization and effectiveness could be greatly enhanced by appropriate "topping up" in administrative training which could be included in or following their degree programs.

Within most Sahelian countries there are, in addition to university programs, institutes of administration (National Schools of Administration), with degrees comparable to B.A. university degrees, which seek to meet the civil service manpower needs of their respective countries. Unfortunately, these institute and university programs rarely concern themselves with middle- and lower-level administrative manpower requirements and grossly neglect the requirements of those who serve at provincial, municipal, and rural levels of government. A crucial need in all Sahelian countries is to provide administrative training programs in interior areas which will not only seek to educate and train but which will also serve as vehicles for provincial levels of government officials.

A profound administrative problem is that inputs into the decision-making system flow almost uniquely downward from the central government with little chance given to provincial government units to inject into the system anything more substantive than responses to central government demands. Therefore, problems which do not fit on central government forms are often not considered. In a situation where more rapid development is occurring in rural areas (and where increasing numbers of problems will not fit on forms), it is imperative that provincial bureaucracies be better qualified to handle their own problems, that the central bureaucracy be able to handle the new inputs which will be generated in rural areas, and that the central government officials become aware of problems, processes, and personalities outside of the capital city.

A program of in-service training seminars in provincial towns was designed by AID for Chad and may prove to be a useful model for other Sahelian countries.[3] Intensive courses have been conducted examining provincial and local administrative management problems, and a number of the course presentations are being given by faculty from the capital city as well as by qualified government officials who teach on a part-time basis. In addition to up-grading administrative officials in the interior, this program has exposed central government officials and professors from universities and institutes to administrative realities in rural areas. None of these training programs has taken persons from the rural areas into the capital city -- even when courses have been structured to last as long as three months. Training conducted at provincial sites has the added advantage of enhancing concern over improper administration practices there and might also provide for better contacts and understanding between the provincial capitals and their outlying regions. The cost of provincial in-service training programs in Chad from 1977 through 1980 is estimated at $600,000. It is assumed that costs in other Sahelian countries would be comparable.

The shortcomings in matters of organization and of politico-administrative structure are in no way surprising, considering that even the most highly developed countries are only beginning to apply modern methods of organization and management. Yet, one might add parenthetically, managerial crutches like zero-based budgeting are no substitute for good administration or decisive leadership. Nevertheless, the shortcomings of the executive in terms of efficiency and expertise are undoubtedly more alarming and more costly in the Sahelian countries. Errors in economic policy, inconsistency, and waste are considerably more harmful since the level of development is lower and the national income smaller. Furthermore, the utilization of technical assistance personnel is not an entirely satisfactory remedy to problems of structure and organization. Foreign experts are, as a rule, either advisers without any real commanding responsibility or subcontractors for technical and limited tasks (preparation of investment projects, etc.) -- the administrative organization and the process of decision-making largely escape their influence.

At times foreign aid may even increase the lack of "executive capacity" in the developing countries. Donor operations are more frequently connected with individual projects than with programs and tend to neglect the key problem of direct and indirect administrative costs. However, the general thrust of these remarks calls for qualification. Surely, the pursuit of strict economic consistency at the interdepartmental level is too ambitious an aim for most of the Sahelian countries including those which, professing a certain degree of economic liberalism, limit state intervention to a strict minimum. Even the most highly developed countries, including the United States, have up to this day been unable to meet the whole set of requirements -- information, personnel, methodology, structure -- for setting up a system of planning-programming-budgeting at the federal government level. That is why the Sahelian countries, even more than the developed countries, must proceed by stages.

It is futile to wish to coordinate the policies and actions of ministerial departments and governmental agencies as long as they are themselves unable to cope with their own problems. It will be well to begin by improving the work at the departmental level and to endow the departments with good decision-making structures. Ambitious, big-push type efforts to realize development administration objectives, more often than not overload the bureaucracy. An evolutionary approach to development makes good sense in many ways, including administration. At the nuts and bolts level symbolized by the development project, Uma Lele states:

> It cannot be overemphasized, however, that at initial stages project expansion must take place at a slower pace than has been the case in the projects reviewed. Thus, considerable attention can be devoted to understanding the rural social structure and the role that it can play and gradually to delegating genuine responsibility of administration to local organizations. Such a participatory, as distinct from a paternalistic, approach to development seems critical for the long-term viability of rural development programs beyond the stage of donor involvement.[4]

The organized experience afforded by development projects can fructify over time in closer intrasocietal ties. This positive "side-effect" illustrates a development truism: it is through effective "modi operandi" and appropriate intervals for the achievement of socioeconomic objectives as much as the actual acheivement of the objectives -- that people experience meaningful development. In other words, the means are as important as the ends. The preoccupation with "results," has detracted from our understanding of the full implications of the process. Indirect benefits, external economies, spillovers, linkages are terms that denote secondary effects which, in reality, may be of primary importance.

The necessity of proceeding by stages also derives from the need for adaptation of policy and structures to the movement and change in society, as it passes at local levels from poverty, and a traditional adaptation to poverty, towards greater individual prosperity and a stronger cash-economy. It is seen as a transition from necessary and multiple intervention by government to break the vicious circle of dependence and powerlessness to a condition where the farmer, in his greater security, can choose among the richer variety of services which a richer economy can offer, and thus cope more independently with farm-management. The most difficult part of this transition, as an administrative problem, is the earliest stage, where government, often weak in personnel and, in the context of a poor society, has to assume the maximum task. For in these early stages even the agencies which later on will share that task -- cooperatives, local government -- are composed either of the weak and poor for whom the help is needed, or of the rich and powerful, whose position often stands in the way of wider progress.

Moving too fast too soon can lead to the resistance associated with the polarities of over exposure and double exposure. By the same token, there are those who argue that abrupt change is more likely to take since opposition is not given a chance to build up in time to arrest the flow of transformation. Although it is not always appropriate to generalize from the experience of one country, the Senegalese attempt to accelerate economic growth by increasing administrative and political efficiency is instructive.

BLAZING THE WAY FOR POPULAR PARTICIPATION

The task of hurdling the more mundane obstacles to Senegal's national development as outlined by the Twenty-five Year Plan were left to Senghor's lieutenant and prime minister, Mamadou Dia. These included reforming the commercial structure which had created the country's dependence on private interests linked to foreign trade; establishing guidelines for controlling production and exchange; and organizing the markets of agricultural products in order to use prices as an incentive for expanding food crops. Since Dia was an economist, he instituted radical reforms designed to curb neo-colonialism in Senegal. However, reforms of such a wide-reaching nature could not help but crystallize opposition on the part of those who profited by the former arrangement. Dia soon felt the wrath of the Senegalese elite and their European supporters. The tensions between Dia and the commercial interests led to a crisis in December 1962, which brought about the elimination of Dia as well as his position. Ironically, Dia, the Moslem, had been supported by many of the Catholic planners of Lebret's Economie et Humanisme group. He was removed by Senghor, a Catholic, who was supported by the powerful maraboutic leaders of Senegal's Moslem majority. Senghor did not abandon the Plan but he was quite willing to proceed at a slower pace. Demonstrative of his political shrewdness, he refused to support an economic revolution which appeared to be too rapid, given the strength and weight of its opponents. By clearly distinguishing his policies from "revolutionary" African leaders like Ghana's N'Krumah, Mali's Keita, and even his former lieutenant, Dia, Senghor has remained in power while each of the former succumbed to coups led by conservative forces.

To date, approximately 40,000 animators have been trained and few villages in Senegal have not been affected by the animation program. These animators have introduced intermediate technology, and they have assisted in the mobilization of volunteers for the construction of roads, schools, and dispensaries. The cooperative movement has grown to the point where over 1500 cooperatives exist at present, handling 80 percent of the country's groundnut crop. Moreover, animation has wrought profound social and psychological changes. Explaining the importance of Animation to the "African Road," Senghor holds: "The transformation of mentalities, the creation of new attitudes oriented towards progress has as its corollary the will to reorganize better than in the past. Suppressing religious and ethnic quarrels, the divisions inherited from the colonial past, the peasants discover their solidarity of destiny."[5] In his "encadrement" of the population -- a total organization and politicization of the society (even down to sports) -- Senghor has made strides in cementing Senegalese society in a bid to achieve national unity.

Prior to independence, Senegal suffered from a schism between an urban elite of a West Indies type and the peasantry. The former sought total integration with France and viewed the peasants as a constraint to French acceptance. These African Frenchmen divided themselves, left or right, on French issues not African ones. Senghor, in gearing himself to the hinterland, successfully moved the political center of gravity to the peasant majority. Pursuing his "populist nationalism" to this day, Senghor has partially bridged the peasant/elite dichotomy in his person and by his politicization of both constituencies. While criticizing the "development without growth" status of the economy, Samir Amin acknowledges that Senghor has succeeded in creating a "strong feeling of national unity", sparing the country of the ethnic and religious problems of other African states.[6] Irving Markovitz affirms: "Senghor as political broker has been the great technician of politics. He has created and balanced great coalitions of the most diverse groups; he has emerged as the calculator of interests, the synthesizer of opposites, and the formulator of the lowest common denominator."[7]

Although the "Animation Rurale" program has been held up to the rest of the Sahel as an extension service exemplar, it suffers deficiencies that can be avoided. Perhaps more attention would be paid to the problem of running a large development brigade if the difficulties were more openly recognized and acknowledged. The need for good coordination even in a purely agricultural program -- let alone in an integrated rural development program -- seems clear enough. The small farmer needs advice (backed by research) in crop and animal husbandry; a veterinary service; improved tools associated with appropriate technology. He needs help with wells and pumps for minor irrigation, and the pumps will need credit, and before he is credit-worthy in commercial eyes. He will need an efficient distribution of seed, fertilizer, and pesticide. He will need all this advice and service in a "package," i.e., at the right time, in the necessary sequence, and without conflicting inputs from the responsible agencies.

If, added to this, the "rural development" elements -- education, health, village industries, etc. -- are thrown in as well, the task of agency coordination becomes formidable indeed. We have already mentioned subjects covered by more than half the ministries which a national government is likely to have. Plainly, these mission agencies cannot be combined into one mega - ministry, and just as clear is the need for the point of unified advice and service to be that which is most proximate to the farmer. But the animator cannot function if he gets conflicting instructions from the "district," the "department" if there is confusion at the "region" level, or the "region" if there is confusion in the capital. This is justification for the demand for better administrative coordination and greater popular participation in government.

In a lucid exposition on administrative reform in Senegal as it pertains to the rural poor, Arthur M. Fell expresses his optimism about an effort to induce popular participation via a major innovation in Senegal's political and administrative structure:

> On February 19, 1972, Law Number 72-02 of February 1, 1972 on the Organization of Territorial Administration appeared in the *Journal Officiel* of Senegal. This legislation launched a major Administrative Reform opening new possibilities for popular participation in the economic, political, and so-

> cial development of the country. Indeed, prior to the Reform, there was no structure in Senegal which permitted effective rural participation in the governmental process. Although regional assemblies existed under the former system, less than a fourth of their members were rural representatives. Moreover, Regional Assemblies only met infrequently, had minute budgets, and lacked real power.[8]

From a prudential point of view, this on-going shift in Senegal's political center of gravity could have unexpected, possibly far-reaching ramifications. The rural denizens will remain for some time to come, weak and embroiled in sorting out their various provincial equations. However, the new strategy could considerably accelerate their ascension to power. The emergent situation is characterized by a greater diffusion of power in a more complex matrix -- departing from the neatness of the bipolar (urban-rural) state. In fact, the fulcrum of power has begun to shift away from the cities to new administrative constructs not entirely of rural persuasion. This quasi-populist trend to strengthen the hand of the rural population derives from the latter's size, which continues to vastly outnumber that of the city dwellers, and to the fact that the former are politically more manageable -- particularly when their basic needs are met. The instability of the cities, on the other hand, with the endless coups, riots, and demonstrations of elites such as students and other members of the intellegentsia pose a tougher problem to get a handle on. In contrast, the relative homogeneity of the social groups populating the countryside permits a Senghor to tailor national programs that are more likely to be accepted by a rural majority. In many ways this transition is a recognition of the apocalyptic ring to Samuel P. Huntington's observation: "Urban instability is minor but universal. Rural instability, on the other hand, is major but unavoidable."[9]

The inadequacy of popular participation at all levels of government led Senghor in 1969 to commission an in-depth study on how to reorganize territorial administration in order to involve the public in areas of decision making which had previously been hermetically sealed off. In particular, there was an awareness of the need to decentralize power in budget spending. "In fact, the establishment of autonomous or self-governing communities was sometimes said to be the goal of African socialist programs. But little had been done in Senegal prior to the Administrative Reform to implement this idea outside of some early efforts by Animation Rurale to encourage greater local participation in the affairs of rural communities."[10] The five-volume study prepared for Senghor by an elite office attached to the Presidency, the Bureau of Organization and Methods (BOM) highlighted four policies: 1) "deconcentration;" 2) decentralization; 3) local participation; and 4) "regionalization" of planning. In March 1971, a working group composed of members of the BOM and concerned ministries, namely Plan, Finance, Rural Development, and Interior, set about the business of outlining a workable plan of action. The timetable for implementation of the Reform has been staggered taking effect in the last two "regions" (comparable to U.S. states) in July 1980 and July 1982. There are several reasons for phasing the Reform including the need for such prerequisites as the publication of a series of laws, decrees, and circulars, the retraining of administrative staff, and a certain amount of experimentation on a case by case basis.

In integrating technical services and popular participation at the various levels of government, the new administrative structure is decentralized and deconcentrated in comparison with the former system (see Tables 26 and 27). In each region, besides a governor, there is a Regional Council whose members are elected by indirect suffrage, one half by Departmental Councils and one half by economic groups and cooperatives. Regional Development Committees composed of representatives from technical and political cadres of the government as well as the Regional Council ensure technical inputs. The next administrative encrustation is the department (there are two or three departments per region), which is headed by a Prefet. A Department Council will now permit greater popular participation as will the Departmental Development Committee. Departments are composed of two or more arrondisements (districts) headed by a Sous-Prefet. At this level too there is a forum for popular participation, namely the District Council, whose members are elected by indirect suffrage by the Rural Community Councils. The various technical services (water and forestry, rural works, community development, and so on) staff the Centres d'Expansion Rurales (CER - Rural Extension Centers) which make available technical expertise at the district level. Finally, at the heart of the reform is the Rural Community, which is composed of several well grouped villages, ideally with a population in the vicinity of 10,000. Fell states:

> The Rural Community is administered by the Rural Council which can have between 12 and 21 members depending on the population of the Rural Community. Two thirds of the Rural Council are elected by universal suffrage and the other third consists of representatives of cooperatives active within the Rural Community. The powers and areas of activity of the Rural Community Council (RCC) are set by law and its actions are subject to approval by the Sous-Prefet. The Rural Council's areas of activity are significant within the context of local government. Most important, the Rural

Table 27 SITUATION BEFORE THE REFORM

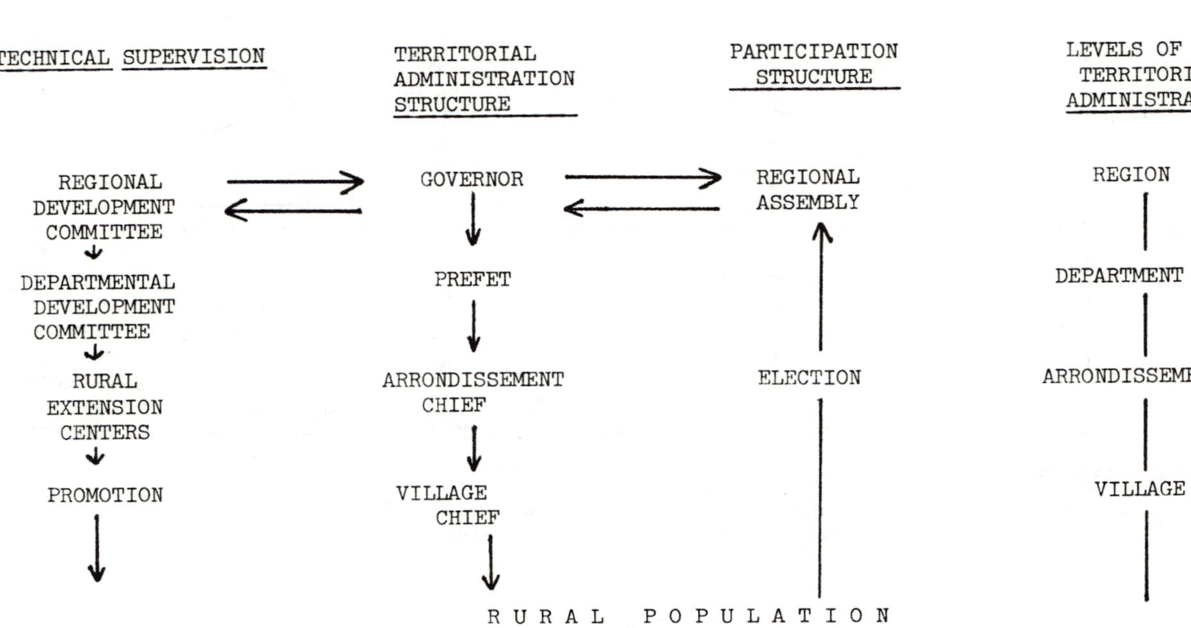
TECHNICAL SUPERVISION
TERRITORIAL ADMINISTRATION STRUCTURE
PARTICIPATION STRUCTURE
LEVELS OF THE TERRITORIAL ADMINISTRATION
REGIONAL DEVELOPMENT COMMITTEE
DEPARTMENTAL DEVELOPMENT COMMITTEE
RURAL EXTENSION CENTERS
PROMOTION
GOVERNOR
PREFET
ARRONDISSEMENT CHIEF
VILLAGE CHIEF
REGIONAL ASSEMBLY
ELECTION
REGION
DEPARTMENT
ARRONDISSEMENT
VILLAGE
RURAL POPULATION

Table 28 SITUATION AFTER THE REFORM

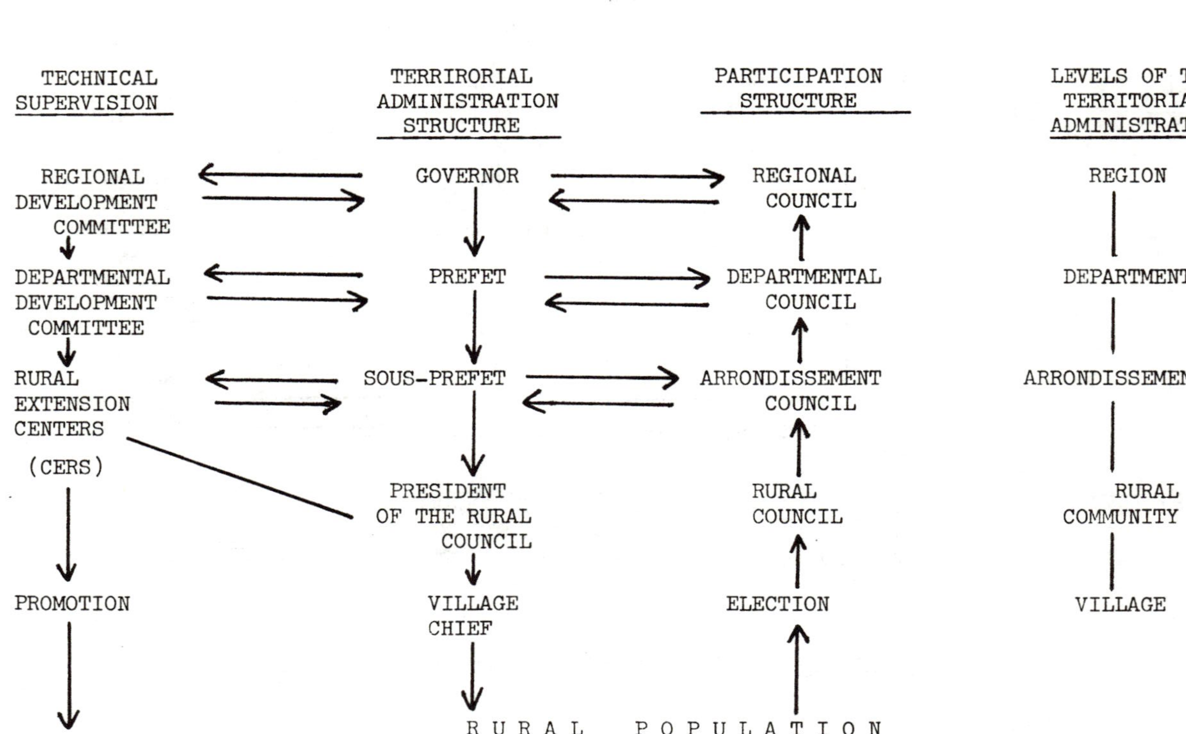
TECHNICAL SUPERVISION
TERRIRORIAL ADMINISTRATION STRUCTURE
PARTICIPATION STRUCTURE
LEVELS OF THE TERRITORIAL ADMINISTRATION
REGIONAL DEVELOPMENT COMMITTEE
GOVERNOR
REGIONAL COUNCIL
REGION
DEPARTMENTAL DEVELOPMENT COMMITTEE
PREFET
DEPARTMENTAL COUNCIL
DEPARTMENT
RURAL EXTENSION CENTERS
(CERS)
SOUS-PREFET
ARRONDISSEMENT COUNCIL
ARRONDISSEMENT
PRESIDENT OF THE RURAL COUNCIL
RURAL COUNCIL
RURAL COMMUNITY
PROMOTION
VILLAGE CHIEF
ELECTION
VILLAGE
R U R A L P O P U L A T I O N

> Community has control over its own purse strings and is provided with financial resources. This is no doubt the single most signifstrings and is provided with financial resources. This is no doubt the single most significan and innovative aspect of the Reform.[11]

Based on word of mouth and general observation, it appears that Rural Communities have so far been relatively effective in spending their budgets. Some observers think they are more efficient than the central government insofar as getting things done with the finances at hand. One Rural Community reportedly built more local roads in one year under the Reform than had been built in that locality since independence under the old administrative system. Popular participation in spending is also making its weight felt with respect to priorities, particularly in the health sector. Rural dispensaries and village maternities are blossoming throughout areas where the Reform has been implemented.

A number of rural development institutions are central to the progress envisaged by undertaking the Reform. The cooperative movement has been given a strong vote of confidence. By participating in the RCCs, where they have one-third representation, cooperatives have had their political prowess greatly enhanced. The existence of an institution known as the "Maison Familiale," a community social and training program centered around a "family house" or community center has been advanced by the Reform as an important vehicle for realizing its participation philosophy. At present, there are some 27 community centers sponsored under this program, and plans are to expand the program throughout Senegal.

A puzzling problem confronted by designers of the Reform involved the extant Rural Extension Centers (CERs). The latter have representatives from various technical services which operate as a multi-disciplinary team within a department. Their mission is to introduce better farming techniques, assist in designing projects, train youth, and carry out health, education, and literacy work, all under the general rubric of "promotion humaine"). Some of these activities resemble agricultural extension work, but that activity is specifically assigned to departmental corporations ("sociétés d'interventions"), which have more financial and staff resources and better ministry backing than the CERs have had up to now. With the advent of the Administrative Reform, the Ministry of Rural Development advocated abolishment of the CERs to avoid duplication of effort. The more influential Ministry of Interior advanced the view that CERs were essential to the success of the Administrative Reform, particularly if the latter was to provide necessary technical support to Rural Communities and enable them to spend their budgets with proper technical guidance. This conflict was resolved by Senghor who, in a letter dated June 18, 1974, stated that both the CERs and the development corporations would be retained to provide maximum support for the Rural Communities.[12]

Perhaps the most significant issue, and the one least given to prediction, is the question of how the Administrative Reform affects the process of development planning. In Senegal, as in other parts of the Third World, socialism, which is viewed as more rational and "scientific" than capitalism, is in vogue because of its emphasis on planning. "But why whould one think that planning is less 'complicated' than market mechanisms?" asks Aristide Zolberg.[13] The answer in part is that centralized planning is a more elitest approach that can be accomplished by a small group of individuals who are capable of exercising their will over the people. Whereas, capitalism requires more widespread participation and less centralized direction.

Senegal's national planning is based on the experience of four-year plans since independence. The Fifth Four-Year Plan (1977-1981) is built around a method of planning by objectives and by project. Readjustment of the plan is a continual process actuated through interministerial finance and investment committees. While national projects will continue to be planned with decision making to be made on a central government level, decision making on local projects is supposed to be lodged at the appropriate local level within the structure of the Reform. Fell observes: "Whether this remains theory or is translated into practice will depend on how well popular participation is able to assert itself at the various levels."[14] In other words, the bottom line is whether the mobilized participation we are witnessing in Senegal can make the transition to autonomous participation.

Inquiry into this metamorphosis calls for an examination of participation in relation to the capacity of traditional societies in terms of concentrating or dispersing power. In the case of many Sahelian communal groups, the "we" or "in-group" feeling is so strong that the groups are "candidates for nationhood." Primordial-political disaffection and assertiveness, based on language, culture, ethnicity, or kinship "threatens partition, irredentism, or merger, a redrawing of the very limits of the state, a new dimension of its domain."[15] These sentiments cannot be ignored since they can seriously distort the preferred relationship between mobilized participation and liberal democracy. Hence, there is always the danger that a communal group may subordinate a political institution to its own interests, thereby not only weakening the level of institutionalization, but also weakening or destroying the legitimacy accorded the institution by other communal groups. Institutionalization usually denotes adaptability, complexity, coherence, and especially autonomy; control of a political institution by a communal group represents political decay, the opposite of development, in Huntington's terms.

"In later modernizing countries the telescoping of modernization tends to spread political consciousness and the possibility of political action through the countryside at a time when urban development and modernization are still at relatively low levels."[16] Is this observation at the core of Senghor's shift toward a rural bias? Senghor is viscerally pervious to the need to bridge the rural-urban income distribution gap. He is particularly concerned with the long-term social consequences of disparate concepts of equity in distribution of wealth and incomes between peasant incomes in the country's interior and those of residents of the more industrialized, commercialized, and capitalized coastal region. One does not have to remain in Dakar for long to become aware of the fact that urban incomes buy costly imports and modern services and place a premium on foreign, more specifically, Western lifestyles. Africanization, a cure-all in Anglophone West Africa, which calls for replacing non-Africans with Africans in existing jobs, is meaningless of and by itself since it cannot be regarded as substantially related to effective domestic shifts in power. True Africanization calls for greater receptiveness to the needs of the rural majority. While Senghor is the assimilationist epitomized, the authentically African culture variable is very important to him. If cultural autonomy is to manifest itself, the countryside is the logical venue. For Senghor, the rural community is an unblemished and solid block of wood to work with. It remains to be seen whether concepts such as "negritude", with its insistence on an intuitive black African method of cognition, will be segregated from compromise and allowed to lead to absurd political ends.

Despite measures like the Administrative Reform, the danger of a participation "implosion" is very real in Senegal. Besides the risk of a military seizure of power once the venerable Senghor leaves the scene, there is the possibility of theocracy "a la" Iran. Senghor grants more audiences to Moslem marabouts than any other interest group in part because he comes from the country's small Christian minority. The marabouts play a key brokerage role between central authorities and the population, particularly in the countryside. Perhaps the earliest indication of Senghor's dependence on the marabouts came in 1958, when the regime opted in favor of a 15 percent increase of salaries, while the farmers took an equal reduction. The marabouts helped to keep the lid down. At the time, it was argued that this was the only way to proceed since an equal rise in farm income would inevitably have brought in its wake further allocation of resources to a pregnant corps of administrators, enlarging its ranks to cope with the material consequences of the farm bonanza. This religious interface with politics, for obvious reasons, is usually played down. However, religion as it is practiced and administered impacts political orders and the level of political participation on many levels. In the Sahel, religion continues to be the pre-eminent source of constituency creation.

Popular participation can degenerate into a rubberstamp

exercise controlled by a few powerful individuals besides the marabouts such as the President of the RCC, who is in charge of the Rural Community and acts as representative of the Sous-Prefet to publish laws and regulations, to enforce police measures, and to execute decisions by the Sous-Prefet concerning public order, security, and sanitation. Indeed, one political commentator has observed: "Increasingly, African systems of government have succumbed to personal rule. This is, of course, nothing new in the history of mankind. The administration of cities in the United States has been in the hands of political bosses primarily because superior economic forces were disinterested in contending for power locally."[17]

The Senegalese elite is not found ensconced in the principal source of national wealth -- groundnut production -- but at the point where the farmer exchanges his crop for money or credit -- in other words, where negotiable value is added. The vaunted public sector elite, because it has been viewed as a separate, effectively autonomous group, has come to be treated, in literature mainly, as a kind of order of knights of the public interest. In reality, given the precarious economic conditions that govern public and private affairs in the Sahel, this elite has often behaved as if it were in the uncomfortable position of a mouse within reach of the cat. More important to its immediate survival than popular participation has been the fashioning of political machines based on a patron-client relationship.

LAW AND DEVELOPMENT

The Sahelian countries are in search of internal equilibrium quite distinct from environmental dislocation. The possibility of mutual gain arising from a situation in which all parties within national orders pursue their interests, although these activities may be antipodal, cannot arise when only one faction, namely the elite, is dominating the interest arena. "To their societies, they (the elite) are Einstein, Ataturk, Rousseau, Lenin, Trotsky, Freud, Napoleon, Darwin, and Newton all rolled into one. They are the god from the machine and the devil."[18] With this kind of preponderance, is it surprising that many Third World countries have not reached the juncture where certain rules of the "rational-pursuit-of-interest-game" are formulated and passionate behavior eliminated? Without a genuine balance or harmony of interests in the social order, a society cannot make the logical extension in statecraft to a consented form of government tolerant of public contestation. In the absence of the option to ideologize and institutionalize a political system secured by countervailing agencies, a conflict-ridden domestic scene has but one fairly predictable "denouement": authoritarianism.

The acid test of vigorous popular participation is the degree to which a political system tolerates, even nurtures, dissent and upholds rights stipulated in lofty language in national constitutions and codes. In many Third World societies, the overarching challenge is to right socioeconomic imbalances resulting from a failure to institute a general acceptance of a common, much less equal, membership. Yet, most of these societies pay considerable lip service to the proposition that all persons are equal before the law. To take these words at their face value and to assist deprived majorities in gaining equality before the law is a major development task that has long been neglected. The law in its capacity to modulate human activities is a vital tool for both social change and a necessary transparancy in the workings of government. The problem, then, is to determine how the principle that the law should apply equally to poor and rich can be put into practice. AID offers a compelling answer. It has begun to fund legal assistance projects in Barbados, Columbia, Dominica, and Grenada. AID recently sent representatives to a meeting of Latin American lawyers who gathered in Santo Domingo to plan strategy for the long uphill battle to achieve legitimacy for the cause of legal assistance and public interest law in Latin America. The Sahel is a good place to begin this campaign in Africa.

To go beyond the grandiloquence of Sahelian constitutions more will have to be known about the Sahel's legal and administrative structures. Sahelian governments must be prepared to dedicate substantial resources if they are to replicate with any degree of success something remotely resembling U.S. neighborhood legal services programs. The need for these kinds of programs is great. For instance, many migrant workers within their own countries and in other countries of the region, including the West African coastal countries, live in unnecessarily squalid conditions because, in many cases, they are unaware of their rights under national labor laws and are unable to communicate in French, the legal "lingua franca." With a concerted educational campaign, Sahelian rural and urban poor can be made more familiar with government in all its incarnations. As matters stand, even with administrative reforms such as Senegal's, there is confusion as to which government roles, executive, legislative, or judicial, are functional to the continuous process of development.

In many parts of the Sahel, rights are treated as privileges, and as such outside the protection of due process. Yet, norms of due process are not applicable only to the enforcement of democratically promulgated substantive laws. Even a corrupt and authoritarian regime may establish substantive laws the administration of which can be criticized as procedurally unfair. Civil service codes of conduct are not very different from our own, but if defendant has the opportunity to tamper with the evidence before the court and to otherwise illegally impede the discovery process, the regime would be subject to legitimate criticism for procedural injustice as well as for undemocratic rule. It is short-sighted to regard procedural due process merely as an aspect of the theory of separation of powers or as a protection of government by popular consent. Thomas C. Grey observes:

> Procedural fairness involves a special moral concern for the correct and accurate decision of disputes which affect substantive rights. Its norms impinge from the outside on decision-making institutions, and require of those institutions more concern for the substantive rights which would be threatened or infringed by erroneous decisions that the institutions (or officials) would otherwise be inclined to show, given the natural balance those institutions are likely to strike between the competing claims of accurate decision, cost, and institutional self-interest.[19]

The rapidly changing social and economic environment in the developing world cannot but affect law, particularly if the law is to be relevant to its matrix. "Law is one of the instruments of social control -- one of the techniques in Toynbee's interaction between challenge and response: man challenged by the Nile waters, by arctic snows, by jungle animals, or by arid desert." For Leland Hazard, "The response to the challenge calls for law emanating from the 'perception' and 'understanding' of rulers."[20] Where the environment compels a change in law that is not forthcoming, foreign aid donors have a duty to intervene. In the past, this kind of performance conditioning has been the road not taken. And it has made all the difference. To qualify this literary flight, the failure to explore the avenue of legal aid to the developing countries is at the very least contributory to assessments of foreign aid like Robert A. Dahl's: "... as a strategy for transforming nonpolyarchies into polyarchies the American foreign aid program must be adjudged a total failure."[21]

There is a recalcitrance surrounding the effectiveness of foreign aid from the donor's perspective that cannot be eliminated easily. The channels of influence for addressing the core dilemma of legal reform are usually remote and indirect. Roscoe Pound, speaking on the safeguards against the abuse of judiciary discretion, noted the need to rely on "taught traditions" and the "trained intuition" of the judges themselves.[22] Donors cannot at a stroke create institutional solutions to the administrative problems facing recipient governments. However, donors can see to it that the personnel in charge of development ventures are influenced by an appropriate set of "taught traditions" and that the latter are in a position to use their "trained intuitions" creatively.

CONCLUSION

Generally, public administration is taken for granted in the Sahel. Yet, the allocation of adequate attention and resources for developing administration itself should be high on the development agenda. When a development plan is formulated, it should include an assessment of the administrative resources required. Greater attention must be paid to the cultivation of administrative personnel, their skills, and attitudes. This obtains "a fortiori" to technical personnel. In the Senegalese experience, the animators are poorly paid and are often considerably dependent on the goodwill of the richer or more powerful members of their village. Their prospects are not good: while obvious failure may be penalized, there is little material reward for good work under trying circumstances. Very much the same could be said of the lowest ranks of extension staff in other countries of Africa and Asia. Something could be done to improve career prospects: at least salary increments could be increased, since the social cost (in a technical sense) of employing otherwise unemployed men, in whom a multi-year educational investment has been made, is very low.

There are no simple answers to this problem, but there are ways of diminishing it. Career structure, pay, and training are one. Another may well be to restructure the service so that the lowest grade of extension officer is employed by the farmers whom he serves. There are difficulties here: the biggest farmers will tend to get the most service and local jealousies or vested interests may play too big a part. But the advantages would be significant -- those who pay the officer would be anxious to see that he earned his keep and would be in a better position to judge his work.

The problem of rich farmer leverage on government workers will be magnified considerably once the large scale irrigation projects in the Sahel get underway. To assess the likelihood of big improvements in productivity as a result of irrigation and to be reassured that small farmers will at least not be made absolutely worse off, one must know more about how irrigation officials at various levels actually make decisions, about the sort of pressures that are brought to bear on them, and their response to those pressures. And one must know, too, what decisions they do not make and the pressures which are not brought to bear on them. Robert Wade states: "Strangely little research has been done on questions of this sort. That they are sensitive questions is obvious, but the reason for their neglect seems to lie more in the traditional identification of irrigation as a subject for engineers, not social scientists."[23]

One would expect that on relatively new schemes the distribution of water would not simply be a reflection of the distribution of power. For the placing of canals on the landscape, and the placing of their outlets, is to a large extent determined by conditions of topography and soil; compared to roads, bridges, factories, canals are more "site-attracted." With respect to the holdings of large and small farmers, their location is likely to be more or less random. In a relatively new project, therefore, one would expect to find especially intense pressures from those with resources to move the distribution system back towards "equilibrium," where the conditions of water service mirror the wider distribution of power. But these pressures may be resisted more strongly than in the case of the distribution of other inputs, such as credit or fertilizer because the zero-sum nature of water distribution in an outlet command is more obvious than in the case of the other inputs: farmers can see who gets the water; they can see that the total is (more or less) limited. The substance of this point is that much of the irrigated area in the Sahel is and will be new, and the performance of irrigated agriculture will depend on the effectiveness of irrigation projects in the early operational stage before some kind of steady mode of operation is reached.

Tendencies toward growing inequalities of irrigation benefits might be offset, in part, by a variety of institutional measures. By closer supervision of lower rank officers; closer connections between performance and promotion; higher salaries and higher penalties. Means must be devised to make it rational for low level officers who have discretionary power to influence costs and benefits, to deny water to those who want it even if it is not their turn. They can be persuaded to flout elementary fairness if the risks of detection are small and the punishment if detected is also small. Hence, much depends on how closely they are (and can be) supervised, what sanctions are available to those in supervisory positions, and how likely these sanctions will be employed.

The supply and quality of technical and administrative resources at times fails to meet the demand function in development efforts. For this reason, it must not be misallocated where is is available, or spread too thin. If the energies of the best and the brightest serving the administrative apparatus are tied up cooking unworkable and infinitely complex systems of exchange control, rationing of imports, allocation of quotas, nationalizing, running inefficient public enterprises, etc. -- if governments attempt to do things which private business, indigenous or foreign, can do more efficiently -- it should be no wonder that those services, indispensable for economic growth, which only the government can perform or which it can perform better, are sadly neglected. In this sense, undue regulation of economic life is often counterproductive. For instance, Sahelian administrators would be well-advised to heed the analyst who has concluded:

> Direct intervention in the cattle markets for the purpose of making the sale of younger animals more attractive to producers does not

> appear to be warranted. Any market interventions witnessed by the research team, such as the cattle parks project, appeared to be only disruptive, impairing the efficiency of the markets. An improved transportations infrastructure, well maintained transit corridors, and an increased demand for young animals as a result of the expansion of fattening projects in the south should alter the price structure in favor of younger animals. Given the price responsiveness of suppliers, the new price structure should call forth more young cattle without any direct market interventions.[24]

Moreover, since any investment consumes a certain amount of administrative work and since that consumption varies considerably in intensity and duration from one sector to another, and according to the extent of entrepreneurial tasks assumed by the state, it is essential for the executive branch as a whole not to overrate its strength and to adjust carefully its role in development to its administrative capacity, so as to avoid being itself the originator of bottlenecks, incoherence, and duplication.

In view of the fact that bureaucracies are immense consumers of law -- since they require rules -- the interface between law and development can be explored in furtherance of a mutuality of interests between bureaucrats and the general population. To resurrect a caveat, the truth can be sifted out from official falsehoods only if governments open themselves to cross-examination so that basic issues of development may be clearly defined, and the war against poverty may not be diverted to improper ends or conducted with undue sacrifice of human rights.[25] In addition to laying bare or, if you will, demystifying the development process via the law, donors can as a matter of policy encourage Sahelian regimes to concentrate on political development. Despite the outward inhibitions of some donors towards this kind of involvement, the bulk of historical evidence suggests that there is little possibility of escaping the consequences of actions taken in the political realm.

In a sense, government and politics tend to perform a gatekeeper function in controlling the various dimensions of the modernization process.[26] Illustrative of the power of politics are some of the abrupt reversals of trends that occurred when colonial governments replaced, or in turn were replaced by, indigenous governments. It was not incongruous that at the Nigerian independence ceremony, immediately after the Union Jack came down, a phalanx of armored cars fired blank ammunition at the crowds encircling the stands. With rare and tenuous exceptions, this field day is still in progress in Africa and grows with intensity as the military resolve that the power vested in them by their guns makes them the final arbitors of matters authoritarian.

9 Conclusions and Recommendations

It is perhaps appropriate at the conclusion of a study like this one to draw attention to principal policy recommendations and to induce cross-cutting lessons that may have wider application. Manifestly, it will not suffice at this juncture of the Sahel's development to simply enumerate topics that could bear further research or to elaborate intellectual abstractions, however germane and tantalizing they may be. Trying circumstances call, above all else, for workable initiatives. The time is ripe in the Sahel for a broad array of policy decisions that will not be immune to the corrosive realities of the development setting. If a good policy fit is to be achieved, built-in flexibility will be necessary to permit minor revision or even major redirection of policies in the course of field implementation. Without unduly fattening up recommendations, it may be useful to summarize in executive fashion the contents of this study.

Few policies are more sensitive to both donor and recipient governments than those that seek to bring about growth with equity. Donors in particular face a dilemma when they champion the uplift of the very poor in parts of the developing world where ruling elites may not be especially given to this cause. Of course, resource transfers can make for temporary relief of hunger or distress. But to engineer a permanent change in the status of the low-end poor is a different matter. Rural poverty is not always simply due to lack of funds or of technology. Frequently, the rural depressors are built into the political and socioeconomic system. Among the assumptions donors bring in tow is the belief that foreign aid can be used to shift the gears of an indifferent national government and definitely turn it around toward rural development. Unfortunately, donors have yet to show the necessary persistence to confirm whether this is a realistic belief, or merely, in the words of Samuel Johnson, an example of the triumph of hope over experience.

Sahelian rural poverty can be attributed mainly to eight significant constraints, each of which is interrelated with the others. Some of the constraints that have been identified include: (1) land, water, and forest resources that are difficult to manage; (2) a low level of technological development in agriculture and livestock production, the primary economic activities of the rural poor; (3) the relative absence of transport and agricultural production and marketing infrastructure; (4) traditional social structures that slow the process of change; (5) highly centralized political, administrative, and institutional structures that impede participation of rural poor in managing their own development; (6) human resource constraints, including poor health and shortages of trained managers and entrepreneures in every sector; (7) government policies that are biased against rural producers in favor of urban residents; and (8) dependence on the export of a few primary commodities for foreign exchange earnings.

For the Sahelian countries a commitment to growth with equity means a commitment to rural development. This commitment requires developing high yielding technical packages for rainfed farming, expanding irrigation and, in some ways most important, improving natural resource management and conservation. Although an agricultural-based rural development strategy is more apt to be equity-oriented than one based on industrialization, equitable growth does not always or necessarily result. For the Sahel, however, the economics of crop and animal production at the present time dictate against plantations, large mechanized farms or ranches and, consequently, most agricultural development programs are small-farmer and herder-oriented.

In the past, benefits of growth have been less than optimal for the rural poor. The benefits accruing to rural people have been limited in terms of the number of small farmers and herders reached and the geographic areas, i.e., higher rainfall zones, covered. Sahelian governments are making a tentative commitment to growth with equity. Their resolve to weight development programs toward the rural poor is mirrored in on-going changes in government policies toward agriculture and industry. These include:

- -- substantial increases in official prices of export crop and staple food grains since the 1968-1974 drought;
- -- increased investment in food and agricultural production by the Sahelian countries;
- -- increased allocation of external assistance to food and agriculture; and
- -- increased allocation of resources to the provision of health services to rural people.

The commitment to growth with equity for the rural poor is tempered by the political exigencies of rapid urbanization and rising demands for jobs and social services in urban areas. Sustained and substantial aid, that can be made available through foreign assistance, is essential to reinforce the nascent commitment to improving the welfare of the rural poor.

Socioeconomic objectives can best be achieved through long-term, broadly integrated programs. These programs place a heavy burden on developing countries for improved planning, management, and mobilization of resources -- and they require close cooperation between developing country governments and donors to augment technical and capital resources. One such program, as we have seen, revolves around the multi-donor Sahel Development Program of the Club des Amis du Sahel. As a new model for international development cooperation and synergy, the Club merits attention. It has succeeded in proposing a viable strategy geared to well-defined objectives, the means for achieving them, a timetable for implementation which has the support of both Sahelians and the international community. On the geopolitical plane, the Club offers a refreshing respite from the cleavages and conflicts that predominate in world order and illustrates the benefits to be derived from endeavors that accent the factors of convergence over those of divergence.

In SDP, we have the beginnings of an innovative effort to realize integrated development. The success of SDP rests on the commitment of donors to finance this significant experimental model for North-South cooperation. It is estimated that the local investment and recurrent costs for a $10 billion program over a ten-year period would be about $6.8 billion. This amounts to 1.4 times total government revenues in the Sahel in 1974 and 21 percent of the region's gross national product.

A necessary expansion of social services requires substantially greater investment than is currently being allocated to the provision of such services in rural areas. In countries as poor as those in the Sahel, widespread local participation in the form of building and maintaining schools, dispensaries, and roads will be essential to reduce the enormous investment and recurrent costs that would be required. Alternate management structures to the village cannot be created in the time available to Sahelian planners. For while the long-term development program in the Sahel aims at the year 2000 as its horizon, some fundamental changes will be undertaken in the agricultural production systems of the area within the next decade. This means, that large cadres of conventional civil servants cannot be trained and, indeed, the creation of such institutional infrastructure in the capitals may not be desirable.

Even were the Sahel to receive "carte blanche" from benefactors unknown, the strategy adopted and the manner in which it was implemented would be critical to the desired outcome. Corruption or serious misreadings of what changes the social matrix will bear could subvert the whole program. For instance, non-site-bound projects are particularly amenable to exploitation by the rich and powerful as illustrated by an example from Nigeria:

> One of the most ironic illustrations of politi-

> cal communalism was seen in the siting of the national secondary schools that were intented to foster political integration. The three ministers who decided their location came from Sokoto, Warri and Afikpo: the schools were allocated to Sokoto, Warri, and Afikpo."[1]

Development planning is inevitably involved in various forms of open and hidden social conflict. As with physical objects, any attempt to move or change social groups and institutions creates friction. An effort to move them far or quickly is apt to create active resistance with the radical repercussion of little or no change at all. This is the danger one courts in the polarity of overexposure. With considered policies, expositors can avert overexposure and catalyze cognitive exposure, i.e., a state that permits conceptually binding bids on the offers of the Twentieth Century.

In few places does the Baconian proposition that knowledge equals power obtain as wholly as in the developing areas. The advantages that accrue to indigenous expositors, i.e., elites, who are often perceived by their peoples as the prophets of Pasteur and Einstein, should not be abused in the polarities of double and under exposure where, to continue the contract metaphor, acceptance of the phenomenally new is aborted by not so much the complexity and fine print of the instrumental state but by the loopholes and the rampant uncertainty that preclude serious contract formation. Yet, this kind of obfuscation is common and leads to the conclusion that the development process lends itself too easily to deception. In many parts of the world, it has become a smoke screen for repression and power blindly and unrestrainedly pursued. In some measure the onus rests on parties that are more concerned with economic than political construction. The authoritarian shortcut to strong government is at times encouraged by outsiders, whose concern with political stability for economic or geopolitical advantage is not infrequently paramount to questions of abuse of power. Moreover, insecure elites (civilian or military) are much easier to manipulate and less likely than popularly entrenched governments to get too big for their britches.

Disconcerting is a smug and condescending view of Third World self-government epitomized in the words of Alexis de Tocqueville: "If men are to remain civilized or to become so, the art of associating together must grow and improve in the same ratio in which the equality of conditions is increased."[2] This argument is widely cited by Third World elites. Prior to his departure from Iran, the Shah informed the foreign press that he would be happy to become a constitutional monarch in the Swedish mold once his country attained Sweden's level of political development. Of course, the problem cannot be reduced to deficiencies in the "art of associating together." In many traditional Third World cultures, human relations are more evolved than in the West, and among Sahelian pastoralists, as we have seen, more egalitarian. The problem, largely, is with foreign-trained elites for whom the Jacksonian idea that every citizen is capable of discharging the normal functions of government is remote and peculiarly American. One might very well ask where Western education systems went wrong? However, this perspective on politics is not new. Samuel P. Huntington states: "Men are reluctant to give up the image of social harmony without political action. This was Rousseau's dream. It remains the dream of statesman and soldier who imagine that they can induce community in their societies without engaging in the labor of politics."[3] That is not to say that Third World leaders are totally oblivious to politics. The government dispensary in the remote Nigerienne town of N'Guigmi, situated on Lake Chad, distributed free medication with pamphlets that duly noted that the medicine came with the compliments of President Hamani Diori. This feeble effort to win political support, needless to say, was inadequate.

Political evolution in whatever direction can be altered dramatically by events that have their origins outside the body politic. The political consequences of drought in the Sahel have been profound. With the overthrow of the Mauritanian government in August, 1978, there is only one civilian government remaining in the group of Sahelian states that formerly belonged to "Afrique Occidentale Francaise" (AOF). Once the venerable Senghor leaves the Senegalese scene, it is anyone's guess as to what kind of government will follow. With or without "coups d'etat," the 1968-1974 drought has heightened awareness of the importance of the rural populations to the ruling groups in each Sahelian country. Correspondingly, the Sahelian Ministers of Rural Development have become increasingly important. So much so that when the Interstate Commission to Combat the Effects of the Drought (CILSS) was established in 1973, it was comprised of the Ministers of Rural Development from each of the Sahelian states.

AVOIDING A BUREAUCRATIC MORASS

While many more comprehensive studies on sectoral problems must be completed, this is no excuse for the bureaucratic phenomenon of paralysis by analysis. The CILSS-Club mechanisms can and should do more to foster a regional outlook across countries and sectors. The danger is that as regional organizations proliferate, their principal purpose will be overlooked. Although it is too early to tell, an incipient sense of what it means to be a Sahelian rather than a Voltaic or a Gambian, Gourmanchay or Hausa, is evident in official circles. The very act of establishing many of these regional organizations stems from a growing awareness of things generically Sahelian. This awareness must be encouraged more vigorously in the future if the momentum of regional cooperation is to be sustained. I am reminded of the admonishment of Louise Weiss, a Gaulist member of the European Parliament, who criticized the builders of Europe for having lost their way in the maze of European institutions:

> The community institutions have produced European sugar beets, butter, cheese, wines calves and even pigs. They have not produced Europeans.[4]

The benefits of Sahelian unity transcend the importance of putting the region on the map geopolitically. Economies of scale require coordination of national industrialization schedules; development of river basins depends on cooperation between riparian states; common challenges in the biological sciences call for a regional science policy; in sum, common challenges reflect the congruence of interests that find Sahelian countries in a shared enterprise of integrated development. However, the politics of exclusion intrinsic to regional arrangements should not preclude Sahelian countries from cultivating stronger ties with other West African neighbors.

The constraints on regional economic cooperation attributable to poor or non-existent telecommunications and transportation links are self-apparent. Viable industrialization projects, even on a very limited scale, in the landlocked countries, will almost always require prior improvement in infrastructure. Yet, existing traffic and trade patterns hardly justify the investment involved, particularly from the vantage point of the coastal countries. The only way the latter can justify expenditures for these regional links is if the inland countries can be seen as expanded markets for the coastal countries' goods.

Large-scale industrial exploitation of mineral deposits may increase the benefits of regional interconnectedness. There is only superficial data on the mineral resources of the Sahel. In Senegal, deposits of iron, phosphate, titanium, salt, and gold are known. Phosphate, titanium, and salt deposits located near Dakar are being worked, but the only inland mines exploited are the gold deposits. Iron deposits also exist on both sides of the Senegal-Mali border. None of the identified deposits in Mali of iron, bauxite, manganese, zinc, and phosphates are being worked. One gold deposit near Bougouni and a salt deposit near the Algerian border represent the extent of mining activities in Mali. In addition to its uranium, Niger has known deposits of iron, tungsten, tin, coal, and salt, most of which are being exploited. Iron ore is mined in northwest Mauritania and provides a substantial source of foreign exchange.

Expansion of transport infrastructure can also be framed in terms of agricultural output. In Mali, a country of 465,000 square miles with only 1,036 miles of paved roads, there is little incentive for farmers to grow crops for the market even where climatic conditions are favorable. The high cost of transporting crops to market areas and the high rate of spoilage makes locally grown crops less competitive with imported foods in coastal areas. Scarce foreign exchange and development resources are, therefore, expended for food imports which further inhibit local agriculture development. The lack of secondary and feeder roads is a major constraint to increasing the access of the rural poor to such sector supporting services as agricultural extension or to such basic social services as health. River transport is limited by the seasonal pattern of rainfall and poor management and other inefficiencies hinder rail transport between Sahelian and coastal countries.

In addition to transport infrastructure, other forms of rural infrastructure are in short supply. The Sahel enjoys 3,000 kilometers of major rivers but very few irrigation schemes. Those which do exist are in poor repair. The harnessing of the seven river systems in the Sahel (Niger, Senegal, Lake Chad, Gambia, Volta, Logone and Chari) is the key to the development of irrigated agriculture by opening up roughly 2 million hectares of potentially irrigable and untapped agricultural soils, and would provide power and transport. Actuating the potential of irrigation downstream from proposed major dams such as Manantali or Selingue will require substantial additional investment in irrigation systems. Physically rehabilitating those systems in disrepair and strengthening the capability of managers and farmers to maintain them would have a significant short-run payoff in increased food and agricultural output.

Achieving broad-based rural development in the Sahel, rests largely on reversing declining staple food trends and increasing productivity in export crops and livestock. This view has been accepted by all of the Sahelian countries and donor members of the Club du Sahel, and their development strategies have been designed accordingly. The hope is that this new emphasis will help stem the on-going exodus from the rural areas to the major urban centers. The consequences of this uneconomic migration are growing unemployment, urban poverty, and increased pressure on governments to step up the provision of social services to city residents paid for in part by taxing the rural areas. Traditionally, the excuse for not channeling more resources into the hinterland rested on the premise that even where there was in place a progressive rural structure, absorptive capacity was very limited. On the other hand, there are those who see this problem as a unique opportuntiy. David Shear states:

> If we assess where the absorptive capacity in the Sahel is greatest, it is at the local level. That is, at the level of the village. The long-term development program for the Sahel, therefore, is focusing on the village as a principal channel for delivery of development assistance. It is this method for administer-

> ing assistance almost directly to the local level which also makes the Sahel Development Program a unique enterprise.[5]

As the pendulum swings in the other direction, we must carefully consider whether overzealous adherence to a doctrine of commitedness to 10,000 villages is no more a commitment to integrated rural development than blind devotion to one metropolis. The present exposition has accented the Sahelian system of systems and there is a danger that rural development could be retarded if it is pursued ruthlessly with inadequate concern for how it relates to the whole. Pursuant to an interactional theory of development, one could invoke what Marion Levy calls the fallacy of misplaced dichotomies. Conceptualization of distinctions in binary form when our subject matter -- human settlements -- vary only in degree, we are told, is not only "the classic misuse of the law of the excluded middle, it also guarantees the begging of important questions."[6] Of course, there is a middle way that bridges the village-city continuum, giving the village a new sense of relevance in the scheme of things while easing pressure on principal cities. I refer to John P. Lewis' spatial centering theory, which suggests the need to enhance the urban ambience of middle-sized towns. It is quixotic to believe that Sahelian villages will continue to hold sway over the minds of men and women whose traditional personality containers are being eroded by the abrasive process of modernization.

In considering the required changes in Sahelian production systems, the Club has concluded that "radical changes have often been achieved by coercion -- which we exclude -- or by an equally radical change in the human environment."[7] The latter option is being expostulated by the Sahelian majority. This change is not in the natural order of things and must be encouraged by policy decisions and appropriate investments. Hence, to recapitulate, policy formulation should ensue along the following lines:

- Investment priorities should be balanced between interests of urban and rural populations rather than promoting rural subsidization of urban industrial investment.

- National planning on a sectoral basis should be broadened to include spatial considerations in the allocation of investments and the design of programs.

- Planning strategies which promote economic growth at one or a few major urban centers should be shifted to a policy that will strengthen the economies of regional cities,

> district centers and market towns through a concerted effort at raising the productivity and incomes of rural populations and developing services and industries supporting rural populations.[8]

Righting inequity is rarely a facile task under the best of circumstances. The demands on government resources of rapidly growing urban centers cannot be ignored. It is to be expected, in the words of Henry Bienen that "Economic development often creates new tensions and gives rise to organized interest groups which make explicit demands on government and party."[9] The bottom line is that Sahelian bureaucracies are frequently not well-informed about the extent of economic disparities and, consequently, lack a good basis for formulating sound policies that address these disparities. While a literature has accumulated over the years on various aspects of the Sahel, hard current data which can serve as a basis for analysis and action is scant. There have been virtually no modern censuses taken in the Sahel, seriously hampering, for instance, the study of rural unemployment. There is no source of data which sheds light on income distribution and rural poverty. Where data exists in provincial and village records, it has seldom been analyzed.

Sahelian bureaucracies are highly structured and their operations often cumbersome. Highly centralized decisionmaking within ministries discourages lateral communication among working level personnel within a single ministry and practically prohibits dialogues between ministries. High-level commissions are created to stimulate intragovernmental exchange and priority program coordination but are ineffective because of interministerial jealousies. For instance, there is discord between the Ministers of Rural Development,who are the country representatives to the Club Council of Ministers, and the Ministers of Planning, who complain that they are not adequately consulted about Club programs which affect national economies. Since the underlying governmental bottlenecks are not addressed, i.e., appropriate delegation of authority, open exchange of information, clearly defined priorities, etc., high-level commissions suffer from competing priorities, technical ignorance, and a general reluctance to either assume or share responsibility with other ministries. Under these circumstances, coordination and collaboration among ministries is difficult and policy making and management are weak.

By involving more bureaucrats in the strategy of development, i.e., recognizing "due process" rights of bureaucrats at all decision-order levels, "esprit de corps" and motivation essential to development can be instilled among those who are charged with direction of programs. Most Sahelian leaders have ignored the value of an activist genre of strategic guidance within their administrations. Bureaucrats, despite all the put downs, do like to think that they make a difference. And in the Sahel, with its limited human resources, they do.

Insufficient attention is paid to the qualifications of the development administrator. Intelligent and well-prepared individuals can contribute an infusion of creativity to the development process. The administrator can play a pivotal role as a solver of puzzles. But he must also be a tester of strategies. Though he may, during the search for a particular puzzle's solution, try out a number of alternative approaches, rejecting those that fail to yield the desired result, he rarely consciously tests the "paradigm" when he does so. Instead, he is like the chess player who, with a problem stated and the board physically or mentally before him, tries out various alternative moves in the search for a solution. Key initiatives to ameliorate administrative capability to respond to development needs promptly and to increase the overall capacity of Sahelian governments to react where necessary, on a sweeping, paradigmatic basis include:

- Expansion of the limited data base on which bureaucrats draw. The new research institute established in Bamako, Mali, under the aegis of the Club is a good first step. Individual governments should bolster their in-house capability to mount research efforts on basic social and economic questions.

- Public inputs are necessary into processes which link central planning with effective implementation at the local level and which facilitate feedback of information from the periphery to the center rather than processes in which planning is separated from implementation and in which the needs of local populations are determined by central authority. "Bottom-up" flows of information and decisions should be emphasized over exclusively top-down direction and control. Where centralized control of the rural development planning process tends to predominate, a situation labeled by Robert Chambers as "planning without implementation" usually emerges.[10]

- In addition to structural changes that could maximize bureaucratic coordination, emphasis should be placed on upgrading the quality of personnel. Such incentives for competent and conscientious work as promotion by merit and other forms of recognition should be more widely instituted.

It has been observed that in the final analysis economic progress does not depend upon plans and planning. "Given actual or potential effective demand, development depends upon the presence and behavior of the agents of production and distribution, whether in the public or private sectors."[11] It is often not a question of raising big new battalions but of getting the right man into the right job, opening the general administrative grade to men of proven technical or managerial ability. However, the quality of work of the executive branch does not depend solely on the personal values of ministers and officials or on the number of qualified administrative personnel. It rests largely on the general structure of government and on the organizational working methods in the ministerial departments. These factors determine the overall consistency of the decisions made and the effectiveness of the actions undertaken. In other words, the rhythm and quality of the procedures of preparation, those of the making and implementing of decisions, have a fundamental bearing on the ability and skills of the administrator.

With a greater transparency in the workings of government, there would be wider scope for self-assessment from within as a function of the acuity of criticism from without, conceivably leading to necessary administrative reforms. Therein is one of the many benefits of public interest law in the Sahel. In transactions with their increasingly intrusive governments, poor Sahelians could benefit from enhanced knowledge of their rights and legal representation to ensure that extant laws are respected at their face value. The function of legal counsel "ex vi termini" is to explain the conditions under which the state can intervene in individual lives. It is quixotic to believe that legal advocacy can and will change anytime soon the external environment of poor countries like those of the Sahel. Indeed, there are in these settings many factors which militate against the independence of law in general and civil procedure in particular. However, positivist advocacy is one of the most stunningly relevant tools for assisting Third Worlders to communicate with their governments, to invoke their rights, and to maximize their autonomy.

THE TEMPTATION TO COLLAPSE PROCESS INTO RESULT

In addition to civil rights, integrated development is concerned with meeting the basic needs of the world's expanding population. This concern arises from widespread humanist values that "man is the measure of all things," that development is for the betterment of people. Also, there is more awareness that a pre-condition for stabilizing world population growth is the attainment of decent standards of living in developing countries, particularly for the most basic of human needs: food and health.

If Sahelians have given agriculture such prominence in

their overall plan, it is because people still go hungry and suffer malnourishment. A study prepared by the World Bank suggests that the Sahelians' choice is sound (See Table 26).[12] It is argued that unless emergency measures are taken to increase agricultural production in the poor countries, their population growth will result in huge food deficits beginning in 1985. The study also shows that, in the medium term, population growth will make it necessary to put all the land still available under cultivation. It endorses the ideas and proposals that appeared in the wake of the great scare over the depletion of grain stocks (mostly American) in 1972-1973. Once the fear was dispelled, very few of these proposals for "providence and assurance" were acted upon. There are continuing doubts in the Sahel, as in other parts of the developing world, that sufficient emergency stocks of grain will be maintained for world emergencies. In 1979, for the first time in five years, world food production was overtaken by consumption, depleting some surplus stocks and confirming Sahelian fears.

Agriculture provides Sahelian leaders with a clear target for a fresh coruscation of ideas that could produce results on a wide scale. For the Sahelian countries (excluding Cape Verde for which there is no data and Senegal for which manufacturing constitutes more than a fifth of export trade), primary agricultural or mineral commodities account for more than 90 percent of exports. The rapid growth of urban centers due to migration is largely attributable to low farm incomes in the countryside. Opportunities there are few, particularly in the off-season, and agriculture remains a low-status way of life. Wage labor in the cities has not been able to absorb the influx of migrants, but the cities maintain their attraction because incomes, even of the urban poor, come closer to average GNP per capita (in the $100-150 range) than do the incomes of small farmers and herders. The income per farm worker is from eight (Niger) to fourteen (Mali, Mauritania) times lower than the urban worker's income. Furthermore, the ratio between agricultural income and urban income deteriorated over the last ten-year period. At the same time, the cost of essential inputs purchased by the farmer increased faster than the selling prices for crops so that the value added on the farm decreased.

Improvement of rural living standards has many different aspects, which are so inter-related that they are both objectives and means to an end. More food production involves restoration of soil fertility and soil conservation; it involves more efficient use of water -- rain, underground, rivers -- improvement of infrastructure and communications, of marketing and storage. Seen in its wider relationships, the rural sector involves much more than just agriculture or those engaged in cultivation. However, substantial increases in agricultural output are essential to move the system, provide jobs, and generate income in the rural sector to buy goods and services. Generally, such substantial increases can be achieved only through improved

TABLE 29

WORLD CEREAL PRODUCTION

Country	Kg Per Head and Per Year	
	1961-65	1974
1. Poorest countries (less than $200 per capita)	145	136
2. Middle-income countries (more than $200)	134	163
3. All developing countries	143	147
4. Developed countries (over $2,000)	510	590
Coefficient of disparity:		
Developed countries/developing countries	3.5	4.0
Developed countries/+poorest	3.5	4.3
Middle-income countries/+poorest	0.9	1.2

SOURCE: World Bank, "Food Problems of the Low-Income Countries", Finance and Development, June 1977.

agricultural technology supported by a variety of activities required to assure access to the benefits of that technology. The planning and management of technology and inputs to achieve greater physical outputs on the farm is the necessary, though not sufficient, element in any rural development program.

Study of the diffusion of technical change in agriculture in the Sahel has been limited at times by the unprofitability of the innovation recommended to farmers. Because it was believed that farmers were rejecting profitable innovations, there has been a major emphasis on studies to discover the barriers to the acceptance of innovation. There are many aspects of Sahelian culture and social organization which are highly conducive to the rapid spread of innovation. There is need for research which will analyze these positive features and provide the basis for policy and programs which take advantage of these positive features for the more rapid spread of innovation. Profitable innovations will often spread among farmers naturally. However, understanding of social processes can provide the basis for greatly accelerated diffusion. For instance, it is important not to lose sight of the fact that agricultural work like religious rites, in the context of the Sahelians' high valuation of social solidarity, are social events, strengthening the bonds of kinship. Obligations to one's kinsfolk to share in agricultural work is a potent means of preserving group solidarity.

The Sahel's agrarian structure is basically wholesome compared to feudalistic counterparts in other regions of the world. Sprawling "latifundia" do not dominate small private holdings, requiring drastic land reform. Empirical data suggest that the communal systems of land tenure in the Sahel have not proved in themselves so inflexible as to preclude adaptation to new conditions. The question of the influence of land tenure in the Sahel is, therefore, not whether traditional systems present "per se" a powerful obstacle to economic development but, rather, whether the new forms arising from the increasing invasion of subsistence economy by an economy based on exchange will lead to economic development without, in the long haul, destroying much of the land for agricultural production, or resulting in abuses detrimental to the social and economic welfare of the community.

The Sahel Development Program calls for the achievement of food self-sufficiency by the year 2000. Assuming a slight increase in nutritional intake and, in comparison with the situation in the Sahel prior to the drought, it will be necessary by the end of the century to more than double the production of staple cereals and livestock, increase the output of rice almost fivefold and that of wheat (almost nil at the moment) to more than 500,000 tons annually.[13]

Principal policy issues in the agriculture sector include:

- Post-harvest losses are high in the Sahel.

Several studies indicate losses generally around 20 percent and, occasionally, as high as 40 percent. Improved storage and processing of foods could contribute greatly to reducing famine and malnutrition. The most recent Sahelian crisis dramatically demonstrated the need for central storage and, especially, for regionally oriented systems. Private enterprise has a role to play, but is frequently being ignored or constrained. Commercial storage in higher risk areas, when coupled with national and regional storage policies, could help to alleviate periodic, drought-caused famine.

- More rational price policies could have an important long-term effect on production and income. The current maze of price supports, controls, and subsidies tend to neutralize each other and act as disincentives to increased production of cereals and cash crops.

- A renewed effort to make farm inputs -- seed, fertilizer, pesticides, and credit -- available to all interested farmers and encourage all farmers in their use could help achieve optimum return on land and work. More research is needed on problems affecting rainfed agriculture. The development of minimum package technology also stands to improve prospects for increasing the productivity of the majority of farmers.

Herders are the second major group of rural poor. They account for about one-fourth the regional population. These pastoralists share the Savanna belt with small farmers and occupy for the most part the Sahel zone of the Savanna belt during the rainy season, moving southward with their animals in pursuit of water and grass as the rains recede. Herders tend livestock, their chief asset, whose numbers in the Sahel before the drought were among the highest in Africa. Within the group of herders is a small population of nomads who inhabit the northern subdesert. These nomadic people tend mainly camels and goats, do not farm and are virtually unreachable by government services.

Herding societies have a relatively flexible social organization which has evolved from the rigors of transhumance in inhospitable surroundings and the need for demographic balance in the herds. Thus, the motive of combining and recombining herds is neither maximization of profit nor the well-being of animals, but survival. The same flexible social organization prevents large accumulation of animals among its members by various redistributive methods such as loans, marriages, and gifts. An intricate, evolved code of relations between herders and farmers requires that herders respect the demands on land during the agricultural season and keep out of major areas of farming activity. However, the nature of the two activities (farming and herding) is complementary. Small farmers who own cattle entrust them during the agricultural season to traditional herders who take the animals on a long migration in search of forage. Farmers usually reciprocate by allowing the herders to pasture their own animals in harvested fields. Cattle eat crop stalks and other residue and the farmers receive manure as fertilizer in return.

Of the two rural groups the life of the herder is the harder, his existence the more precarious. Invariably all of the "quality of life" indicators are dismally low -- in health, nutrition, mortality, education, transferable skills, and income. The number of cattle, the herders' principal asset, which perished during the 1968-1974 drought was tremendous, variously estimated at 20-50 percent of pre-drought figures in Mauritania and Niger, 20-40 percent in Mali and Chad, and 10-20 percent in Upper Volta. Furthermore, what the drought did not destroy, accelerated slaughtering did. These losses and changes in the age and sex composition of livestock herds will affect production of meat and milk for many years. By 1977 only the Gambia had replenished cattle herds to pre-drought levels. A return to normalcy will be gradual. Due care will have to be exercised in controlling grazing to expand carrying capacity of the land and to increase meat production.

Changes in the agriculture of the Sahel highlight the integral nature of integrated development within the "seamless web" of social reality. As with other open-ended notions like "art" or "politics," in the study of modernization the interest of facts lies in their variety, and the power of ideas rests not on the degree to which it homogenizes the disparate variables, but the degree to which it can order them. The social science community on the whole has a much larger and substantive role to play in the development of assistance strategies than has been the case heretofore. The social scientist has historically been an examiner of local systems in a static sense. In many ways, this has permitted the creation of a valuable critical analysis of local institutions. The time has come, however, for the addition of certain further responsibilities. These responsibilities relate to the target groups in development schemes. It is no longer adequate for social scientists to study local cultures without examining conceptual tectonics. Inputs in the development process, including capital accumulation and health care, must be perceived as vehicles to integrated development germane to the process in proportion to the stock placed by them in the conceptual systems of transforming societies. Development cannot afford to collapse result into process. To contend that the major stumbling blocks to integrated development are in the main non-economic is not to deny that these obstacles could not be hurdled with the aid of propititious economic measures. Unquestionably, trade and commerce, the urbanization that accompanies industry, the impartiality of the market, lead to a valuable cross-fertilization of ideas, to exposure, and to re-orienting and re-shaping of the sociocultural environment. Yet, it is important to add parenthetically that intensive studies of incremental capital output ratios, difficult though they are to be precise about, agree in showing wide variations by country in the amount of capital needed to get the same increase in output.[14]

In the words of John Stuart Mill:

> Human nature is not a machine to be built after a model, and set to do exactly the work prescribed for it, but a tree, which requires to grow and develop itself on all sides, according to the tendancy of the inward forces which make it a living thing.[15]

The development of human skills, institutions, and attitudinal change is a more intricate matter than the mere injection of capital. It may be cheaper, but it is certainly more difficult. Whereas in the colonial period human difficulties appeared to Third Worlders as exogenous and political, they have now become endogenous, socioeconomic, and to that extent more emphasized in a political matrix that, under the new circumstances, can not insulate itself in pursuit of stability.

Personal and inarticulate aesthetic considerations can at times be more effective in the conversion of perpetuators to the ways of the modern paradigm than the most articulable technical arguments. Michael Polanyi has underscored the centrality to human development of "tacit knowledge," i.e., knowledge that is acquired through practice and that cannot be articulated explicitly.[16] The peasant who embraces a new technique must often do so in defiance of the evidence provided by problem-solving. He must, that is, have faith that the new approach will succeed with the many large problems that confront it, knowing only that the traditional method has failed with a few. A decision of that kind can only be made on faith since it is based less on past achievement than on future promise.

Because the unit of cultural achievement is the solved problem, and because social groups know well which problems have already been solved, few perpetuators will be persuaded to adopt a viewpoint that opens problems that seem neutralized. This impulse of society to protect the rightness of its prior decisions is widespread. Among economists it is known as the sunk cost fallacy. In psychology, this tendency to cleave to states of the world previously "invested in" is called cognitive dissonance. Nature itself, through some erratic behavior, may undermine societal security to the point that prior achievements seem problematic. Thus, the opportunity for change presents itself. The Sahel, today, is at such a juncture. The Sahelians have, in many areas, the advantage of substituting evolution-toward-what-we-wish-to-know with evolution-toward-what-we-do-know.

In the human resources sector, special importance should be attached to policy formulation relative to education and health. Sahelian students continue today to spend most of their school time accumulating and encoding what A.M. Whitehead referred to as "inert ideas that are merely received into the mind without being utilized, or tested, or thrown into fresh combinations." Many Sahelian political and educational leaders have criticized the present schooling system for disorienting young people from the realities of Sahelian life and for failing to respond to the needs of Sahelian society.

If the education system is to become germane to Sahelians, it must not simply produce farmers -- but good farmers equiped with knowledge that can make them function with a degree of confidence. To this end, a number of Sahelian countries are re-examining the curriculum, the functions and the organization of schools in agriculturally-based societies. There is a growing awareness that if the school is to play its proper role, it must inculcate in students and, at the very least, not deprecate appropriate social attitudes of living and working in rural communities. To this extent, education can contribute to controlling urban swelling.

The importance of education to development is nowhere more clearly demonstrated than in the area of health. Many Sahelians in the hinterland need to be informed about transmission of maladies and convinced that, for instance, snail vectors are a serious hazard to their health. Schistosomiasis is the best-known health problem resulting from irrigated agriculture, though Sahelians in rural areas are generally unaware of its transmission. The snail vectors live in canals and along the banks of lakes and sluggish rivers. Transmission can be reduced by decreasing the snail population but preventing the snail from infesting open water sources is almost impossible. Thus a more feasible alternative is to limit human-snail contact. Because human behavior patterns are a central factor in the transmission of vector-borne diseases, education is a directly effective way of limiting the spread of disease. Instruction of adults and children in schools and training facilities about the daily practices that spread disease should be considered whenever implementing large-scale projects that touch on this kind of problem. At the United Nations Water Conference in Mar Del Plata, Argentine, the revelation was made that 70 percent of the world's population is without safe and dependable water supplies. More than two billion men, women, and children are exposed to infectious diseases because of the lack of safe water. There are 250 million new cases of water-borne diseases a year and 25,000 people die daily from them. There is evidence that providing safe drinking water is as much a social phenomenon as a technical one. In the Sahel, a great deal has to be learned about water hygiene, including institutionalized water supply and waste disposal. More than 2000 years ago, the Chinese believed that drinking cold water could make you sick. If a host did not have tea, boiling water was served, even on the hottest days. Where Sahelians believe that murky water is more "nutritious" than clear water, as do the Gourmantchay of Upper Volta, an educative process should be initiated without delay.

An education that is relevant to the needs of poor, rural people can increase self-confidence with a multiplier effect on an individual's willingness to fully tap his resourcefulness and make contributions to his community. Self-awareness with any acuity, a prerequisite for cognitive exposure, is a derivative of education. In a speech at the University of Dakar, an institution he was instrumental in founding, Senghor reminded the Senegalese elite that their education would have to bear the imprint of Negritude: "E-ducation, by its very etymology, means being torn from self and from one's milieu, assimilation of self to foreign elements ... But education is first of all a return to self ... It is evident that in order to assimilate, one must have the strength to assimilate, one must be. And a people cannot be by denying itself."[17]

Among the 8 Sahelian countries, there are roughly 37 distinct linguistic/ethnic groups. Consequently, the governments of the Sahelian countries have, without exception, indicated that priority consideration should be given to reform of their primary school systems as a step toward national unity. Nonetheless, education in the Sahel falls short of serving the needs of the rural majority. Few of the Sahelian countries have yet achieved more than an estimated 10 percent adult literacy rate; the estimated rate for all Africa is 17 percent. While Senegal has managed to enroll 23 percent of school-age students, other Sahelian countries average out at an enrollment rate closer to 10 percent against 27 percent for all Africa. Given the dent that education makes in national budgets (approximately 22 percent), fiscal and social costs in terms of the education system as a development tool exceed social benefits. Farm families in rural areas that are benefitting from crop production projects have greater access to education than do farm families in more remote areas. The more isolated among the rural population are reached by local language radio broadcasts. Many of these northern-tier herders and nomads adhere to Islam and receive childhood training in Arabic. On the other hand, religious literacy alone is insufficient for equipping these people for the inevitable demands of more complex life. Moreover, these societies traditionally shun women from even this kind of training, rendering them the least educated group in the Sahel.

Previous attempts at reforming the primary school systems have largely been confined to decree promulgations without adequate preparation. As a result they have led to high costs, to disappointment and to unproductive disruption of the existing systems. All the same, creation of functional learning systems at the national and local levels will be essential to the success of Sahelian development. The building of these systems should proceed on three fronts simultaneously:

1. In primary and functional education, through adapting the primary school system to present day requirements, including the need for functional education of the parents of school children. A major part of this reform would be the introduction of lessons and materials in indigenous languages, rather than in French;

2. In non-formal education, working through radio, extension techniques, traditional institutions and experimentation with modern technology to reach producers and their families;

3. In specialized human resources and management training, to meet the needs for trained manpower in agriculture, livestock, fishing, health, water resources, and other key areas.

In creating these functional learning systems across the Sahel, planners will need to be guided by periodic estimates of changing manpower needs and availabilities. Similarly, planning of health and social services requires reliable data concerning population growth and distribution combined with an accurate assessment of health and disease patterns. Unless national censuses, surveys, and epidemiologic studies in the Sahel take special account of the following three factors, considerable uncertainty will remain concerning purported future demographic patterns:

1. Migration: nomadism, rural settlement, and also rural-to-urban population shifts;
2. Isolated rural populations; and
3. Changing fertility and age-specific mortality rates.

Less than 20 percent of the Sahelian population have access to modern health care, making this one of the most serious problems confronting rural development. For the present, Sahelian health services are inadequate for the task before them. Even a cursory examination of health expenditures shows the lion's share of resources going for facilities, personnel, and urban curative health care. Outreach and preventive services which have the greatest potential for affecting vital rates are sadly neglected. Few disease control programs have been initiated, although a significant effort to free higher rainfall areas from river-blindness is underway in Upper Volta. Aside from malnutrition, major debilitating diseases in the Sahel are malaria, measles, and intestinal diseases with concentrations of schistosomiasis, trypanosomiasis, and onchocerciasis in some areas. Programs to control these diseases are expensive, complex, and beyond the means of these countries.

It has been posited that the use of village health workers in the development and collection of health and vital statistics offers an effective mechanism by which to develop a health information system. Moreover, it is possible to train village practitioners and selected village residents to enhance their skills in prevention and to provide simple diagnoses and treatment of common health problems and, thus, to facilitate their effective intervention in the health status of the community. At the local level, the common disease patterns of infants and young children -- respiratory infections, diarrhea, malaria, and malnutrition -- are the major killers and can be effectively managed at the village level, along with a wide variety of prevalent infectious and parasitic diseases. Village health workers, as they continue to serve their communities, can expand the scope of their knowledge and problem-solving skills.

An important goal of the health sector is the programmatic linking of water delivery projects with village-based health services. Pilot rural water supply projects will shed light on the degree of maintenance and utilization of water delivery systems. These data will provide a much needed insight into potable water delivery and future development options. Recognition of the significance of problems of allocation, proprietary rights, and priorities for access to water (especially when it is a scarce commodity) and solution of some of the problems of basic resources (e.g., river basin agreements) and of providing maintenance and operating funds, offer reason to expect redoubled effort and additional funding to be more successful in improving water availability than has been the case in recent experience.

Increased emphasis on environmental impact analysis is necessary in the Sahel, especially in the health sector. More information is required on the impact of population distribution (often influenced by development initiatives) on the environment and how each development activity ultimately relates to the health status of the individual and to the ecological integrity of the country and/or region. In Chad, the Bol Polder (a pilot irrigation project) was assessed by AID to determine the effect of irrigation on various water related diseases (schistosomiasis, malaria, etc.). It was disclosed that the incidence of a number of parasitic infections increased and, in fact, the general disease situation was exacerbated. Further research should develop criteria for determining appropriate technology for water projects that would include possibilities of recycling water supply and waste water management with resource recovery at the village level (e.g., fish farming), social and physical environmental considerations, and codification of water rights and changes necessary if supply is to be altered.

Ecological degradation is serious throughout the Sahel and a science policy which encourages technological inputs that maximize resource conservation should be adopted. It is often possible to save significant amounts of water by better farm management. Cultivation practices are significant factors in shaping the flux and storage of water within the soil in farmland areas. Spray and trickle techniques are capable of distributing water very sparingly. Improved coordination in the application to farm problems of the several specialities related to the effective use of water is essential.

Less than half the world's drier zones are unproductive deserts for climatic reasons, but useable land is being converted to waste by the influence of man and livestock. About sixty million people live directly on the interfaces of deserts and arable lands, and the basis of their livelihood and living standards is in jeopardy.[18] Once lost to desert encroachment, land is reclaimed for human benefit only at tremendous cost.

The Sahel Development Program is pervious to the problems of deforestation and ecological disequilibrium in the Sahel. The situation will continue to deteriorate for a good many years because of the magnitude of firewood requirements and the demand for agricultural and pastoral land of a growing population. The Club has set ambitious reforestation targets designed to meet requirements for firewood and construction timber, better management and protection of grazing land, conservation of soil, and protection of wildlife. The outcome of the first phase firewood production sub-program (1978-1982) is expected to be 110,000 hectares of new forest and improved management of 877,000 existing hectares.[19] In the case of several countries, this program will not suffice to make up the shortfall caused by increased energy (wood) consumption. To recapitulate:

- When water supplies are limited, a population density that seems low on paper can be overwhelming on land. The effective use of water for both crop and livestock production requires policies that stress conservation of this precious resource.

- Attaining environmental balance requires striking a technological balance. A coherent science policy for the Sahel as a whole could contribute to progress on this and many other fronts by encouraging allocation of resources to specific R & D objectives with regional relevance and by increasing cooperation within technology networks.

- Small-scale technologies may be the solution to the Sahel's energy needs, and consequently, an important means of decelerating Saharan encroachment. Sahelian governments should actively incorporate these technologies into rural development programs.

Policy recommendations -- were it otherwise -- are easier to make than to implement. Given the intractability of the environment-energy trade-off, the adequacy of any one of these recommendations will turn on the effectiveness of its intervention strategy.

MAINTENANCE OF AIM -- A JOURNEY OF ONE THOUSAND MILES

Because integrated development is "the very stuff of politics -- the kernel of crucial decisions" in the developing countries, it places great demands on the policymaker who cannot afford to be less than conversant in the development process. In addition, the policymaker is torn by the perennial competition, and one endemic to all governments, between the urge for comprehensive measures in addressing complex issues and the urge to respond piecemeal to the momentary crisis at hand. Even the most closed governing systems have chinks, creating innumerable uncontrollables and a need for symbolic, rather than real, performance. The influences which congeal to exert pressures for the enactment of measures with immediate returns often do the cause of integrated development a disservice.

Speed kills in development too. William Letwin remarks: "If rapidity of economic growth were not costly in terms of other human objectives everyone should endorse it without qualification; as it is, no reasonable man can prefer it to the exclusion of all other goals. It is one of many objectives, and must be weighed against the rest."[20] Many dimensions of social and economic development must be laboriously acquired "ex post" and "en route." Thus, progress can frequently be halting and circuitous. Societies may involuntarily enter into a traumatic state of double exposure in which they are buffeted by strong tensions between residual and modern values. In the interim, social cleavages are exacerbated and economic contradictions grow. With a smaller pie, elites are less generous, and the chances of a "revolution from above" diminish proportionately to shrinking resources.

Albeit, in a number of Third World countries (especially those, including several of the Sahelian countries, that fall under the rubric of the Fourth World) average and total incomes remain abysmally low, some of these countries could do a better job on the distribution and employment fronts and, therefore, need to change or amend some of their modes of agricultural and industrial expansion. However, even with improvements in domestic policies, developing countries require reinforced economic expansion to cope more effectively with their internal equity problems. John P. Lewis states:

> There is no way they (the developing countries) can meet their welfare needs simply by reshuffling existing income -- or by accenting new (non-economic) dimensions of social ambience. If they would be more egalitarian, they need more aggregate growth and more growth-supporting investment, so that they can spread income increments over a broader base.[21]

Unfortunately, foreign investment in a program in the Sahel which could foster the policies delineated herein is not assured. On the U.S. front, President Carter's determination to trim the federal budget while making substantial aid commitments elsewhere, especially in the Middle East, will make it difficult to obtain the backing of the Administration and Congress. Support in Congress for long-term aid, especially for the expensive drought-proofing process is problematic for a number of reasons. To begin with, Congress has been disillusioned because in some quarters it was expected that a full-fledged development program would result from the initial $5 million contribution. In effect, this was only a down-payment which helped finance a set of plans. The result of this advanced planning has been projections of far larger sums of money than were expended at the height of the 1968-1974 drought. In the absence of the vivid media coverage of the Sahel when outright crisis conditions prevailed, Appropriation Committee members will not have the specter of famine-stricken children on their consciences. Moreover, at a time when, Thelma is just as likely to be associated with the disco group as with the battle cry of the civil rights movement, it is difficult to detect domestic, grass-roots lobbies that could prod concerned principals into approving SDP installments over time. Despite evident faltering on Capitol Hill, there has been no call to arms by sympathetic ethnic groups or private voluntary organizations. Although black Americans have been airing numerous gripes with the White House, follow-up on SDP is not one of them.

The Administration and the Congress must be reminded that the Sahel fits current criteria for foreign assistance rather snugly -- it is the poorest region of the world by any test. Participation in the transformation of the Sahel affords an opportunity to demonstrate U.S. commitment to human needs so basic as to be human rights. In the final analysis, the costs of sitting out a major international effort, requiring careful coordination and burden sharing, outweigh the benefits. An unwillingness to cooperate with other donors, including OPEC, would undermine the credibility of U.S. commitment to easing

North-South tensions. Naturally, the brunt of disappointment would be felt by Sahelians and could possibly ramify throughout Africa. According to Constance Freeman, SDP is being viewed by Africans as a litmus paper test of U.S. policy towards that continent:

> Current U.S. relations with black African countries, while significantly better than those of the past decade, remain tenuous. Africans are still skeptical about the degree and character of U.S. interest in their problems and have, in many cases adopted a "wait and see" attitude. Substantial U.S. involvement in the Sahel, an area in which this country has little short-term political interest, would demonstrate to Africans that the United States is sincerely interested in their major goal -- long-term development. Conversely, an unwillingness to participate would send a negative signal to Africans in the face of repeated U.S. assurances of U.S. support for African interests. It might also be interpreted as an unwillingness to participate in a program in which Africans themselves are increasingly taking the lead. Finally, the Sahel program provides a useful format in which to provide substantial assistance to African "moderates" as many Sahelian countries fall into this category.[22]

Whatever course it elects to pursue, the United States must make its decision without further delay. By waffling, false expectations are created in the Sahel, where there are signs of frustration as a result of less generous resource transfers to date than were anticipated. Although some might argue for procrastination in addressing this question and subtlety in breaking the news to the Sahelians, there are limits to what I have referred to as paralysis by analysis. These bounds were reached with the submission of recommendations generated in the initial planning process. The question now is whether to fish or cut bait.

Were the U.S. to pull out of SDP, it is unlikely that the Club-inspired pattern of development would unravel. Conversely, if the decision is affirmative and, this possibility cannot be ruled out, it will be necessary to rethink U.S. foreign assistance. Since the inaugeration of the Congressionally mandated "New Directions" policy in 1975, AID has allocated the bulk of its resources to efforts aimed at providing services to the poor majorities in developing countries. As a result of this legislation, AID has not participated in the construction financing of infrastructure projects in the belief that such projects have little or no "trickle down" of benefits to the rural poor. Ancillary arguments given in support of this legislation are that enough financing by other donors is available to meet infrastructure needs and that the relatively modest U.S. aid budget is better spent on programs providing a more direct link to the rural poor. However, as pointed out in an AID Policy Paper,

> If country commitment is strong enough to assure that the benefits of development assistance will actually support rather than subvert programs toward basic needs objectives, U.S. assistance could expand to include activities which, though they may operate more indirectly, are necessary to meeting basic needs over the longer run.[23]

To realize such integrated development objectives as basic human needs, the economic growth vector must literally be bent and woven into a pattern of distribution of income that permits the low-end poor access to vital goods and services. To augment the supply of services and to facilitate access to them is normally a governmental function. In the Sahel, this function encompasses expanded infrastructure. In other words, road construction and river basin development are concatenated variables central to a permanent improvement in living standards of the poor majority.

Foreign aid (American or of other provenance) can also do something else. It can alleviate the long-standing and severe political development problems that underlie national and regional tensions. As John Dunn observes: "... it takes today a real ideologue, whether of the right or of the left, to see with any confidence a happy political future for the Sahel."[24] By relieving economic pressure on the system, aid can strengthen the resolve to make prolonged, at times, painful changes. However, it will not do to accept the tacit assumption that with foreign aid the more diffuse forms of economic and social change will almost stealthily prevail over the follies and irrational stubborness of politics. The infectious optimism Functionalist theorists reserve for an ascendant habit of international cooperation notwithstanding, donors may occasionally need to engage in the unpopular, unilaterally conceived, business of policy and performance conditioning. Nonetheless, the emergence of multilateral aid organizations like the Club du Sahel and CILSS marks a turning point in Sahelian regional integration. These transnational bodies -- existing under international auspices, employing personnel of many nationalities, and operating within national jurisdictions -- endow enterprises like the Sahel Development Program with the staying power to achieve integrated development. In this journey of one thousand miles, foreign aid distilled is largely a matter of maintenance of aim.

Notes

CHAPTER ONE

1. John W. Sewell, "The Sahel Is Not a Wasteland," The New York Times, June 22, 1976.

2. Jacques Giri,"Scientific and Technological Cooperation with the Sahel Countries; The Experience of the Club du Sahel," OECD, STCD/S/78.5, March 15, 1978, mimeo.

3. See Noel V. Lateef, "The African Greenhouse," War on Hunger, November 1977.

4. "Drought in Africa: Acts of Man," The Economist, June 11, 1977, p. 56.

5. Framework for Evaluating Long-Term Strategies for the Development of the Sahel-Sudano Region, Massachusetts Institute of Technology, 1974; An Approach to Recovery and Rehabilitation of the Sahel Region, United Nations Sahel Office, 1975; World Bank Approach to Economic Development of Sahel, IBRD, 1975; Perspective Study of Agricultural Development in Countries of the Sahel Area, FAO, 1974; and Progress Report on the Drought-Stricken Regions of Africa and Adjacent Areas, UNDP, 1976.

6. See Noel V. Lateef, "The Sahel's Uncertain Future," The Progressive, June 1975.

7. Guillaume Boudat, Desertification de l'Afrique tropicale seche (Paris: Anasonia, 1973), p. 505.

8. A.I.D. internal memorandum from Goler T. Butcher to John J. Gilligan, August 8, 1977, p. 4.

9. Although information is scanty, that which exists indicates that human mortality related to the drought was much less than was at first feared. This was due not only to relief efforts but also to the tenaciousness and skill which the people of these countries have developed to survive a catastrophe of this magnitude. For an extensive discussion of the methods they used, see John C. Caldwell, The Sahelian Drought and its Demographic Implications, Overseas Liaison Committee, American Council on Education, Paper No. 8, December 1975.

10. See Elliot Berg, "The Recent Economic Evolution of the Sahel," Center for Research on Economic Development, University

of Michigan, June 1975, p. 30.

11. Caldwell, p. 67.

12. Albert O. Hirschman, The Strategy of Economic Development (New Haven, Yale University Press, 1958), p. 176.

13. Ibid., p. 5.

14. In a 1966 policy document prepared for AID and the State Department, Ambassador Edward Dorry recommended reduction of U.S. bilateral assistance to Africa. The Sahelian countries were not included among the 10 countries earmarked to continue recieving aid.

15. James K. Bishop and J.D. Esseks, "U.S. Aid to the Sahel," ASA Paper, 1976, mimeo., p. 4.

16. The reports are reproduced in AID press releases of August 21, 1973 and October 23, 1973.

17. John P. Lewis, Quiet Crisis in India (New York: Doubleday & Co., 1962), p. 1.

18. U.N. Public Affairs Office Release, June 6, 1974.

19. Interview with President Leopold S. Senghor, Dakar, Senegal, June 2, 1977.

20. Quoted in Sanford J. Ungar, "The Real Reasons For Our Africa Role," The Washington Post, June 18, 1978.

21. Interview with President Hamani Diori, Niamey, Niger, May 12, 1972.

22. See "An African Policy," The Washington Post, April 25, 1976.

23. Lewis, p. 6.

24. Rajni Kothari, "Sources of Conflict in the 1980s," February 1977, mimeo.

25. NAS, "More Water for Arid Lands," Washington, D.C., 1974, p. 12.

26. Brookings Institution, "Reappraising Foreign Aid," Washington, D.C., July 1977, mimeo., p.23.

27. Richard N. Cooper, paper presented at M.I.T. Conference on NIEO, May 1976, mimeo.

28. Gunnar Myrdal, "The Conditions of Economic Integration" in Robert Lekachman, ed., National Policy for Economic Welfare at Home and Abroad (New York: Columbia University Press, 1955), p. 173.

29. William Letwin, "Four Fallacies about Economic Development" in David E. Novack and Robert Lekachman eds., Development and Society: The Dynamics of Economic Change (New York: St. Martins Press, 1968), p. 33.

30. "Making the Sahel Bloom," The Baltimore Sun, May 7, 1976.

CHAPTER TWO

1. Richard Higgot and Finn Fuglestad, "The 1974 Coup d'Etat in Niger: Towards an Explanation." The Journal of Modern African Studies, September 1975, p. 383.

2. Samir Amin, Neocolonialism in West Africa, (Harmonds-

worth: Penguin Books Ltd., 1973) p. 66.

3. Karl Deutch, "Theories of Imperialism and Neocolonialism" In Steven J. Rosen and James R. Kurth eds., *Testing Theories of Economic Imperialism*, (New York: D.C. Heath and Co., 1974) p. 32.

4. Tony Smith "The Underdevelopment of Development Literature," *World Politics*, Vol. XXXI, January 1979, p. 288.

5. Johan Galtung, "A Structural Theory of Imperialism," International Peace Research Institute Publication, No. 27-1, p. 87.

6. Klaus Knorr, The Power of Nations, (New York: Basic Books, Inc., 1975) p. 255.

7. Amin, p. 165.

8. One U.S. dollar = 275 Francs CFA.

9. *Rapport Jeaneney*, "La Politique de Cooperation avec les pays en voie de developpement;" (Paris: Documentation Francaise, 1963).

10. Interview with Diori.

11. "Le Chef d'Etat au sujet de l'uranium," *Les Temps du Niger*, April 4, 1973, p. 1.

12. "Le Prix de l'Uranium," *Jeune Afrique*, No. 717, October 5, 1974, p. 31.

13. Higgot and Fuglestad, p. 396.

14. *Le Monde*, May 6, 1974, p. 13.

15. "Une Confiance Excessive," *Jeune Afrique*, No. 795, April 2, 1976, p. 23.

16. Amin, p. 274.

17. René Dumont, "The Third World in Mortal Danger," *Development Forum*, I, 6, August-September 1973, p. 2.

18. Seymour Martin Lipset, *Political Man: The Social Bases of Politics* (Garden City: Doubleday, 1963), p. 70.

19. Mamadou Diarra, *Les Etats Africains et la Garantie Monétaire de la France*, (Dakar: Les Nouvelles Editions Africaines, 1972), p. 60.

20. "France's Role in Africa," *West Africa*, February 19, 1979.

21. "La Crise de la Cooperation," *Le Monde*, December 2, 1972.

22. E. Wesley F. Peterson, "French Economic Relations with the West African Monetary Union," Woodrow Wilson Association Monograph Series, No. 7, Princeton University, 1975, p. 22.

23. A book which typifies the views of many Sahelians is Basil Davidson's *Can Africa Survive? Arguments Against Growth Without Development* (Boston: Little, Brown and Company, 1974). Recently R.D. McKinlay and R. Little in an article entitled: "A Foreign Policy Model of U.S. Bilateral Aid Allocation," (*World Politics*, October 1977, Vol. xxx, No. 1), examine the foreign policy utilities inherent in dependency through the optic of an analytic model of U.S. aid allocation.

24. Henri Bourguinat, "Les groupements economiques regionaux des pays en voie de developpement: pour une reevaluation,"

Etudes Economiques Ouest Africaines No. 12, BCEAO, May 1977.

25. W. David Hopper, "The Development of Agriculture in Developing Countries," Scientific American, September 1976, p. 142.

26. FAO, CIFA Report of the Consultation of Fishery Problems in the Sahelian Zone, Committee for Inland Fisheries for Africa (CIFA) Occasional Paper 4, 1975, p. 13.

CHAPTER THREE

1. Barend A. de Uries, "New Perspectives on International Development," Finance and Development, Vol. 5, No. 3, September 1968, p. 25.

2. Ibid., p. 26.

3. Cited in Albert O. Hirschman, The Passions and the Interests (Princeton: Princeton University Press, 1977), p. 55.

4. Ibid., p. ii.

5. Jacques Giri, "An Analysis and Synthisis of Long-Term Development Strategies for the Sahel," OECD, March 1976, mimeo.

6. Inis L. Claude, Jr., Swords Into Plowshares: The Problems and Progress of International Organization, (New York: Random House, 1969 Third Ed.), p. ix.

7. Maurice J. Williams, Development Cooperation-Efforts and Policies of the Members of the Development Assistance Committee -- 1977 Review, OECD, November 1977, p. 133.

8. Club des Amis du Sahel, "Strategy and Program for Drought Control and Development in the Sahel," May 1977, mimeo., p. 8.

9. AID transcript of Ottawa Meeting of the Club des Amis du Sahel, April 1977, mimeo., p. 2.

10. CILSS Directive No. 12/CM/8, Bamako, January 1976, mimeo., p. 1.

11. Mahbub ul Haq, The Poverty Curtain: Choices for the Third World (New York: Columbia University Press, 1976), p. 70.

12. See Clive Gray, "Working Group for the Study of Recurrent Costs of Development Projects in the Sahel," CILSS - Harvard Institute for International Development, May 18, 1979, mimeo.

13. Paul Marc Henry, Programme integré de developpement dans le Sahel, Vol. 4, (Paris: Norbert Beyard France, 1974), p. 127.

14. GAO, "The Sahel Development Program -- Progress and Constraints," ID - 78 - 18, March 29, 1978, p. 5.

15. Ron Kornell, Internal Memorandum, "Mid-east Trip -- Report to Arab Financial Institutions, Club du Sahel, March 17, 1978.

16. AID, "Sahel Development Program; Annual Report to the Congress," February 1979, p. 7.

17. Goler T. Butcher, "Africa: New Successes and New Challenges," Agenda, April 1979, p. 23.

18. GAO, "U.S. Development Assistance to the Sahel -- Pro-

gress and Problems," ID-79-9, March 29, 1979, p. 3.

19. Jim Kelly, "Review of the Regional Development Strategy for the Sahel," AID Memorandum, April 5, 1979, p. 2.

20. Butcher, Action Memorandum for the Acting Administer April 10, 1979, p. 1, Attachments A, B, and C.

21. Lucian W. Pye and Sidney Verba, eds., Political Culture and Political Development (Princeton: Princeton University Press, 1965), pp. 38, 51.

22. Claude, p. 352.

23. Paul S. Reinsch cited in Claude, p. 350.

CHAPTER FOUR

1. See Edward F. Denison, Why Growth Rates Differ, Washington: The Brookings Institution, 1967.

2. AID, "Excerpts from Various Documents on Health Programs in Africa; a Submission to the National Medical Association," January 1975, p. 4.

3. Ibid., p. 37.

4. Ibid., p. 55.

5. Family Health Care, Inc., "Health Impact Guidelines for the Design of Development Projects in the Sahel," Contract No. AID/afr-C-1138, April 13, 1979, p. 20.

6. ECA/FAO, Women's Unit, "The Health Status of African Women," mimeo, 1974, p. 73.

7. David Shear, "The Role of the Village in Sahelian Development," April 1978, mimeo., p. 25.

8. AID, "Development Assistance Program FY 75: Upper Volta and Niger," March 1975, p. 20.

9. Lee M. Howard, "Key Problems Impeding Modernization of Developing Countries -- The Health Issues," AID, 1970, p. 72.

10. James Grant, presentation made before SID World Conference in Ottawa, May 1971, mimeo.,p. 3.

11. P. Abela, "The Growth of the Education System in the French-Speaking States of Tropical Africa," Paper for the European Regional Conference SID, Cologne, May 4-6, 1970.

12. David Shear and Roy Stacey, "The Sahel: An Approach to the Future," War on Hunger, May 1975, p. 13.

13. Louis Malassis, The Rural World: Education and Development (Paris: The UNESCO Press, 1976), p. 115.

14. UNESCO, "Guide pratique d'alphabetisation fonctionnelle," 1972, p. 14.

15. Ibid.

16. See Benjamin Bloom, Stability and Change in Human Characteristics (New York: Wiley, 1964).

17. O.K. Moore, "Some Puzzling Aspects of Social Interaction" in J. Crawford, ed., Mathematical Models in Small Group Processes (Stanford: Stanford University Press, 1962).

18. Frederick Harbison, Lecture at Princeton University, May 1, 1973.

19. PECTA, "Employment in the Sahel" February 1977, p. 4.

20. David Turnham, The Employment Problems in Less Developed Countries (Paris: OECD, 1971), p. 122.

21. Ronald G. Ridker, Employment and Unemployment Problems of the Near East and South Asia (Delhi: Vikas Publications, 1973), p. 40.

22. Michael Lipton, Why Poor People Stay Poor: Urban Bias and World Development (Cambridge: Harvard University Press, 1977).

23. Lewis, Quiet Crisis in India, pp. 192-195.

24. Ibid.

25. Michael A. Cohen, et al., "Urban Growth and Economic Development in the Sahel," World Bank Staff Working Paper No. 315, January, 1979, p. 4.

26. AID, "Manpower Planning in the Sahel," ADO-Ougadougou, 1976, p. 2.

27. ILO, "Sharing in Development," Geneva, 1975, p. 14.

28. OAU, "The Unemployment Problem in Africa," Addis Aba, 1977.

29. See ILO, "Time for Transition," Geneva, 1975.

30. ILO, "Sharing in Development," p. 43.

31. M.L. Dantwala, "Definition of Unemployment and Problems of its Measurement in Developing Countries," In The Challenge of Unemployment to Development and the Role of Training and Research Institutes in Development (Paris: OECD, 1971), p. 30.

32. Turnham has suggested a technique whose operational procedure would be: "... (i) to calculate average income among fully employed workers; (ii) to take one-half or one-third (and potential full-time) workers whose income falls below this level and (iii) examine the circumstances of this group-activities (and the lack of them); status-employees/self-employed, etc.; sociological and demographic features -- race, family size, sex, age and so on. A practical yardstick of the employment situation is then the size of the proportion of low paid workers and a worsening or improvement in the situation would be judged by reference to increases or falls in the proportion over time." See Turnham, op. cit., p. 51.

33. See Lewis, p. 45.

34. Mahhub ul Huq, "Employment in the 1970s: A New Perspective," speech delivered at SID World Conference in Ottawa, May 1971, mimeo, p. 2.

35. See John W. Mellor, The New Economics of Growth (Ithica: Cornell University Press, 1976).

36. "Strategy and Program for Drought Control and Development in the Sahel," p. 63.

37. Club du Sahel, "Sur le plan humain," Dakar, March 1977.

38. Club du Sahel, Human Resources Team Report, 1978, p. 12.

39. Ibid.

40. Club du Sahel, "A Strategy for Realizing Sahelian Human Resources Potential," 1976, p. 3.

41. Pan American Health Organization, "Childhood Mortality," Washington, 1973.

CHAPTER FIVE

1. Thomas S. Kuhn, The Structure of Scientific Revolutions (Chicago: The University of Chicago Press, 1970), p. 210.

2. See Barrington Moore, Jr., Social Origins of Dictatorship and Democracy (Boston: Beacon Press, 1966).

3. The indexical strategy consists of several rather arbitrary indices of social progress -- literacy, miles of paved road, per capita income, complexity of occupational structure -- against which the society in question is measured. The typological approach involves setting up ideal-type stages, and conceiving change as a quantum-like breakthrough from one of these stages to the next. In the world-acculturative approach, modernization is conceived in terms of borrowing from the West, and change is consequently measured by the degree to which values, ideas, and institutions which were, supposedly, perfected in the West have diffused to the society in question and taken root there. And in the evolutionary approach certain world-historiical trends -- increasing social over energy -- are postulated as intrinsic to human culture, and a society's movement is measured in terms of the degree to which these trends express themselves. Clifford Geertz, Islam Observed (Chicago: The University of Chicago Press, 1971), pp. 57-59.

4. Mellor, The New Economics of Growth, p. 294.

5. See Leon Festinger, A Theory of Cognitive Dissonance (Stanford: Stanford University Press, 1957).

6. Hirschman, The Strategy of Economic Development, pp. 185-186.

7. Geertz, p. 64.

8. The"negative capability" was originally defined by Keats as the capability "of being in uncertainties, mysteries, doubts, without any irritable reaching after fact and reason." F. Scott Fitzgerald elaborated on this idea in The Crack-Up (1936): "The test of a first-rate intelligence is the ability to hold two opposed ideas in the mind at the same time, and still retain the ability to function. One should, for example, be able to see that things are hopeless and yet be determined to make them otherwise." George Orwell referred to this concept as "doublethink," graphically expounding it in 1984 (1949). Orwell gives us a less fictional example of doublethink in "Notes on Nationalism": "All nationalists have the power of not seeing resemblances between similar sets of facts. A British Tory will defend self-determination in Europe and oppose it in India with no feeling of inconsistency." George Orwell, England Your England (London: Secker and Warburg, 1953), p. 42.

9. Michael Polanyi, The Logic of Liberty (Chicago: The Chicago University Press, 1958), p. 4.

10. David E. Apter, Ideology and Discontent (New York:

The Free Press, 1964), p. 40.

11. David E. Apter, "Political Religion in the New Nations," In Geertz, Old Societies and New States, p. 70.

12. Leopold S. Senghor In Sylvia Washington Ba, The Concept of Negritude in the Poetry of Leopold Sedar Senghor (Princeton: Princeton University Press, 1973), p. 180.

13. Garrett Hardin, "The Tragedy of the Commons" In Bruce A. Ackerman, ed., Economic Foundations of Property Law (Boston: Little, Brown and Company 1975), p. 4.

14. Michael M. Horowitz, "The Sociology of Pastoralism and African Livestock Projects," Institute for Development Anthropology,Binghamton, New York, December 1978, p. 24.

15. Christopher L. Delgado, "Village Livestock Intensification in Southeastern Upper Volta," Center for Research on Economic Development, University of Michigan, 1978, p. 1.

16. Michael M. Horowitz, ed., "Colloquium on the Effects of Drought on the Productive Strategies of Sudano-Sahelian Herdsmen and Farmers," Institute for Development Anthropology, Binghamton, New York, September 1976, p. 70.

17. V.R. Potter, "The Tragedy of the Sahel Commons," Science, 1974, p. 185.

18. H.A. Oluwasanmi, "Land Tenure and Progress," Journal of African Economics, June 1971, p. 42. Cf. James C. Riddel and Kenneth H. Parsons, "Land Tenure Issues in African Development," Wisconsin Land Tenure Center, June, 1978.

19. David C. McClelland, The Achieving Society (Princeton: Van Nostrand Co., 1961), p. 404.

20. See Noel V. Lateef, "A Techno-Environmental Analysis of Zarma Social Structure," Bulletin d'IFAN, Dakar, 1975.

21. W. Arthur Lewis, Theory of Economic Growth (New York: Harper & Row, 1965), p. 12.

22. McClelland, p. 401.

23. Fred I. Greenstein, "The Benevolent Leader: Children's Images of Political Authority," American Political Science Review, Vol. 54, 1960, pp. 934-43.

24. See especially Kathleen Cloud, "Sex Roles in Food Production and Food Distribution Systems in the Sahel," December 15, 1977, mimeo, The Center for Educational Research and Development, University of Arizona, and Achola O. Pala, "African Women in Rural Development: Research Trends and Priorities," Overseas Liaison Committee Paper No. 12, December 1976.

25. Jim Kelly, "Review of the Regional Development Strategy for the Sahel," AID Memorandum, April 5, 1979, p. 6.

26. W. Arthur Lewis, op.cit., pp. 23-57.

27. Teihard quoted in Irving L. Markovitz, Senghor and the Politics of Negritude, (New York: Atheneum, 1969), p. 34.

28. L.S. Senghor, Pierre Teilhard de Chardin et le politique Africaine (Paris: Sevil, 1962), p. 34.

29. Senghor quoted in Markovitz, p. 132.

30. J.L. Hymans, Leopold Sedar Senghor (Edinburgh: Edinburgh University Press, 1971), p. 196.

31. L.S. Senghor, On African Socialism (New York: Praeger, 1964), p. 58.
32. Interview with Senghor.
33. Senghor, On African Socialism, p. 79.
34. Ibid.
35. Ibid.
36. Ibid.
37. Albert O. Hirschman, A Bias for Hope (New Haven: Yale University Press, 1971) p. 337.
38. Edward Shils, "On the Comparative Study of the New States," In Clifford Geertz, ed., Old Societies and New States (New York: The Free Press, 1963), pp. 19-20.
39. Ibid., p. 16.
40. See Noel V. Lateef and Nelda L. Lateef, "Zarma Ideology," Bulletin d'IFAN, Dakar, 1976.
41. Samir Amin, Neocolonialism in West Africa (Harmondsworth: Penguin Books Ltd., 1973), p. 70.
42. Robert N. Bellah quoted in Apter, Ideology and Discontent, p. 24.
43. Apter, Ibid., pp. 24-25.
44. Simon Kuznets, Modern Economic Growth (New Haven: Yale University Press, 1966), p. 7.
45. Ibid., pp. 6-7.
46. Ibid., p. 12.
47. Quoted in Dennis Thompson, The Democratic Citizen (Cambridge: Cambridge University Press, 1970), p. 60.
48. William Pfaff, "Reflections: Economic Development," The New Yorker, December 25, 1978, p. 46.
49. Ibid.
50. Kusum Nair, Blossoms in the Dust (New York: Praeger, 1962), p. 193.
51. Talcott Parsons and Edward A. Shils, eds., Toward A General Theory of Action: Theoretical Foundations for the Social Sciences (New York: Harper & Row, 1962), pp. 76-77.
52. Ali A. Mazrui, "From Social Darwinism to Current Theories of Modernization," World Politics, No. 1, October 1968, p. 82.
53. W. Arthur Lewis, op. cit., p. 15.
54. McClelland, The Achieving Society, p. 195.
55. Albert O. Hirschman, Development Projects Observed (Washington, D.C., The Brookings Institution, 1967), p. 35.
56. Ibid., p. 160.
57. For a humanistic analysis of the potentialities of urban areas, see Harvey Cox, The Secular City (New York: Macmillan, 1965).
58. Quoted in Badouin Danière, "Scènes du nationalisme," L'Afrique et le Tiers Monde, June 1977, pp. 53-54.

CHAPTER SIX

1. Paraphrased from John P. Lewis, Quiet Crisis in India.

2. There has been a tendency to accept some of the basic premises of the two-sector models without observing the caveats regarding the mutual interdependence of the sectors and the inherent dangers of undue imbalance. For a detailed discussion of early two-sector models, see W. Arthur Lewis, "Economic Development with Unlimited Supplies of Labor," The Manchester School, 22 (May, 1954); Gustav Ranis and John C.H. Fei, "A Theory of Economic Development," American Economic Review, 51 (September, 1961); Bruce F. Johnston and John W. Mellor, "The Role of Agriculture in Economic Development," American Economic Review, 51 (September, 1961). Subsequently, a number of highly sophisticated extensions of the earlier models have been developed. See, for example, Gustav Ranis and John C.H. Fei, Development of the Labor Surplus Economy: Theory and Policy (Homewood, Illinois: Richard D. Irwin, Inc., 1964) and P. Zarembka, Toward a Theory of Economic Development (San Francisco: Holden-Day, 1972).

3. See Jacob Viner, "The Economics of Development" in Jacob Viner, International Trade and Economic Development (Oxford: Clarendon Press, 1953), p. 6.

4. William Letwin, "Four Fallacies about Economic Development" in David E. Novack and Robert Lekachman, eds., Development and Society: The Dynamics of Economic Change (New York: St. Martin's Press, 1964), p. 25.

5. W.W. Rostow, "The Stages of Economic Growth" The Economic History Review, August,1959 p. 46.

6. W. Gerald Matlock and E. Lendell Cockrum, "A Framework for Agricultural Development Planning, Vol. II," Center for Policy Alternatives, MIT, Cambridge, Mass., December 31, 1974.

7. Charles P. Humphreys and Scott R. Pearson, "Choice of Technique, Natural Production, and Efficient Expansion of Rice Production in Sahelian Countries," Food Research Institute, Stanford University, June 13, 1979, pp. 78-81.

8. "Compte Rendu, Seminaire sur la mise en valeur des 'terres neuves' au Sahel," Ougadougou, Club du Sahel, October 10, 1978, p. 3.

9. W. David Hopper, "The Development of Agriculture in Developing Countries," Scientific American, September 1976, p. 142.

10. AID, "Range Development and Management in Africa," 1974, p. 14.

11. Edward D. Eddy, III, "Integrated Crop and Livestock Production in Niger's Southern Pastoral Zones," Center for Research on Economic Development, University of Michigan, Ann Arbor, Michigan, 1978, p. 9, 13.

12. "Range Development and Management in Africa," p. 43.

13. IBRD, "Proposal for a Cooperative Effort to Rationalize the Livestock Industries of the Sahel," 1974, p. 5.

14. MIT, "A Framework for Evaluating Long-Term Strategies for Development of the Sahel-Sudan Region," December 1974, p. 108.

15. Ibid., p. 22.

16. CIFA Report, p. 218.

17. Roger Revelle, "The Resources Available for Agriculture," Scientific American, September 1976, p. 121.

18. National Academy of Sciences, "Water in Agriculture," 1976, p. 11.

19. Ibid.

20. Steven Franzel, "An Interim Evaluation of Two Agricultural Production Projects in Senegal: The Economics of Rainfed and Irrigated Agriculture," Working Paper No. 28, African Rural Economy Program, Department of Agricultural Economics, Michigan State University, East Lansing, Michigan, June 1979, pp. 50-51.

21. See William R. Cline, "Policy Instruments for Rural Income," Princeton University - Bookings Institution Project on Income Distribution in Less Developed Countries, January 1975, mimeo.

22. Rostow, p. 47.

23. Leopold S. Senghor, On African Socialism (New York: Praeger, 1964), pp. 157-158.

CHAPTER SEVEN

1. Barbara Ward, "Giving Ground," The Economist, August 31, 1977, p. 34.

2. M.I.T., "Inadvertent Climatic Modifications," 1970, mimeo, p. 12.

3. "The Gambia: The Need for a National Tree Planting Programme," Ministry of Agriculture, Banjul, August 1977, pp. 2-3.

4. "L'Etude de la desertification de l'Afrique tropicale seche," Bois et Forets des Tropiques, March 1973, p. 44.

5. Roger Revelle, "Requirements for Energy Resources and Rural Applications in the Developing Countries," In Norman L. Brown, ed., Renewable Energy Resources in the Developing World (Boulder: Westview Press, 1978), p. 127. "Strategy and Program for Drought Control and Development in the Sahel," p. 79.

6. Ibid., p. 130.

7. T.C. Delwaulle, "Le role du Forestier dans l'amenagement du Sahel," Bois and Forets des Tropiques, April 1974, p. 25.

8. Overseas Development Council, "Report to the Rockefeller Foundation," Washington, D.C., 1977, p. 5.

9. AID, Development Assistance Program 1976-1980, November 1975, p. 81.

10. U.S. Bureau of Reclamation, "Senegal River Basin: Water Resources Development Analysis", January 1975, p. 7.

11. Ibid., p. 9.

12. UNDP/FAO, "Groundwater Resources in the Lake Chad Basin," Vol. 1, 1973, p. 43.

13. Ibid., p. 45.

14. Gary Nelson, "Why Irrigation Projects May Become Enduring Monuments of Failure", Focus, March 1977, p. 24.

15. Ibid.

16. C.K. Kline, D.A. Green, R. L. Donahue, and B. A. Stout, Agricultural Mechanization in Equatorial Africa, (East Lansing: Michigan State University, 1969), p. 29.

17. "Sahel Food Crop Protection Project," Project Paper, AID, 1975, mimeo., p. 38.

18. John W. Mellor, "The Impact of New Technology on Rural Employment and Income Distribution," Ithaca, AID - Cornell University Project, January 1973, p. 1.

19. B.N. Ikigbo, "Report of Commission I," Dakar, A.A.A.-S.A. Second Conference, March 1975, mimeo, p. 1.

20. "SODEVA Project Paper," Project Paper, Dakar, AID, 1974, mimeo., p. 12.

21. Robert Toute, "Intensive Systems in Peasant Agriculture, A Case Study: Senegal," Dakar, IRAT, 1976, mimeo., p. 6.

22. Victor Lateef quoted in "Annual Budget Submission FY 1977," Dakar, AID, July 1975, p. 3.

23. Harvey Brooks, "Critique of Appropriate Technology," forthcoming.

24. John W. Mellor, "The Impact of New Technology on Rural Employment and Income Distribution," Ithaca, AID - Cornell University Project, May 1976, p. 19.

25. Chandra H. Soysa, "Sharing of Traditional Technology," Focus, 1977/1, p. 3.

26. Orville Freeman quoted in Noel V. Lateef, "Mutual Benefits of Science and Technology Collaboration with the Developing Countries," Department of State, August 1978, p. 123.

27. Kuznets, Modern Economic Growth, p. 6.

28. Samuel C. Gilfillan, The Sociology of Invention (Chicago: Follet, 1965), p. 10.

29. William W. Lockwood, The Economic Development of Japan: Growth and Structural Change, 1868-1938 (Princeton: Princeton University Press, 1954), p. 198.

30. See Harvey Brooks and Eugene B. Skolnikoff, "Science, Technology and International Relations," Presented at the NATO Science Committee 20th Anniversary Commemoration Conference, May 1978, mimeo.; Noel V. Lateef, "Paving the Way for Technopolis," Bulletin of the Atomic Scientists, November 1979; and Michael J. Maravcsik, "Science and the Developing Countries," NSF, October 1977, mimeo.

31. Vernon W. Ruttan, "Induced Technical and Institutional Change and the Future of Agriculture," New York, Agriculture Development Council reprint, December 1973, p. 9.

32. See Jack Baranson, "North-South Transfer of Technology: What Realistic Alternatives are Available to the U.S.?," Prepared for the Department of State, December 1977.

33. See Gustav Ranis, "Technology Choice and Employment in Developing Countries: A Synthesis of Economic Growth Center Research," Center Discussion Paper No. 276, Economic Growth Center, Yale University.

CHAPTER EIGHT

1. Shear, "The Role of the Village in Sahelian Development," p. 5.
2. Hari Mohan Mathur, "Administrative Training and Rural Development," _Focus_, March 1977, p. 29.
3. See "Report on a Study of the Education and Training Component of the Mali Livestock Sector Grant," AID, November 1975.
4. Uma Lele, _The Design of Rural Development: Lessons from Africa_ (Baltimore: The Johns Hopkins University Press, 1975), p. 99.
5. Senghor quoted in Markovitz, p. 144.
6. Interview with Samir Amin, Dakar, Senegal, January 3, 1977.
7. Markovitz, p. 32.
8. Arthur M. Fell, "Administrative Reform in Senegal: The Rural Community," Club du Sahel Paper, No. 1115, July 10, 1978, p. 1.
9. Samuel P. Huntington, _Political Order in Changing Societies_ (New Haven: Yale University Press, 1968), p. 72.
10. Fell, p. 8.
11. Fell, pp. 5-6.
12. Senghor, Correspondence to the Prime Minister, June 18, 1974.
13. Aristide R. Zolberg, _Creating Political Order: The Party States of West Africa_ (Chicago: Rand McNally, 1966), p. 63.
14. Fell, p. 12.
15. Clifford Geertz, ed., "The Integrative Revolution," _Old Societies and New States_ (Glencoe: The Free Press, 1963), p. 111.
16. Huntington, p. 32.
17. Henry L. Bretton, _Power and Politics in Africa_ (Chicago: Aldine Publishing Co., 1973), p. 171.
18. Pfaff, p. 48.
19. Thomas C. Grey, "Procedural Fairness and Substantive Rights," in Robert M. Cover and Owen M. Fiss, eds., _The Structure of Procedure_ (Mineola, New York: The Foundation Press, Inc., 1979), p. 103.
20. Leland Hazard, _Law and the Changing Environment_ (San Francisco: Holden-Day, 1971), p. 5.
21. Robert A. Dahl, _Polyarchy_ (New Haven: Yale University Press, 1971), pp. 212-213.
22. Roscoe Pound, _Justice According to Law_ (New Haven: Yale University Press, 1951), p. 29.

23. Robert Wade, "Administration and the Distribution of Irrigation Benefits," Economic and Political Weekly, November 1975, p. 1743.

24. Eddy, p. 13.

25. Noel V. Lateef, "The Development Smoke Screen," The Churchman, December 1979.

26. See William Mullen, "Pestilence, Ignorance, Red Tape Mean Disaster in Sahel Region," Chicago Tribune, April 19, 1976.

CHAPTER NINE

1. J. O'Connell, "The Political Class and Economic Growth," The Nigerian Journal of Economic and Social Studies, Vol. 8 (November 1966), p. 137.

2. Alexis de Tocqueville, Democracy in America (New York: Knopf, 1955), p. 2.

3. Huntington, pp. 10-11.

4. Quoted in Ronald Koven, "A European Parliament," The Washington Post, July 18, 1979.

5. Shear, "The Role of the Village in Sahelian Development," p. 29.

6. Marion J. Levy, Jr., " 'Does It Matter If He's Naked?' Bawled the Child," in Klaus Knorr and James N. Rosenau, eds., Contending Approaches to International Politics (Princeton: Princeton University Press, 1969), p. 93.

7. "Strategy and Program for Drought Control and Development in the Sahel," p. 63.

8. See John P. Lewis, pp. 181-217.

9. Henry Bienen, Tanzania: Party Transformation and Economic Development (Princeton: Princeton University Press, 1967), p. 13.

10. Robert Chambers, "Planning for Rural Areas in East Africa: Experience and Prescriptions," in David K. Leonard, ed., Rural Administration in Kenya (Nairobi: East African Literature Bureau, 1973), pp. 15-18.

11. Interview with Boubou Hana, Niamey, Niger, December 7, 1972.

12. World Bank, "Food Problems of the Low-Income Countries," Finance and Development, June 1977, p. 16.

13. "Strategy and Program for Drought Control and Development in the Sahel," p. 50.

14. See Denison, Why Growth Rates Differ.

15. John Stuart Mill, On Liberty (Northbrook: AHM Publishing Corp., 1947), p. 59.

16. Michael Ploanyi, Personal Knowledge (Chicago: Crowell, 1958), pp. 149-157.

17. Senghor, Address given at the University of Dakar, June 1965.

18. Barbara Ward, "Giving Ground," The Economist, August 13, 1977, p. 36.

19. "Strategy and Program for Drought Control and Develop-

ment in the Sahel," p. 72.

20. Letwin, p. 38.

21. John P. Lewis, "Oil, Other Scarcities, and the Poor Countries," World Politics, Vol. 27, October 1974, p. 76.

22. Constance J. Freeman, "Desert Encroachment Prevention: The Sahel Development Program," Testimony before the Subcommittee on Foreign Relations, U.S. Senate, June 1978, mimeo., pp. 31-32; see Leon Gordenker, International Aid and National Decisions (Princeton: Princeton University Press, 1976).

23. "A Strategy for a More Effective Bilateral Development Assistance Program," AID Policy Paper, March 1978, p. 9.

24. John Dunn, West African States: Failure and Promise (Cambridge: Cambridge University Press, 1978), p. 3.

Index

DATE DE RETOUR
IM-5

BIBLIOTHÈQUE CHAMPLAIN
3 9365 00114120 1